THE NEW COMPLETE NORWEGIAN ELKHOUND

Trollbakken's Tussi
Winner of hunting and show prizes, Norway, 1984.
Owned by Guttorm Risdal.

THE NEW COMPLETE

NORWEGIAN ELKHOUND

by OLAV WALLO

with the assistance of Karen Elvin

THIRD EDITION
First Printing — 1987

HOWELL
BOOK HOUSE INC.

230 Park Avenue, New York, N.Y. 10169

Library of Congress Cataloging-in-Publication Data

Wallo, Olav, 1898 –
   The new complete Norwegian elkhound.

   1. Norwegian elkhounds.   I. Elvin, Karen.
II. Title.
SF429.N6W35   1987   636.7'53   87-3543
ISBN 0-87605-243-X

Tusen takk Karen Elvin
for your great help in
assembling my book.

Olav

Is this moose for real?   *— Hirtle photo.*

Contents

Ch. Vin-Melca's Nimbus, the all-time top Elkhound show winner, with 63 all-breed Bests in Show and 177 Group Firsts, including two at Westminster. Owned by Patricia V. Craige and Harold Schuler and handled by Mrs. Craige.

Tyra av Kotofjell, a Best in Show winner in Norway, bred by Birger Grønvold and owned in America by Olav Wallo.

Publisher's Foreword

IT IS with great pleasure that we present this third edition of what is universally recognized as the classic book on the Norwegian Elkhound.

The Complete Norwegian Elkhound, by Olav Wallo and William C. Thompson, was first published in 1957. Mr. Thompson died in 1968. The second edition, written by Mr. Wallo and titled *The New Complete Norwegian Elkhound,* was published in 1970.

Now, with the invaluable assistance of Karen Elvin, Olav brings us this grand new edition. The first change in more than 16 years, it is more than just a revision—it is really an all-new book. While the authors have been careful to retain the excellent features that have given the book its revered status, everything has been updated and much that is new has been added. The book has been completely reset and over 180 new pictures are included.

Olav Wallo and this book have been honored many times, here and in Norway. What must stand as one of the finest tributes ever paid to a breed book author, and one of the greatest outpourings of love, came in 1978 when the Norwegian Elkhound Association of America dedicated its Seventh National Specialty Show in his honor.

Olav, who in his lifetime has been an airline pilot and an inventor, was born in Norway at the turn of the century and came to America in 1922. Today, more than 65 years later, there is still the Norse cadence in his speech and the Norse love of the great outdoors in his heart. This love guided his choice of American home, atop a high hill in Bloomington, Minnesota, with a sweeping view of the Minneapolis skyline—"a place where the wilderness still whispers, where deer, beaver, raccoon and fox are welcome freeloaders, and where birds of all sizes and colors wing above."

11

When land developers began to lay waste the woodland beauty of his environs, Olav took up the cudgels with true Viking fury. He became co-founder and co-chairman of the Nine Mile Creek Citizens Committee, and from 1966 to 1974 served on the Bloomington Natural Resources Commission. In recognition of his work in this cause he received the Distinguished Service Award from the city of Bloomington in 1975 and three years later was named the Outstanding Senior Citizen of Hennepin County. In addition, he has been very active in humane work and is a charter member of the Minnesota River Valley Audubon Society.

Many other tributes decorate his hobby room. They include greetings from King Olav of Norway, from President Herbert Hoover, from the Government of Canada, and for his work in behalf of his home state there are salutes from Hubert Humphrey and Governors Wendell Anderson and Rudy Perpich.

Through the years the warmest link to memories of his youth midst the forests, fjords and mountains of Norway has been the dog that he first knew there as a hunting companion. Recognized as one of the top authorities on the Norwegian Elkhound throughout the world, Olav is particularly proud of being an honored member of the Norsk Elghund Club, a distinction that few have been accorded.

In America his association with the breed began with the gift of an eight-weeks-old puppy from his wife, Lola. His early Elkhounds were good hunters, but with the first litter came the realization that if he was to have dogs of the type he remembered and treasured, he must turn his eyes "back home."

The opportunity came with a hunting vacation in Norway in 1946, during which Olav established close rapport with some of the most important breeders there. In follow up, two years later he received from Norway Ch. Stella, in whelp to Trygg av Skromtefjell, a very handsome dog and a good hunter. Out of the litter came "handsome youngsters of a new type—lighter coat, higher on leg and not as massive as so many Elkhounds in this country. This was the hunting type."

The "hunting type" became established as the desideratum of the breed and Olav Wallo's Runefjell Kennel was a prominent force in its establishment and promotion. In all, the kennel imported 22 notable dogs from Norway over the next 25 years and produced 30 champions.

The Runefjell Kennel had as its motto: "*Honor, Protect and Improve the Breed*," and it was lived up to in every way. Now, in preparing this revision, this same motto has been Olav's—and our—guideline.

—ELSWORTH S. HOWELL
Publisher

12

Olav Wallo handling a quartet of champions from his Runefjell Kennels to Best Team in Show at Minneapolis 1958 show, under judge Ernest E. Ferguson. The four dogs, from l. to r.: Ch. Runefjell Gunar, Ch. Runefjell Dagney, Ch. Isabell av Runefjell and Ch. Sigred av Runefjell.

Ch. Borghill av Runefjell, bred and owned by Olav Wallo.

A 1939 card picturing Elghunds of the Stavsetras Kennel in Trondheim, Norway, owned by Charles Stavseth. Note the excellence of quality.

Preface

MY interest in and admiration for the Norwegian Elghund goes back many years. Although its saga is well-known to the Scandinavian people, I hope others will enjoy knowing more about the National Dog of Norway.

To see dogs of this breed hunting in the field or forest, or posing in the show ring, has always been a thrill. I like the simple natural true personality of this great hunting dog whose original characteristics and appearance remain unchanged. He has all the fine qualities that a breed could possibly inherit.

His story in the United States goes back more than seven decades, from a slow start with a few secluded breeders and owners to the rank he enjoys today—46th in popularity of the 129 breeds recognized by the American Kennel Club. This is a good place to be—not too high up on the scale, and not too far down.

Because it is the name by which it is officially registered in America and England, throughout this book the breed is identified as the Norwegian Elkhound.

But I feel uncomfortable with this unfortunate and inaccurate translation of the dog's true name ELGHUND. Elg (which should be translated as *moose,* not *elk*) and hund (meaning *dog* as in Dachshund). The Norwegian Elghund is a wonderful name; it is easy to pronounce and the sound is music to the ear.

The breed is not a hound; it doesn't look like a hound, it doesn't hunt like a hound and it doesn't run like a hound.

In the dog shows in Scandinavia, it is a member of Group I, the *Spetshundar*. This Group includes Alaskan Malamutes, Siberian Huskies, Finnish Spitz, Greenlanders, Samoyeds and many more. The array of these

Puppies of the Vin-Melca Kennels, 8 weeks old.

sturdy, straightforward Northern breeds makes the Spetshundar Group a beautiful, thrilling sight at every dog show.

In the American show setup, these breeds are scattered, lost and strangers in the seven Groups. They belong together. Hopefully, some day the American Kennel Club will recognize the injustice that has been done through the years in not assembling these breeds within one Group. For the judges, it would certainly make more sense and would make deciding among them more equitable. For the breeders and owners, it would be a grand homecoming—a family reunion. This, and giving it its true name of Norwegian Elghund, is something I hope the leaders and protectors of purebred dogs in America will give thought to.

I am grateful for the cooperation of the many authorities who have contributed articles, and of the many fanciers who have submitted photographs of their dogs.

OLAV O. WALLO

1

The Saga of the
Norwegian Elkhound

FROM out of the hazy mists of prehistoric time came the man and the beast—walking not as friendly, devoted pals, but as deadly enemies. Neither asked quarter, nor gave it. Again and again the scene repeated itself: a wounded moose in flight, and following in its bloody trail came the beast and then the man, ready to fight over the prey.

Later, the man, king of the forest and the thinker, captured the young beast, fed it, and taught it to hunt, track, and trail. The two grew to work as a team, and when the beast located wild game, the man came and killed it.

Hunting was best in the spring of the year, when the snow melted in the day but froze at night. The snow crust would carry the man and the beast, but the heavy moose would sink into its depth. The beast would growl and snarl in front of the moose, and fight to hold it back, so that the man could attack with his spear and his bow and arrows. That night, moose meat would cook over the fire. The beast could not bark in those days; his only expression of glee or sorrow was a wolf-like howl.

Many a snow has melted in the mountains since that time. Progress has rolled forward, the man has become civilized, and the beast is now the dog.

In Denmark's flat woods, where the *Veidefolket* (gypsy peoples) hunted and roamed, the *Torvmosehund* (swamp dog) was found. It is generally believed that he was the forerunner of our Northern breeds, including the Norwegian Elkhound. It is also assumed that the people migrated into Scandinavia from the South. Some came as free men, others

Two Elkhounds holding moose at bay.

—Photo, Ola Bjorneby.

as hunted. They roamed the wild country, hunted and trapped, and lived off what the valley gave, for the land was rich in wild game and fish.

Some time ago, an interesting discovery was made at Hov Farm, north of Oslo. In a water-logged country, at a depth of 17.5 meters, an elk-revier (horn) was found. It is probably the oldest to be discovered thus far, being dated by radiologic science to be about 8,000 years old. The horn is in good condition, which is believed to be due to the fact that it had been dropped by the elk in a bog.

Very little is known concerning the origin and the ancestry of the *Veidefolket*. But in their wanderings they left behind *modings* (rubbish dumps) that have provided a wealth of information for the modern archeologist. In these *modings,* not only in Denmark but also in Southern Sweden, tools and weapons have been found, and it has been established that both big and small game were hunted with *Torvmosehund*.

After the time of the *Veidefolket* came the Viking period, when the freeborn Norsemen sailed the open sea, and the dog was the steady companion of the hardy man. In battle on land or sea, the dog was an honored member of the crew. Should the commander be wounded in battle, he would be carried on board his Viking ship. His dog, dead of course, would accompany him as the burning ship set full sail on a straight course far out to sea to Odin's and Thor's kingdom, the Valhalla, home of all brave and courageous Vikings. No leader would be welcome to Valhalla if he came with scant earthly possessions. Odin is quoted as saying that they should come to Valhalla with the same amount of wealth as they had on the pyre.

In another period of the Viking regime, the king or commander would be buried with full accoutrements—with his ship, weapons, tools, and even his dogs; this was the case at Vistehulen, Jaeren, in the southwest part of Norway. There, Professor Brinchmann of the Bergen museum found relics of the stone age, including four skeletons of dogs, two of which were very similar in bone structure to modern Elkhounds. Expert archeologists presume that this grave dates back to from 4000 to 5000 B.C.

Then there were such other finds as the dog skeletons in the famous Gökstad ship, and the clay bowl in the grave at Vallöby, which bore in bas-relief a hunting scene with Elkhounds.

Next, Christianity came to Norway and the Viking period ended. With its passing, the Elkhound retrogressed. Christianity came not as peaceful, hymn-singing guidance, but as harsh, rough dominance. Many of Norway's great leaders left the country and settled in Iceland and Greenland. Many who could not leave and would not turn Christian were thrown into the dog den, there to be torn to pieces by vicious dogs, presumably large dogs imported from Southern Europe.

Some centuries later came the black death. Valley after valley was swept clean of people. The dead were not buried because there were no survivors left to dig the graves. Farmhouses rotted and fell to the ground. As nature took over, brush crept over fertile fields, turning them into a wilderness.

The year 1696 was a tragic one for the Finnish people, for the severe, killing frost early in August froze the lakes and rivers and ruined the crops. Hunger and famine were in store for these Suomis folks. Of the 450,000 Finns, an estimated 100,000 left their homes and began the arduous journey westward across fjords, through endless forests, and over mountains—a long wandering in the face of an onrushing winter. How many reached Norwegian soil is not known, but many a nameless grave was dug in the wilderness and forgotten.

In Norway, the Suomis people mainly settled in the deep forests, where they cut timber, built homes, grubbed the fields, and hunted. From the Norwegian government they received title to the land.

Between Oslo and Ringerike there was at that time the vast area of Krokskogen, a deep forest settled by the Finns, which was much like their native land. Even today in Krokskogen one finds many names of Finnish origin.

At that time Krokskogen was noted for its big game, such as moose and bear, and for large game birds, such as *tiur* and *orrhane*. It is a well-known fact those great hunters from Finland also used the Elkhound to hunt big birds. Even today, far removed as he is from this period, an Elkhound, seeing a big bird in a tree, will sometimes stand beneath and let bubble from his throat a sound that is like small silver bells ringing. The bird will be so fascinated that he will not notice the hunter, even at a short distance.

It was a common thing with my Elkhound, Fram, purchased from Eidsvold in 1918. A friend of mine, John Martinsen, shot two *tiur* in Sorumsmoen over Fram in 1919, and after that Martinsen and Fram made many trips to Krokskogen and Hollaia. Martinsen stated that it was the most fascinating hunting that could be experienced, and he should know for he was one of the best moose hunters in Ringerike at that time. How many *tiurs* were shot over Fram could never be learned. But one thing is certain, Martinsen did not borrow Fram for company alone.

Some Elkhounds have inherited these unusual gifts, and will hunt birds as the breed has done from way back in time. Mr. and Mrs. Eugene Caza, of Lake Elmo, Minnesota, told me of this experience with their bitch, Dama av Dalysen: "When Dama was about nine months old, we took her pheasant hunting. She flushed some birds out of the bush for us, and one flew up into a tree. While we were getting a bead on the pheasant, Dama ran up to the tree and sounded out with a loud, clear voice that seemed to us like the ringing of bells. The pheasant was captivated by her call, enabling us to

22

walk up close and shoot. From that time on, Dama always greeted us with a beautiful call that sounded like ringing bells, and she also used it to help us get our game whenever we went hunting."

The saga of the Norwegian Elkhound is rich in folklore. One of the most interesting legends is that of Tore Ullin and his Elkhound Bram. It all started at a midsummer dance on Myrvold Mountain, where young and old came to dance, play and drink for two days. From Kvernbro Valley came Kransen, a raw-boned fighter always handy with the knife, hated by most women and a friend of no man. Tore, from a neighboring valley, was a handsome, friendly young man, the strongest of them all. On the second day, the two got into a fight and Tore killed Kransen. From that time on, he was a hunted man.

Tore fled northward at night, alone except for Bram who he took with him. They came to a beautiful valley, and here Tore the Hunted and his dog lived in a hole in the mountain for many years. For food, they hunted— summer and winter. In the deep snow and frost of the winter evenings, Bram's tail became encrusted with ice and snow, and he dragged it after him like a broom. So Tore took the tail and curled it on the dog's back, and tied it with a leather thong. From that time on, according to the story, the Elkhound has had a curly tail.

In Norse history, the years from 1825 to 1845 are referred to as the Wolf Period. At that time, thousands of wolves swarmed into Norway from Finland and Northern Sweden. Long, lanky, bony, and hungry, they hunted in packs, killing everything in their way, including wild game, cattle, and people. Many outlying districts had to be abandoned, because the inhabitants dared not go outside for days and farm stock were killed right in the barns. In one valley, the wolves even killed 15 horses.

For the Norwegian Elkhound, the big-game hunter and also the guardian of home and livestock, these were trying times. Although he was a good fighter, the Elkhound always had to fight against great odds. Usually he wore an iron collar with sharp spikes pointing outward. In spite of this, many an Elkhound was torn to pieces by his deadly enemy.

In the south central part of Norway, the night of February 14, 1842, for many years was called Wolf Night (*Graabine*) for that was the occasion of the big fight between a pack of wolves and nine of the toughest Elkhounds in the Norderhove Valley. The dogs' leader was Fanarok the Fearless, the greatest fighter of them all. His little brother, Purven, was the runt of the litter and not much of a fighter or hunter. Fanarok was his brother's pal and guardian. And heaven help the poor creature that picked on Purven.

The night before the fight, Fanorok was locked securely in the barn to protect the cattle, while Purven, the housepet, somehow got outside. Fanorok, hearing the screams of the helpless Purven as he was being torn to pieces by the wolves, pounded on the heavy door trying to get out to help his unfortunate brother—but to no avail. The next morning Fanarok looked over the place where Purven was killed. Some frozen blood in the white snow and a few fur pieces shivering in the wind were all that remained. Fanarok slowly smelled them, and then, when he found Purven's collar, he was sure of what had happened. He raised his great head and in the frosty morning sent a call to his breed, a call of sorrow and hatred, a challenge to his gang.

From farm after farm came the answer. These Elkhounds were strong, seasoned hunters. They had tangled with the roughest moose, so the biggest bear could not scare them. They had felt the rush of air when the moose struck with his front hoofs only inches from their heads. They had leaped at the ferocious bear as he reared on his hind legs with his neck bent like a swan's.

As night approached and a full, bright moon rose over the frozen landscape, a lonely Elkhound in the middle of small Lake Juveren, where the snow was shallow and the footing good, howled his sorrow to the world and to the cold moon. Not far away, eight of his recruits waited in a swamp.

They did not have long to wait. A pack of wolves soon appeared on the lake following their leader and fanning out in an attempt to encircle the Elkhound. The latter raced straight for the slough where his pals waited.

The wolves, in close pursuit, also headed for the slough. But there they were in for a big surprise. The attack came so fast and so furious that they had no time to organize their defense. Open jaws with sharp fangs cut and ripped. With tremendous speed the Elkhounds swarmed over them and tore at the wolves' bodies. Some of the wolves were slammed down. Jaws strong as steel traps clamped shut on throats and did not reopen until the wolf, four legs helplessly fanning the air, dropped lifeless. Growls and screams could be heard for miles. More and more wolves appeared on the lake where they smelled blood.

Men came from farms and cabins. Armed with guns, axes, swords, and other weapons, they stood side by side in the deep snow at the shoreline. It was doomsday for the wolves! And many an account was settled! Most of the men were dealing out heavy blows in the middle of the fray, while others on the outskirts quickly dispatched the wounded wolves seeking to escape on crushed legs. The men, boiling over with many years of hatred and revenge, had no mercy.

The fight raged on for hours; then the wolves realized that they were trapped. They ran from one side of the lake to the other, but could find no path of escape. The men on the shoreline moved inward. The circle shrunk more and more. This was the end.

When the first beam of the February sun rose over the frozen landscape, 27 wolves were stretched out on the snow. For years after, the valley was free of the wolf plague. For the Norwegian Elkhound it was a

24

grand day. As for the men of Norderhove, they proudly wore wolf coats from Norway's greatest wolf fight.

After the Wolf Period the woods of Norway were very quiet. No big or small game was left. Only in Osterdalen and Hedmarken did a small herd of moose remain; the rest had been killed by wolves. Just a few Elkhounds remained and it was difficult to find good specimens among them. Only in a few secluded valleys did the better strains exist. Then man—breeder, hunter, friend—came to pick up the pieces and give the breed new life.

When the giant fell, emptiness prevailed over the wilderness.

(photo, B. Kolby, Norway)

25

ARTISTS' VIEW OF THE NORWEGIAN ELKHOUND

There are many examples of the artists of the world using dogs as subjects and the Elkhound is no exception. Wherever there are dog fanciers, there are renderings of their favorite breeds in many media.

The Elkhound has been honored by selection as the featured breed on both coins and stamps in his native Norway, as seen on the facing page.

In commemoration of the fiftieth anniversary of the Norwegian Elkhound Association of America in 1984, a special medallion was designed for presentation to all those attending the show. This is pictured at center of the facing page.

The distinctive carving created by artist Arne Tjomsland as a Norsk Kennel Klubb honorary award is pictured on Page 28.

Norsk Kennel Klubb Honorary Award

Outside the cave, a stone age man sat by the fire, fingering some sharp flints and a small piece of oak, weather-dried by wind and storm. On the other side of the fire a dog slept, tired after the day's hunt and full-fed on the day's prey—sleeping with his body but not with his senses. His pricked ears, always on guard, searched for the smallest sound. His nostrils vibrated and sucked in all the smells, even in his sleep.

Suddenly, all alive, the dog stood up on straight legs with withers bristling and all muscles tense. From down in his throat gurgled forth warning of a wolf pack far in the wilderness. The dog knew that a wolf never ventured close to smoke from a fire, but it is a dog's task to announce the presence of quarry or enemy. It is the hunter's job to kill. With his simple tools, primitive understanding and overall vision, the man carved the image of the dog as he saw it. He had no gift for details and no use for them, but he knew the dog from the long day and night hunting that had made them a team.

The pictured carving was created by artist Arne Tjomsland as an award to be given by the Norsk Kennel Klubb to persons who have in a deserving way promoted good-will toward the club and dogdom. H.M. King Olav, of Norway, was the first person to receive this wonderful trophy.

2

Norwegian Elkhounds in Norway

T HE year 1865 is memorable in Elkhound history as the year in which Bamse Gram, destined to be the trail blazer and model for the breed for years to come, was whelped. Later known as Gamle Bamse Gram, he was owned by Consul Jens Gram, of Ask, Ringerike, a well-known sportsman and hunter.

No pedigree goes back further than Bamse, and even though there was a good strain of bitches in Ringerike at that time, he must be given credit for the unusual quality of the stock in that district later. Bamse, who was one of the first free-running Elkhounds (*loshund*), was described as follows: "Body coarse and a trifle long, not long-legged, wide head, large erect ears, dark eyes, gray color with a mixture of dark to nearly white, and some brown on the legs."

The first bench show in Norway was held at the *Contraskjaeret,* in Oslo, on June 28-29, 1877, under the auspices of the *Norsk Jeger og Fiskerforening,* a Norwegian hunting and fishing club. On hand were 124 hunting dogs, including 15 "Bear and Elk Dogs." Arne Omsted, Jens Gram, and N. Anker officiated. All the Northern breeds were shown in the same class. Peter Carlsrud's Grant took first prize and Thorvald Buttingsrud's Sikker was awarded second prize. Although Bamse Gram was present, he could not receive first prize because his owner was one of the judges.

The second bench show was held on June 25-26, 1880, with 180 dogs, including 28 Elkhounds. No first prize was given. A. Strande's Fin (a

Gamle Bamse Gram.
Owned by Consul Jens Gram, Ask, Norway.

Ch. Skrub av Glitre.

T. Hemsen, with Senny II and her offspring.

Kaisa av Tallo, at one time rated "as the best bitch I ever had" by Norwegian authority Olav Campbell.

Excellent hunting type. Jerv av Elglia, winner at Oslo, 1936. Owner, Olav Campbell.

Ch. Stella. Bred by H. Berg, Norway. Owned by Olav Wallo.

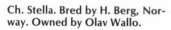

ever shown, and as a producing sire he rated along with Gamle Bamse Gram. It is pointed out that Skrub carried 50% of the blood of Senny II.

T. Hemsen, who was an honorary member of the Norsk Elghundklubb, finished three champions in 1928: Ch. Skrub av Glitre (dog), Ch. Peik II av Glitre (dog), and Ch. Bringe II av Glitre (bitch). Starting with Senny II, Hemsen won consistently with his dogs up to 1949. More than a dozen of his well-known strain came to America.

Hans Christiansen (Gjetemyra Kennels) raised three champions, all with Ch. Skrub av Glitre in their pedigrees: Ch. Binna av Gjetemyra (bitch), Ch. Laila av Gjetemyra (bitch), and Ch. Roy av Gjetemyra (dog). Ch. Binna went to the Skromtefjell Kennels of Sven Mjearum, long-time secretary of the Norsk Elghundklubb, who bred her to Boy av Glitre, a son of Ch. Skrub av Glitre. Later he mated her to her grandson, Falk av Skromtefjell. Through the many generations in the Skromtefjell line, one will find a high percentage of Ch. Skrub av Glitre and Senny II.

One of the oldest and best known kennels in Norway was Elglia, owned by Johnny Aarflot, a popular international judge of Elkhounds. He judged the breed three times in America, and his opinions were earnestly sought. Undoubtedly his most famous dog was Ch. Saga of Elglia (Ch. Skrub av Glitre ex Mausi), whelped on St. Patrick's Day 1929. She had litters by Ch. Skrub av Glitre and by Bjonn. In 1936, she was imported to America by Thomas White, where she had six champions to her credit.

Olav Campbell (av Tallo Kennels) raised Ch. Trysil-Knut av Tallo, 467L, and many other good hunting dogs. He, too, bred to Ch. Skrub av Glitre with his Binna back in 1931. Olav remains very active with the breed and both he and his son have judged the parent club Specialty in America, as well as many important shows throughout the world.

Mention should be made of Erik V. Enberg (Elgstolen Kennels) in Oslo. Best known were his Elgstolens Buster, the sire of many good ones and a proven hunter with many moose to his credit, and Elgstolens Jerv, the famous hunter and field trial winner. Their pedigrees were strong in Gjetemyra blood.

Victor Jensen (Homanskogen Kennels) also had Gjetemyra stock, for he started with Ch. Laila av Gjetemyra, 8351. C. F. Langes (av Honn Kennels) specialized in hunting dogs. Charles Stavseth (Stavsetra Kennels) sent several fine dogs to America, including Ch. Stravsetras Lars, by Fyr, 62A. Nor can one forget Ivar Bo (Kirkemo Kennels) with his Ch. Grei av Kirkemo, 460C, and Harold Sommerstad (Glennas Kennels) with Ch. Glennas Dolly, 1782 K, Ch. Glennas Skrub, 1781 K, and Ch. Jerva, 3448H.

Also prominent in the 1950s were the dogs of Consul E. A. Cappelen Smith (Fjeldheim Kennels), Reidar Stromme (Sorvangen Kennels), Toralf Raanaas (Ryfjeld Kennels) and Sten Abel (Listua Kennels). Others active in the breed included Carl Opseth, T. Amundsen, Thorstein Brenneng,

Ch. Steig av Jarlsberg, bred by
Gerd Berbom, and owned by
Hildur Almo.

Ch. Klegglia's Storm, owned by Birger
Gronvold, Kotofjell Kennels, Norway.

Ch. Tass, 62/4360, select stud dog,
owned by Signe Furuseth.

Ch. Grei av Kirkeno, bred by Alf
Opsahl, Norway, and owned by
Ivar Bo.

Carl Michaelson, A. R. Arneson, P. Larson, S. J. Naess, and Jacob P. Holseng.

One thing that contributed greatly to the advancement of the Norwegian Elkhound was the planned breeding program. Periodically, stud dogs were selected by a supervisory committee of the Norsk Elghundklubb.

Gerd Berbom, who returned to Norway after living in England for a number of years, brought back with her the lovely bitch, Ch. Anna of the Hollow, 1390D. Her Jarlsberg Kennels had three of its stud dogs on the club list at the same time: Ch. Steig of Jarlsberg, Eng. & Nor. Ch. Bamse av Jarlsberg and Brisk av Jarlsberg. Ch. Steig was the standout. He was a masculine dog of exceptional quality, well-known as a hunting dog, and the sire of 10 champions, 7 in Norway and 3 in America. His son, Buster, won the first Best in Show in Norway at the Annual International Show in Oslo on May 30-31, 1953, defeating 891 dogs of all breeds including 68 Elkhounds. Steig's American champions were Am. & Can. Ch. Paal av Jarlsberg, Pelle av Jarlsberg, and Precilla av Jarlsberg.

In the 1960s, Elkhound registrations in Norway numbered about 800 a year: 790 in 1962, 778 in 1963, 819 in 1964, 754 in 1965 and 719 in 1966. The breed ranked fourth in Norsk Kennel Clubb registrations, with the Poodle in first place and the English Setter taking over the Elkhound's second place spot. Although the number of Elkhound breeders and exhibitors was higher than ever before, the other breeds had grown at an even faster pace.

Well-known kennels producing high standard dogs in the '60s included: *Grafjell,* owned by Jon Rua; *Elgens,* Kristian Svestad; *Ryfjelds,* T. Raanaas; *Kalagerasens,* Peder Kalager; *Klegglias,* Kr. Bleka; *Kotofjell,* Birger Gronvold; *Suteras,* Christian and Oscar Svae; *Tuftetuns,* Ingvar Granhus; *Oftenasen,* Magne Aftrat; *Valpasen,* Aagot and Elizabeth Harbitz; *Tortasens,* Jacob P. Holseng; and *Sokomdal,* Arne Furuseth.

A top stud of the period was Klegglias Storm, 61/7943, bred by Kristian Bleka and owned by Birger Gronvold (of *Kotofjell* prefix). One litter by Storm ex Lotte av Kotofjell included Varg, Fell, Lussy, and the famous Driv av Kotofjell, all dogs of exceptional quality.

Driv av Kotofjell, owned by Reidar Stromme, enjoyed fantastic success in the show rings of Scandinavia. He was the first dog to win the "Bamse" trophy, offered by the Norsk Kennel Clubb and competed for at 6 NKK shows each year, and was honored as "the foremost winning dog of the year."

The Tortasens Kennels, owned by Jacob P. Holseng, was another that enjoyed success in selective breeding. From this kennel came world-famous Nor. & Am. Ch. Tortasens Bjonn II, a distinguished winner and a stud dog of considerable merit even before his exportation to the United States, and Bjonn's dam, Ch. Moa, the first bitch to win a Group at an NKK show.

In the 1970s there was a decline in Elkhound registrations, dipping as

37

Nor. Ch. Kuppern (Koppang, 1977). —*Photo, Olav Campbell.*

Nor. Ch. Bella (10027/71), dam of several AKC and Norwegian champions. Owned by Dag Jarn Aalerud.

"King," Ivar Hoelseter. (Best young dog, Jessheim 1975).
—*Photo, Olav Campbell.*

low as 504 in 1971. This was in part due to the formation of a second Elkhound association in the 1960s—the Norsk Elghund Klubb—which advocated registration through the Norsk Jakthund Registere (Norwegian Hunting Dog Registry) rather than the Norsk Kennel Klubb.

New kennel names included: *Glenna,* H. Sommerstad; *Gjetemyra,* Hans Christiansen; *Ruskasen,* Rolf Saetermoen; *Sorvangen,* Reidar Stromme; *Venabu,* Else and Even Riiser; *Grunsetmarka,* Johan Olbergsveen; *Vardetoppen,* H. Sjaastad; *Bjerkedalen,* Per Mauntvedt; *Vindfjell,* Johan Berg; *Elgens,* Kr. Svestad; *Nedreberg,* Kr.Berg; and *Camalot,* regst. Dag Jorn Aalerud and Mrs. G. Misbeek (of the U.S.).

Three young males dominated the show scene in 1971 and 1972—one was to become Int. Ch. Burre (10707/69), by Nor. Ch. Finn ex Deisi, owned by Else and Even Riiser; a second was Nor. & Sw. Show & Field Ch. Ruffs, (68/4275), sired by Nor. & Sw. Ch. Fjall; and the third was Nor. Ch. Buster, (5468/68), sired by Ch. Kalagerasen's Bamse, owned by Eric Enberg. All three were named to the official stud dog list and all three were used extensively in breeding.

In 1973, Bella (10027/71), also sired by Nor. Ch. Finn, was the top winning Elkhound in Norway—in fact becoming the top winning Elkhound bitch in Norwegian show history.

April 1974 dates the beginning of spectacular show careers for two litter brothers, sired by Ch. Noraskog's Milo ex Triksi. They were Int. Ch. Max (13913/72) and Int. Ch. Karat (13911/72). Both dogs were multiple specialty winners, both completed the requirements for International Championship at all-breed shows, both were highly respected hunters, and both were named to the official stud dog list.

The year 1977 was a year of great celebration for the Elghund's friends. The old Norsk Elghund Forbund (League) and the not so old Norsk Elghund Klubb settled their differences and formed the *Norsk Elghund Klubbers Forbund.*

So far that has worked very well. To date, 15 affiliated Elghund Klubbs located in different parts of the country have joined the organization: Follo & Ostfold; Oslo-omradets; Vestfold; Telemark; Agder; Buskerud; Hallingdal-Valdres; Vestoppland; Gudbrandsal; Hedmark; Osterdalen; Norto Trondelag; So. Trondelag; Troms; and Nordland.

The Board of Directors consists of five elected men. The Forbund has elected a breeding committee consisting of three men. These members are well qualified to supervise that program. They have a thorough knowledge of the different pedigrees for males and females and that is of great importance. They also must select the stud dogs. The male must be an excellent hunter and a fine show dog. The rule is that after the stud dog has sired 50 puppies, the committee is to evaluate the offspring. If the puppies are up to expectation, then the stud is again installed. But, if the offspring are not up to expectation, a new stud dog is chosen. For the female

Snella av Suteraas, owned by Ole
Svae.   —*Photo, Per Henriksen.*

Rask (8231/69), owned by H. Sjaastad,
Vardetoppen Kennel.

Show and Field Ch. Karat
(13911/72), multiple Specialty
winner and Official Stud Dog.

Venabu's Gant, owned by Else and Even Riser.
    —Photo, Henriksen.

Hunting champion Garm av Sokomdal (5653/76), owned by Odd Blegen. Winner of the 1980 Three Country hunting competition between Norway, Sweden and Finland.

Gay av Suteraas, owned by Ole Svae.   —Henriksen.

41

Elghund, the rules are the same. She must be a good hunter and also hold her own in the show ring.

To qualify as a champion dog or bitch in Norway, an Elkhound must win three Firsts in Winners class with Certificate, under at least two different judges, and must also score a 1st, 2nd, or 3rd prize at a Field Trial. This last requirement was introduced years ago, and is to a great extent the reason for the relatively small number of champions.

Show dogs are not trimmed or clipped. Even the whiskers are not cut. The nails are expected to be worn down from work afield. A top Elkhound should be able to hunt in the forenoon and be shown in good form in the afternoon. It is a good plan to give the dog a bath prior to the show, if necessary. He should be in good weight so as to present the desired square appearance with wide and deep loin.

Twice a year the Norsk Elghund Klubbers Forbund has judges' seminars both for show judges and for field trial judges. That is the time when every judge must write a critique over every one of 15 Elghunds presented to them. Afterward, the papers are collected and every critique is evaluated. If there are any differences in the critiques, then a discussion will follow. In that way the judging will be more synchronized.

Some time ago it was decided that when an Elghund judge reaches 70 years of age, he must retire. But the club soon found out that was a great mistake. Some of the men were pioneers in Elghund progress. They had the knowledge, experience and foresight. So now they are back again in the show ring and welcome they are.

The first National Specialty of the new Norske Elghundklubbers Forbund was held on February 19, 1978. The judges were Karl Storholm, Olav Campbell and Kjell Oybakken, and they drew 124 gray Elghund entries. Of special interest was the *Brukshundklass* at this show, a class in which only dogs who have obtained hunting prizes may compete. The entry of 18 male Elghunds in this class was the largest ever at a Norwegian show. Norwegian Show and Hunting Ch. Aesop (517/73) was the winner in this class and went on to win First Best in Race for the entire show. The critique by Olav Campbell included the following comments: "The dogs presented here represent some of the very best Elghunds to be found in Norway today. They confirm that we have the breeding stock which makes it possible for us to excel in the quality of our Elghunds (both in outer appearance and in hunting abilities) as compared to other Scandinavian countries; also, in comparison with countries where the people consider only exterior appearance, for example, Great Britain and the United States where they register 7 to 8 times more gray Elghunds per year than in Norway!"

For many years, some people throughout the world have been privileged to purchase fine Elghunds from Norway. Of course the

Trine, Best in Show winning bitch in Norway and Sweden. Owned by Odd and Astrid Strand.

Tuppa av Sokomdal (14827/74), owned by A. Furuseth, Best in Trial at the Follo & Ostfold hunt, 1976.
—*Photo, Olav Campbell*.

DRIV AV KOTOFJELL

Whelped May 26, 1964
NKK #64/6069 - Norwegian Show Champion
                    Norwegian Hunting Champion
SKKR #14573/66 - Swedish Show Champion
                    Swedish Hunting Champion
DSK #302885W - Danish Show Champion

Norsk Gullhund 1966 (Best in all-breed international
                    dog show, NKK, 1966).
Breeder: Birger Grønvold (Norway)
Originally owned by Reidar Stromme (Norway) and
then by Werner Andersson (Sweden).

In the Elghund world there is no international title as such—thus far it has been impossible to assemble the superstars from the countries that raise the breed at an international show. But surely if there was such a title, no one would have merited it as much as Driv.

Norwegians don't sell their best hunters, for they would be very expensive. As a rule, the Elghunters must go through strenuous months of long training, and then the grueling Elghunt. Besides, there are few places where the dogs could be used to hunt moose. However, out of the same litter could come a handsome show dog and these are obtainable.

Hip dysplasia and night blindness are for the most part unknown diseases for the moose hunting Elghunds of Norway. There are few countries in the world where people could produce these healthy, strong, handsome dogs. That is something we should keep in mind and appreciate.

One thing is for sure. We must guard the hunting type of Elghund in the United States and never go back to the roly-poly type we had in the '40s. It would also be to our benefit to engage excellent Elghund judges from Norway now and then. In that way we would know we are on the right tack.

Greta of the North, CD, at Sourdough Gap, Mt. Ranier. Owner, Jerry McClenaghan.

3

The Norwegian Elkhound
in the United States (I)

JUST when the Elkhound first came to America is not definitely known, but the earliest record of the breed in this country apparently is the registration of three Elkhounds in the 1913 American Kennel Club Stud Book:

Koik 170389 (Rap II ex Bibbi), whelped March 1909, gray

Bimba 170390 (Bamse ex Bibi), whelped June 1910, gray

Laila 170391 (Hay ex Binna), whelped July 1910, gray

These three imports (bred by O. Hykket, Carl Olmstead and B. Larsen respectively, all of Oslo, Norway) were owned by Gottlieb Lechner, Weiser, Idaho.

The offspring of these dogs were widely distributed. Some of them went to R. D. Williams, Lexington, Kentucky, who mated them with his own dogs. In his Rookwood Kennels were Norseman, Trondhjem, Svelikin and others. His stock was acquired by two pioneer breeders of Elkhounds in America—Walter Channing (Brixton Kennels, Dover, Massachusetts) and Bayard Boyesen (Vindsval Kennels, Winchester, New Hampshire).

Registrations were few in the early years—only 22 Norwegian Elkhounds were registered by the AKC in the first ten years.

In 1913, the Norwegian Bear Dog, Lady Hilda, won First in the Open class at Los Angeles. In 1914 the Norwegian Elkhound Mich Mich won First in the Open class at Mineola, Long Island, and three years later Gretchen won at the same show.

But it was not until 1924 that the American public got its first real

Mrs. Herbert Hoover and Ronnie av Glitre.

Ch. Rurig av Romsdal and Ch. Ragnhilde av Romsdal, owned by Miss Alice O'Connell.

Ch. Brodd II av Elglia, Skrubb of Green Meadow, Ch. Marko of the Holm and Ch. Martin of the Hollow. Owned by Green Meadow Kennels.

impression of the breed when the imported Ch. Grimm of Lifjell 385780 (Smik ex Lova) was placed fourth in the Miscellaneous Class at Westminster. At the next two Westminster shows the Elkhound was exhibited in its own breed classification and Grimm was Best of Breed. Grimm and his litter sister, Baldra of Lifjell, had been imported in 1923 by Walter Channing.

In 1924, Bayard Boyesen imported five Elkhounds from Norway: two dogs—Ch. Heika av Glitre and Rugg, and three bitches—Heia, Bringe av Glitre and Lydi. Heika, carrying 50% of the blood of the famous Norwegian bitch, Senny II, sired five champions including Ch. Vakker av Vindsval, who was Best of Breed at Westminster four years in succession. Heika was of ideal type, powerful and compact with wedge-shaped head, straight short back and perfect tail carriage. Rugg, a son of that grand old hunter Smik, was famous in the show ring as well as in big game hunting in Norway. Heia, a massive bitch of tremendous bone and substance, was credited with six bears in one winter. Bringe, a daughter of Senny II, was winner of the "Prize of Honor" for 1921.

In 1925, Walter W. Bagge of Des Plaines, Illinois, imported Baruse, a brother of Rugg. Dr. Leon Whitney, famous author of books on dog care and breeding, brought over the bitch Finna (in whelp to Tas). On the West Coast, William H. and Cedelia Maxwell of Lakeside, Washington, imported Senny V from Norway and raised and sold many Elkhounds.

The first import from England on record was Bon Bjerke who came across the Atlantic in 1928. The following year W. F. Holmes of England sent over the first of many Elkhounds bearing the "of the Holm" suffix, Oscar of the Holm. These imports greatly improved the native breeding stock.

The first import from Scotland was Ch. Vingo of Inverailort, bred by Mrs. C. H. J. Cameron-Head. He sired more than a score of fine Elkhounds, including five Kettle Cove champions, three of which were from imported Goro of the Fjiords. Vingo was the first Elkhound to win Best of Breed at both Morris and Essex (in 1933) and Westminster (in 1932). The good-headed, imported Ch. Binne av Glitre repeated the feat and so did imported Ch. Bjonn. Bjonn, who sired two Lindvangen champions in 1935, had a well-proportioned body and excellent tail but is reported to have had a rather narrow skull.

From Canada came Bringe av Solskin and from Sweden came Rapp av Gra, owned by George H. Earle III, then Governor of Pennsylvania. It is said of Rapp, who was Best of Winners at Westminster in 1938, that he had good substance but that his tail was not tightly curled.

Elkhounds were associated with other famous people. For instance, imported Ronnie av Glitre, 929110 (Skrub av Glitre ex Bringe II av Glitre), bred by T. Hemsen, Norway, was owned by President Herbert Hoover—a gift to the President from the people of Norway, a precious token for what he did for his friends over there in their hour of need after World War I. The President transferred one of his Elkhounds, Belleau of Elglia, to famous naval Commander C. E. Rosendahl. Another Elkhound fancier was the King of Sweden, who owned Ch. Pang. Then too, there was Lady Halifax, who was the wife of the British ambassador to Washington and the first President of the British Elkhound Society.

That famous Alaskan musher, Arthur Walden, owned Elkhounds. He said that pound for pound they would out-pull any other dogs, provided that the snow was not too deep for the Elkhound's short legs. A Maine race driver stated that his best dog was an Elkhound, fifteen pounds lighter than the others.

Many of the early Norwegian pedigrees of Elkhounds are somewhat confusing in that there were no less than eight Frams, twenty Fins, six Finns, and goodness knows how many Bamses. Evidently the bloodlines of Skrub av Glitre, Burmann, and Bjonn were much sought after. At least a dozen progeny of Skrub were imported, of which three became American champions. Eight imports were sired by Burmann and ten by Bjonn. No less than 119 Elkhounds were imported prior to 1940, the high in annual importations being 20 dogs in 1933. This, of course, provided a great variety of type and bloodlines for the foundation stock in America.

Oliver F. Holden, Chester, Connecticut, imported a number of Elglia dogs from Johnny Aarflot. Wade Stevenson brought over Ch. Stavsetras Lars from Charles Stavseth, Norway. About the same time the Bradley Martins, Westburg, New York, purchased dogs in England and Norway for their Thistleton Kennels, the name of which was later changed to Balmacaan.

A major importer was the Green Meadow Kennels, owned by W. Scott Cluett and his sisters Edith and Florence, situated in the picturesque Green Mountains at Williamstown, Massachusetts. In the late '30s they housed two dozen Elkhounds including seven champions: Ch. Brodd II av Elglia, Ch. Jerv av Elglia, Ch. Marka of the Holm, Ch. Marko of the Holm, Ch. Martin of the Hollow, Ch. Fourwents Brighde, and Ch. Sonja av Vindsval. All were imported except Sonja. Brodd II and his brother Jerv had moose-hunting records in Norway. Brodd II was Best of Breed three times at Westminster and again at Morris and Essex. Although he was not a large dog (19 inches at the shoulder), he was very stylish and well-proportioned.

Ch. Martin of the Hollow, bred by Mrs. L. F. G. Powys-Lybbe of England, was one of the most influential sires of early American Elkhound history. He produced ten champions (from seven bitches), then a record for the breed. He was described as a very good dark-eyed dog, with nice body and feet, but a little long and carrying a bit of brush on his tail. Martin's

50

Ch. Saga av Elglia (Ch. Skrub av Glitre ex Mausi), owned by Thomas H. White.

Haar Vel's Rusken av Oftenasen. Bred by Magna Aftret, Norway. Owned by Patricia V. Craige and Velma B. Cook.

Ch. Gaupa av Tallo at 1 year of age. A 1950 import from Norway, she was bred by Olav Campbell and owned by L.J. Yettergaard (Avogaard Kennels) in California.

Ch. Tortaasen Ola, bred by Jakob P. Holseng, Norway, and owned by Olav Wallo.

Ch. Bamse av Oftenasen. Bred by Magne Aftret, Norway, and owned by Mr. and Mrs. Henry M. Glasgow, Katrine Glen Kennels.

son, Ch. Olaf av Kongsberg (bred by Robert P. Koenig of Zionsville, Indiana) was sire of nine champions. Olaf's half brother, Rolf of Lindvangen (bred by Priscilla S. Litchfield) was sire of eight champions.

As early as 1927, Lawrence Litchfield, Jr., New Canaan, Connecticut, his wife, and his daughters became interested in the breed. He served as Secretary and then as President of the Norwegian Elkhound Association of America for many years. Later he became vice-president of Alcoa, and moved to Pittsburgh. His Lindvangen suffix figured in the pedigrees of more than twenty champions, and he was a very popular judge of the breed. Mr. Litchfield remained a staunch friend of the Elkhound until his death in 1967.

The Kettle Cove Kennels of Amory Coolidge, Magnolia, Massachusetts, supplied breeding stock to many of the kennels starting in the thirties. Among them were the Romsdal Kennels of Miss Alice O'Connell, Minneapolis, Minnesota. From Ch. Kettle Cove Cora came her Ch. Ragnhilde av Romsdal, the first Elkhound to obtain the Companion Dog (C.D.) title in an obedience trial. A kennelmate, Ch. Rurig av Romsdal, C.D., completed his bench championship in four consecutive shows within nine days and at less than one year of age. Ragnhilde was the dam of four champions, including Miriam Phillips' and Dorothy Pile's Ch. Tronheim av Joywood, Olav Wallo's Ch. Graydal av Joywood, and Barbara Thayer's Ch. Raerta av Romsdal and Ch. Popover of Stonewall.

In 1937, A. Wells Peck and his wife, Catherine, imported Ch. Fourwents Paal from England to head their kennel at Litchfield, Connecticut. Paal became the sire of five champions.

The Pecks' Pitch Road Kennels made some of the most notable Norwegian Elkhound importations to this country, including Ch. Koltorpets Paff from Sweden, Ch. Carro of Ardmere from England, and the celebrated Norwegian-Swedish-Canadian-American Ch. Tortasen's Bjonn II from Dr. Jasper Hallingby in Norway. Bjonn was the first Norwegian Elkhound to win the prestigious Hound Group at Westminster. Whelped in 1952, by Ch. Bamse ex Ch. Moa, he was bred by Jacob Holseng, and was an official stud dog of Norway before his exportation. He was used extensively for breeding in America and produced an impressive line of handsome Elkhounds that included Best in Show winners.

Mr. Peck was for many years the Norwegian Elkhound Association of America's delegate to the American Kennel Club, and he and Mrs. Peck were very active in support of the breed for over three decades.

After judging the Elkhounds at the 1940 Morris and Essex show, Bayard Boyesen said, "There is in all breeds of animals an undefinable quality that marks out the great from the excellent or merely correct. Ch. Binne av Skromtefjell fairly teems with this quality. It might be said that her tail could be more central and that her hind gait could be a bit wider; but this bitch combines in rare degree perfect type and exquisite finish with

Two of the Elkhounds imported from Norway in the 1920s by B. Boyesen (Vindsval Kennels, Mass.). At left, Ch. Heika av Glitre, bred by C.T. Johnsrud; at right, Rugg, bred by Hans Fosse.

Ch. Blakken av Norskfjell, bred and owned by L.M. Tollefsrud.

Ch. Fjeldheims Tito, bred by L. Cappelen Smith (Norway) and owned by Olav Wallo.

Ch. Borgny av Runefjell, owned by Luther Tollesfrud.

the most solid substance." He also observed "The Elkhound is a dog without extremes." Boyesen had to retire from dog activities because of a heart ailment, and his Vindsval Kennels, a landmark for twenty years, was dispersed. He died August 7, 1944.

Other kennels that were discontinued permanently or temporarily during the war were: Kettle Cove, Green Meadow, Balmacaan, Thistleton, and Seven League.

Joseph W. Beatman, later Secretary of the Norwegian Elkhound Association of America, supervised the training of dogs for the Coast Guard in World War II. At first Elkhounds were accepted for Dogs for Defense and some were sent to the Canal Zone, but later only bigger dogs were enlisted. Some Elkhounds were trained as search and rescue dogs whose task it was to locate injured persons and signal their whereabouts by staying with the victim and barking. The Elkhound's method of hunting doubtless suited him well to this task.

Active in Norwegian Elkhound circles from 1932 to 1951 were Mr. and Mrs. Thomas H. White, Cleveland Heights, Ohio. In 1936, Mr. White imported that famous Norwegian Champion, Saga av Elglia, who had three times won the coveted "Prize of Honor" of the Norsk Kennel Klub. This bitch possessed a strong head, heavy bone, tight tail, and beautiful light gray color, and was the producer of six champions.

In his capacity as Secretary of the parent club, Mr. White—an aircraft executive— did much to promote the Elkhound. It was a great shock to the fancy when his private plane crashed in the Potomac River on October 26, 1951, carrying him, his wife, and his daughter-in-law to their untimely deaths. They were on their way to have luncheon with General George Marshall, who had just been given an Elkhound puppy named "Nato" by the high school children of Norway in appreciation for his part in the North Atlantic Treaty Organization.

Barbara Thayer Hall (Stonewall Kennels) began with Elkhounds in 1934. Of the dozens of Stonewall champions, the greatest was probably Ch. Boreas of Stonewall, who died in 1954 at 15 years of age. He was a large, majestic, medium-gray dog with a marvelous disposition and was a good producer, siring four champions. Mrs. Hall showed some red Elkhounds at Westminster in 1941.

In 1949, 13-year-old Patricia Vincent of Norfolk, Virginia acquired her first Norwegian Elkhound, a puppy whose heritage was of Stonewall and Lindvangen lines and who grew up to be Ch. Ulf's Madam Helga, C.D. In 1952, Helga won her C.D. in three trials, bringing her young owner the *Dog World* Award of Canine Distinction. But more important, Helga marked the beginning of what is surely the most famous of American Norwegian Elkhound kennels. (See the story of Dr. and Mrs. Craige's Vin-Melca Kennels in Chapter 4).

In 1951, L. J. Yettergaard (Avogaard Kennels in Fallbrook, California)

The foremost sire of champions in AKC history, all breeds, with more than 200 champion offspring— Ch. Vin-Melca's Howdy Rowdy. A son of BIS-winner Ch. Windy Cove's Rowdy Ringo, Howdy Rowdy was himself a multi all-breed and Specialty Best in Show winner. Pictured with owner Patricia Craige (Vin-Melca Kennels).

Ch. Vin-Melca's Rebel Rouser (1958-1965), outstanding show bitch of her day and a great producer. Her mating with the Pecks' famous Ch. Tortasen's Bjonn II in 1961 set Vin-Melca on course to the eminence it has enjoyed for close to three decades.

Ch. Lady Kazana of Greenwood, first Norwegian Elkhound bitch to go Best in Show in America. Owners, Mr. and Mrs. Winston Scott.

Am. & Can. Ch. Viking, Am. & Can. CD, whelped 1954. Imported from Norway, Viking became a most influential sire. Owned by Mrs. Halvord Hoff.

imported Ch. Gaupa av Tallo (bitch) and Ch. Skrub II av Skromtefjell (dog). Mr. Yettergaard, who was born in Norway, spent many years at sea as a master mariner and when he retired there was no question as to what breed of dog he wanted to own—it had to be the national dog of his native land. He also purchased Ch. Paal av Jarlsberg from Earl Brunsvold.

An important breeder of this era was Dr. Margaret Ascher Beach (Ringstead Kennels), a veterinarian of Forestville, Ct. Dr. Beach donated one of her dogs to Seeing Eye, Inc. as a guide to a blind young woman. She was the breeder of Ch. Bjorgulf Sigurdssen, a great show dog with 9 Group wins and 19 other Group placements, owned by Joseph Beatman.

Other Norwegian Elkhounds to win Best in the Hound Group prior to 1952 included Ch. Binne av Glitre, Ch. Stavsetras Lars, Ch. Thor av Lindvangen, Ch. Tronheim av Joywood, Ch. Vingo of Inverailort, Ch. Gard of Pitch Road, Ch. Thorwald of Kongsberg, Ch. Torfinn av Runefjell, Ch. Bjorn Ringessen of Stonewall, Ch. Sigurd av Roughacres, Ch. Dyre Vaa Trim, Ch. Fraboo, Ch. Gray Rock av Pomfret, Kari's Bena, Rugg av Runefjell, and Ch. Trond III.

Mrs. Nellie B. Wood Hilsmier of Fort Wayne, Indiana, first owned Chows but is better remembered for the many Borzoi and Norwegian Elkhound champions that came from her Woodhill Kennels. Her Ch. Nordic av Woodhill and Ch. Vica av Woodhill were the first Elkhounds to own both American and Canadian championships. Mrs. Hilsmier also owned a sister to Vika, Ch. Ola av Zimmies, who established a record at the time as the dam of ten champions. Seven of these were from the half-brother and sister matings of Ola to Nordic, and the other three were from the mating of Ola to her grandson, Ch. Rugg av Woodhill. These dogs were linebred to the English import Ch. Martin of the Hollow through Ch. Olaf av Kongsberg and Ch. Marcia av Kongsberg.

One of the top winning Elkhounds of the 1950s was Ch. Trond III, owned by Norman T. Fuhlrodt of Des Moines. He was the winner of 16 Group Firsts.

Another top dog of the decade was Ch. Tari's Haakon, C.D., a son of imported Ch. Fourwents Rugg av Aalesund, owned by Florence H. Palmer (Torvallen Kennels) of New Hampshire. Haakon was Best of Breed at Westminster three years in succession, at Chicago International two consecutive years, and at Morris and Essex once. Mrs. Palmer was for many years the treasurer of the Norwegian Elkhound Association of America. Her energies and abilities contributed to the success of such NEAA projects as the annual financial contribution to veterinary research at Cornell University and the club's committee to study the problem of progressive retinal atrophy (PRA) in the breed.

Another breeder who contributed much to the research on PRA was Miss Elsie Healey of Litchfield, Ct. Miss Healey devoted herself to the breeding, housing, raising and care of a PRA test litter of Elkhounds for the research by Dr. D. Cogan of the Howe Eye Clinic in Boston. She was the breeder of such memorable champions as Ch. Kay's Kima of Dragondell and Ch. Leif of Dragondell, CDX, TD.

Leif, the first Norwegian Elkhound champion to acquire the Tracking degree, was owned by the Honorable William A. Timbers, former chief U.S. district judge in Connecticut. Mr. Timbers' Elkhounds frequently accompanied him to court sessions, and an order to "Clear the court!" did not include them. Judge Timbers is a past president of the NEAA, and was for years one of the Board of Directors of the American Kennel Club (including service as its Chairman). He and Mrs. Timbers retain their keen interest in the breed.

Mrs. Edna Mae Bieber (Thornbeck Kennels) is another who served the Norwegian Elkhound well. Her columns in the official American Kennel Club publication, *Pure-Bred Dogs,* provided very informative reading for Elkhound enthusiasts and she helped considerably in alerting breeders to the research being done on PRA. The roll-call of Thornbeck champions included Ch. Thornbeck Lon of Stonewall, Ch. Thornbeck Tyra, Ch. Thornbeck Tristram and Ch. Thornbeck Trygvason. Mrs. Bieber judged at several Norwegian Elkhound specialties.

The Pacific Northwest is an active area of interest in the Norwegian Elkhound. Pioneers of this interest were Mr. and Mrs. Borger O. Lien. Their Northgate strain lies behind many pedigrees there.

In 1952, Mrs. Winston W. Scott of Seattle, Washington acquired the bitch that was to become Ch. Lady Kazana of Greenwood, foundation for a leading kennel of its day—the Greenwood Kennels. Lady Kazana was sired by Napoleon of Northgate, a fine dog purchased by Mrs. Lien from a California kennel, and her dam was Lady Tina, bred by Mrs. Lien and owned by a Mrs. Bryant of Mercer Island, Washington. Lady Kazana was never beaten in the ring by a female. As a producer, she was equally outstanding. Two of her descendants became Best in Show winners (Ch. Baard of Greenwood and Lady Linda of Greenwood), making the Greenwood Kennels the first American kennel to produce two Norwegian Elkhound Best in Show winners. Two littermate offspring not only made championships in quick order, but also acquired the Utility Dog degree with high scores. These were Ch. Just Torvald That's All, UD (owned by Louis H. Priner) and Am. & Can. Ch. Norska of Greenwood, Am. & Can. UD (owned by Lili P. Fowler).

Mrs. Halvord Hoff, owner of the Keyport Kennels in Paulsboro, Washington, was born in Norway, so her love for Elkhounds was a natural one. She purchased her first Elkhound, Ch. Vicki, from Mrs. Lien. After owning Vicki for a while, she decided to add a male. She wrote to Peter Jakob Holseng in Norway, and bought a son of Ch. Bamse ex Ch. Moa. This dog, Am. & Can. Ch. Viking, Am. & Can. CD, was to make as strong an impact on the breed in the Northwest as his brother, Int. Ch. Tortasen's

Ch. Gra-Val's Rolf, first Norwegian Elkhound to win Best in Show in the United States. Bred by Grace E. Vail. Owned by David N. Klegman (Calif.).

Ch. Windy Coves Rowdy Ringo. Purchased as a pet, Ringo's spectacular success in the show ring launched Georgia M. Cole's Branstock Kennels.

Am. & Can. Ch. Wabeth's Gustav, an outstanding winner and producer, bred and owned by Mr. and Mrs. Walter D. Moore. Gustav had 5 all-breed Bests in Show (3 in U.S., 2 in Canada) and sired more than a dozen champions.

Bjonn II, did in the East.

Viking, whelped in 1954, was a key dog in the excellent quality of the Northwest Elkhound. His offspring included such famous dogs as Am. & Can. Ch. Wabeth's Gustav, Ch. Trygve of Keyport, Ch. Wabeth's Bjarne, Ch. Princess Moa of Keyport, and Ch. Ragnaar av Fowlerstad. The innumerable number of champion grandsons and granddaughters included Ch. Gus 'N Zorei's Etterman and Ch. Baard of Greenwood. Also imported by Mrs. Hoff were Ch. Jennie of Skromtefjeld (from Norway) and Ravenstone Brand (from England).

Lili Fowler's (Fowlerstad Kennels at Seattle, Washington) first Elkhound was a Lady Kazana of Greenwood daughter, Am. & Can. Ch. Norska of Greenwood, Am. & Can. UD. Norska was a consistent winner and had a tremendous personality. Mrs. Fowler often took her Elkhounds to children's hospitals, and the youngsters were particularly delighted with Norska's ability to solve problems in arithmetic, barking the correct number in answer to Lili's questions. (She barked according to given signals.)

Mrs. Fowler was very active in the Washington State Obedience Club, and served as its president for two years. Her Am. & Can. Ch. Ragnaar av Fowlerstad, Am. & Can. UD (obtained from Mrs. Halvord Hoff), was sire of Ch. Er-Sue Rikke av Fowlerstad, and grandfather of Ch. Dagne and Ch. Sunde—both of whom had high degrees in Obedience.

Mr. and Mrs. Worth Fowler owned Ch. Baard of Greenwood. Baard, a dog of good size, well-built with a proud carriage, was the fifth Elkhound in the United States to win Best in Show. He was shown extensively, and compiled a record that did much for the breed. It was his success that paved the way for Elkhound wins of the Group and Best in Show in the Northwest. Mr. Fowler served as president of the Norwegian Elkhound Association of America for two years.

Georgia M. Cole's Branstock Kennels housed and bred several fine Elkhounds. Ch. Norda Fylgie of Branstock was the nation's top Norwegian Elkhound bitch for 1965. Georgia Cole, together with Dr. Milo T. Harris, owned Ch. Windy Cove's Rowdy Ringo, a top winning Elkhound of the mid-1960s.

The Norwegian Elkhound was making its impress in California and important in this advance was the Highland Kennels, co-owned by Gladys and Guy Cutter and Craig Tanden. The roll-call was long: Ch. Highland Branstock Renegade, Viking Ruff, Silver's Mikar, Silver's Ladic, Rhondi of Highland—and many more, all champions. The "Three Musketeers"— Gladys, Guy and Craig—did pretty well.

Norwegian Elkhound interest was already strong in the Midwest. When Miriam Phillips purchased the Elkhounds from Alice O'Connell's Romsdale Kennels in Minneapolis, she took over the oldest Norwegian Elkhound establishment in Minnesota. Miss Phillips' Joywood Kennels at

Litter of 14 pups at two weeks, with dam Dyre Vaa Karen II. Sired by Ch. Prins Fron of Maple Leaf, CD. Owned by Mrs. Borger Lien.

Ch. Branstock's Joker Joe, prominent winner owned by Georgia M. Cole.

Am. & Can. Ch. Baard of Greenwood, all-breed Best in Show winner. Bred by Mrs. Winston Scott and owned by Mr. and Mrs. Worth Fowler.

Wayzata, Minnesota went on to establish a long, illustrious history of its own. Joywood Elkhounds were especially celebrated for their hunting ability. Ch. Trondheim av Joywood, CD, whelped in 1941, was the first Elkhound to win a Group in Minnesota. Like his dam, Ch. Ragnhilde av Romsdal, CD (the first Elkhound to win CD in the United States), "Trony" was an Obedience star, too. He was the sire of champions and Obedience titlists and the strain he represented was a very important influence in the Midwest.

Miss Phillips was active in the organization of the Norwegian Elkhound Association of Minnesota, which became the first affiliate club to the parent Norwegian Elkhound Association of America. The first international Norwegian Elkhound Convention was held in connection with the 1959 Specialty of the Minnesota club, at which Mrs. Kitty Heffer of England was the judge. Miriam Phillips continued her love of Elkhounds until her death in 1978. A fund in her memory was established by the Minnesota club to provide funds for education of Elkhound owners and breeders.

Few kennels have enjoyed a success as spectacular as that achieved by the Crafdal Farms at Stow, Ohio. Owned by Bob and Glenna Crafts and registered in 1958, in less than a dozen years it became the largest establishment for Norwegian Elkhounds in America and set many records (for its time) in winning and breeding. In this span 190 Elkhounds bred at Crafdal were finished to championship, 24 of them in the year 1966 alone, and Crafdal entries won 5 all-breed Bests in Show, over 100 Group Firsts and many Specialties.

Crafdal's top winner, and one of the breed's all-time top producers of champions, was Am. & Can. Ch. Trygvie Vikingsson. "Tryg," whelped June 1955, was one of the first litter bred by the Crafts. He was the top winning Elkhound in America through 1959, 1960 and 1961, scoring 3 all-breed Bests in Show, 21 Group Firsts and 10 Specialties. Am. & Can. Ch. Tryglik Turi and Am. & Can. Ch. Thor Mors Thunder also won Best in Show.

Mr. and Mrs. Crafts took special pride in handling their own dogs in the rings. Bob, whose breed participation included service as president of the Norwegian Elkhound Association of America, died in 1969. Mrs. Crafts retired from the dog game in 1976, but continues her interest in environmental concerns and keeps several Elkhound companions with her always.

The Pomfret Kennels of Mrs. Susan D. Phillips at South Royalton, Vermont was a small but productive kennel which produced several fine dogs that won at shows in their own right. Most outstanding of these was Ch. Gladjac Royal Oslo, the winner of the 1962 Norwegian Elkhound Association of America Specialty Show—the first National Specialty. This show was judged by Johnny Aarflot and Ch. Gladjac Royal Oslo went on

4

The Norwegian Elkhound in the United States (II)

IN THIS CHAPTER you have a roll-call of kennels active in the current Norwegian Elkhound show scene in the United States. Arrangement is alphabetical, based on the owner(s)' last name.

In looking back over nearly 80 years of Elkhound history in America, we learn much from tracing the overlapping and intertwining of pedigrees. Of course, the pedigrees we are most familiar with are those of the prominent show winners. As we follow the role that the important dogs of the past play in the pedigrees of many of today's dogs, we realize what a debt is owed to yesterday's breeders who cared enough for the breed's welfare to try to always breed true to the standard.

It is pleasing to observe how many breeders have persevered for long years with Norwegian Elkhounds as their primary interest. The longevity and dedication of these breeders makes significant the contribution their dogs are making to today's bloodlines. Thus, in the summary that follows one will find the names of kennels already long familiar to the fancy as well as names of newer breeders who are picking up the pedigree threads out of which our present breed tapestry is woven.

Anderson, Patricia and Jim — *Hammerfest* — Brainerd, MN

When their first litter of Elkhounds turned out to be one happy wiggling female puppy, Pat and Jim devoted a litter's worth of time to her. She ultimately became Am. & Can. Ch. Hammerfeste's Jente To, Am. & Can. UD. Their experience training for the Obedience ring has led them to prominence with subsequent Elkhounds, Ch. Camalot Trulle Super Special, Am. & Can. CDX and Camalot Trykk Everlastin Luv, Am. & Can. CD. In addition to their Elkhounds, the Andersons have been instrumental in establishing the Finnish Spitz breed in this country and own the first dual-titled Finnish Spitz in the U.S. Both Pat and Jim have served as officers of the Norwegian Elkhound Association of Minnesota and Pat was elected President of the Finnish Spitz Club of America in 1985.

Ausse, Craig and Kathy — *Craika* — North Olmsted, OH
With breeding base of stock from Camalot Kennels that incorporated the correct hunting type and good Elkhound temperament, the Ausses' champions include Ch. Camalot Trulle's Spec'l Delite, Ch. Camalot Tryste's Carbon Copy, and Ch. Harka's Aramis. A breeding of Spec'l Delite to Ch. Sangrud Kolle's Tomten produced a litter of exceptional pups including Ch. Craika Sangrud Tomten's Toby. All the Ausses' pups are raised in the kitchen with all the tender loving care the family can muster.

Backer, Bob and Lynn — *Rob-Lyn Elkhounds* — Palatine, IL
Rob-Lyn's Ch. Lurich Sasste Prince of Hoy, a multi Best of Breed and Group placement winner and winner of the 1977 Northeast Illinois Norwegian Elkhound Specialty, was chosen by Field Enterprises to represent the breed in a book for children. Rob-Lyn's champion roll includes Ch. Houndhaven's Zephyrus.

Balder, Kim — *Asgaard* — Grandville, MI
Mainstay of the Asgaard Elkhound clan is a very special bitch, Ch. Titanic's Holly Holy—a specialty Best in Show winner and an outstanding producer. Holly was a breed winner and Group placer even at the advanced age of nine years, and she won the Veteran Bitch Class at the 1986 NEAA Specialty. Her daughter, Ch. Asgaard Sugar 'N Spice (owned by Sharon Poulin) was Winners Bitch at the 1980 NEAA National Specialty, repeating the win of her dam in 1978. Another Holly daughter, Ch. Asgaard's Critic's Choice, is also producing well for the Balders.

Blackburn, Ruth D.V.M. — *Tantalum* — Dalhart, TX
Dr. Ruth Krueger Blackburn received her D.V.M. degree from the University of Minnesota and while a student there, acquired an Elkhound from Miriam Phillips of Joywood Kennels. Ruth was active in the affairs of the Norwegian Elkhound Association of Minnesota for a number of years until she moved for professional opportunities to work with Dr. Wayne Riiser, early researcher in the area of Canine Hip Dysplasia. Her interest and love of Elkhounds continued, even after a move to Utah, marriage to Mont Blackburn and three children occupied her life.

When time and circumstances permitted, Ruth again brought an Elkhound into her life—Elbamoor Betsy's First Flag acquired from Doris Transue. "Ten," as she is known, produced a good litter bred to Ch. Sangrud Kolle's Tomten. Two pups from this litter have already received Group placements and Specialty wins—Tantalum Tomten's Anders and Tantalum Tomten's Alpha. Ruth is ever a student of the breed and uses her video camera to study judging at shows, dogs at home, pups as they grow and kennels she visits on her extensive travels in her van. Ruth's genuine interest in the welfare of Elkhounds is contagious and one cannot help but enjoy the breed a little more after meeting Ruth and her Elkhounds.

Blair, Martha — *Martrick* — Delaware, OH
In the wake of its foundation stud, Ch. Martrick's Viking Venn, Martrick has produced some impressive champions in the Ohio area. Mrs. Blair has been especially interested in researching the red color gene in Elkhound pedigrees.

Am. and Can. Ch. Titanic's Holly Holy, owned by Kimm Balder (Asgaard).

Ch. Martrick's Vikings Venn, owned by Martha and Richard Blair (Martrick's).

Marbran's Beefeater, bred and owned by Thomas Braly.

Braly, Tom and Marilyn — *Marbran* — Los Angeles, CA

Tom has served as president of the Norwegian Elkhound Association of America, and he and Marilyn have been hard workers for the Norwegian Elkhound Association of Southern California. Although they do not breed many litters, preferring to devote time to their dogs mostly as family pets, over the years they have owned some outstanding winners.

Brennan, Joan and Terri — *Tiro* — Norco, CA

Joan and Terri Brennan are one of several mother-daughter teams operating Norwegian Elkhound kennels, and their Tiro Elkhounds show the love and care that both devote to the dogs. Terri began handling dogs in the show ring at a very young age and was a top competitor in Junior Handling. Their Ch. Tiro's Satin Lady and Ch. Vindarne's Fire 'n Ice were fine producers. Combined with the Rikkana bloodlines (through Ch. Rikkana's Brother Love), their bitches have produced some good looking youngsters. Joan and Terri have long been active in the Norwegian Elkhound Association of Southern California and Joan was chairman of the NEASC Specialty that followed the 1982 NEAA National Specialty.

Britt, Connie — *Starranne* — Denver, CO

Connie has had Norwegian Elkhounds since 1967 and has been an exhibitor since 1974. She is owner of the Best in Show winner, Ch. Zachary of Starranne. Active in local kennel clubs, Connie also finds time to serve on the Board of Directors of the NEAA and served as chairman of the 1980 NEAA National Specialty held in Denver.

Brooks, Margaret — *Bjorndal* — Durango, CO

Few Elkhounds have the chance to grow up as close to nature as do the Bjorndal dogs. Situated in a beautiful setting in western Colorado, the Brooks find the breed ideal for the ranch life of their family. Their interests include Obedience work with their Elkhounds, and over the years Margaret has served as a trainer for the local Obedience club. She has worked closely with Charles and Ann Christiansen of Middensted Kennels to produce good Elkhounds and offspring of Ch. Bjorndal's Middensted Pika, CD, have figured in both Bjorndal and Middensted pedigrees. The Brooks also raise Morgan horses.

Carter, Nick and Carol — *Elgshire* — Cypress, TX

The Carters are justly proud not only of the championships and Obedience titles scored by their dogs, but also of their hunting ability. It started in 1970 with purchase of an Elkhound, Lady Natashia, acquired primarily as a family companion and protection dog. They soon discovered that she had show potential as well and within a year Lady Natashia had earned her CD degree and her championship. Ch. Woodsprings Cytoezar, CD and Ch. TNT Snara Cael of Elgshire, CD formed the foundation of Elgshire Kennels. Elgshire's Beowulf, owned by George Mathews of Florida, hunted boar and deer there. The Carters also co-owned Ch. Solv Kriger av Bifrost with Mike and Penny Wilkes.

Chisholm, Diane and Jerry — *Surtsey* — Burton, OH

In 1967 the Chisholms acquired their first Elkhound, who became Lady Margareta, UD. She achieved her Utility Dog title before the age of three and Diane

Ch. Zachary of Starranne, multiple Best in Show winner. Owned by Connie Britt.

Ch. Vindarne's Fire 'n Ice av Tiro, owned by Joan and Terri Brennan (Tiro) and Sandra Whittle.

Ch. Normark TNT Promise's Moose, owned by Bob and Diana Coleman (Normark).

says, "Fortunately she was trained before anyone told us Elkhounds are hard to train." At age ten, "Nana" was still an active, useful dog, hunting vermin on a regular basis. The first champion for the Chisholms was Ch. Thor V-Kari, CDX, who won Best of Opposite Sex from the Veterans' Class at the Garden State Specialty Show when she was eight years old. All the Elkhounds at this small kennel are house dogs and the goal of these conscientious breeders is to breed sound dogs with sound dispositions.

Christiansen, Charles and Ann — *Middensted* — Georgetown, CO

The Christiansens' small kennel is situated high in the Rocky Mountains where the dogs are conditioned by daily exercise on the mountainous slopes. The founding stock of their kennel combined the Crafdal and English Ravenstone lines in Ch. Tora of Middensted. A breeding to Edna Bieber's Ch. Thornbeck Frey produced Ch. Matchless of Middensted, and another to the Scottish import Ch. Melreva Knute produced Ch. Foltz Tauni of Middensted. Tauni was BOS under Norwegian judge Ralf Campbell at the NEAM Specialty in 1975, and at 12 years of age and in better condition than many younger dogs won the Veterans' class at the 1984 Specialty under Ralf's father, Olav Campbell. More recently the Christiansens have shown a fine young dog, Ch. Middensted's Diamondgill Rolf. They have had a long standing interest in genetics and Charles has published some interesting pedigree studies on such problems as Progressive Retinal Atrophy and Dwarfism in the breed.

Claus, Betty and Freeman — *Redhill* — Tustin, CA

Getting their start as approved judges of Norwegian Elkhounds, Betty and Freeman have branched out and are approved to judge many other AKC breeds. They were the proud owners of Ch. Vin-Melca's Saga of Redhill, and they have bred some fine champions including Ch. Redhill Tuff Stuff. They have worked hard for the NEAA in several capacities; Betty has served as Recording Secretary and as the official delegate to the AKC. Generous hosts, they have frequently entertained exhibitors at the Southern California specialty shows. In conjunction with the 1984 National Specialty, they invited all exhibitors to their home for a gala farewell party to cap that event.

Coleman, Diane and Bob — *Normark* — Convoy, OH

Starting with dogs of Crafdal lines, the Colemans have bred a successful line of Elkhounds and pride themselves on showing their own dogs. Many of the pups they have sold have also been handled successfully by their owners. A top producer is their Ch. Normark TNT Promise's Moose, CD, with several champion offspring to his credit. Moose's dam, Ch. Crafdal TT Mist-Imp Promise is also a top producing bitch. One of Moose's offspring, Ch. Normark TNT Promise's Sjera, was exported to Israel where she became the dam of the first native-born Israeli Elkhounds. Along with their breeding program the Colemans work with the local 4-H program helping children train their dogs and learn about dog care.

Coplin, Herbert — *Stormevaer* — Hubbard, OH

Stormevaer Kennels, owned by Herbert Coplin, was started in 1970 with stock from the Crafdal line. Later, dogs were purchased from Vin-Melca Kennels and handler Jack Patterson campaigned Ch. Vin-Melca's Hex av Norflamma to many show ring wins. Mr. Coplin owns several Newfoundlands as well as Elkhounds.

70

Ch. Folte Tauni of Middensted, owned by Chas. and Ann Christiansen (Middensted).

Ch. Middensted Diamondgill Rolf, owned by A. and C. Christiansen.

Ch. Vin-Melca's Saga av Redhill, owned by Freeman and Betty Claus.

Ch. Elgshires Solitaire, CD, bred and owned by Nick and Carol Carter (Elgshire).

Ch. Vin-Melca's Vagabond, top winning dog of all breeds in America for 1970; winner of 25 all-breed BIS and over 80 Groups (including Westminster '70 and '71). Owned by Patricia V. Craige.

Craige, Patricia and Dr. John — *Vin-Melca* — Carmel, CA

From its beginning in 1949, with 13-year-old Patricia Vincent showing her Cocker Spaniels and Norwegian Elkhounds in Junior Showmanship, up through today's continued winning, the story of Vin-Melca Kennels is one of the most successful and remarkable in all dogdom.

No other Norwegian Elkhound kennel has racked up the number of show wins and records achieved by Vin-Melca. With the assistance of her veterinarian husband, Dr. John, Pat Craige has maintained a breeding and campaigning program that has kept Vin-Melca dogs at the top of national show dog rating systems for many years. The number of top dogs produced and campaigned by the Craiges, and by those who have acquired Vin-Melca dogs, and the enormous amount of travel, work and time represented in accomplishing these records, is staggering.

Pat's success began with Ch. Ulf's Madam Helga, CD, who she trained and exhibited in Obedience as well as breed competition. After graduating from college, Pat acquired an eight-weeks-old puppy from Pitch Road Kennels who became Ch. Vin-Melca's Rebel Rouser, a top producer with six champions to her credit. Her descendants have been the mainstay of the Vin-Melca pedigrees. Rebel Rouser was herself a Group winner and was listed in the Top Ten of various rating systems from 1960 through 1964. Her son, Ch. Vin-Melca's Vickssen, established a fine show record and was an all breed Best in Show winner as well as a Specialty Best in Show winner.

Vickssen became the sire of a very special dog bred by Fred and Lois Turner and campaigned by Pat Craige, Ch. Vin-Melca's Vagabond. Vagabond was named

Ch. Vin-Melca's Vickssen, all-breed BIS winner, No. 1 Elkhound in the U.S. for 1966 and 1967. Sire of three BIS winners. Owned by Patricia V. Craige.

Ch. Vin-Melca's Last Call, all-time top winning Elkhound bitch with 14 all-breed BIS and 8 Specialty BIS. Co-owned by Pat Craige and Dody Froehlich.

Number One dog of all breeds for his show record in 1970—the only Elkhound to ever achieve that status.

Vagabond's half brother, Ch. Vin-Melca's Howdy Rowdy, also bred by the Turners, holds the breed record as Top Producing Sire with well over 200 champion offspring to his credit. Sired by Best in Show winning Ch. Windy Cove's Rowdy Ringo, out of the Turners' fine bitch Ch. Vin-Melca's Vikina, Howdy proved to be a prolific producer and contributed to the bloodlines of kennels all across the country. His own show record included five all-breed Bests in Show and Best of Breed at the 1968 National Specialty. In 1975, at the age of ten, Howdy Rowdy was Best of Breed at the Norwegian Elkhound Association of Northern California specialty show from the Veterans class—over an entry of more than a hundred dogs, most of whom were sired, grandsired or great-grandsired by him. At this writing he stands as not only the top Norwegian Elkhound sire of champions, but also the Number One sire of champions for all breeds in AKC history.

More top honors go to the wonderful Ch. Vin-Melca's Nimbus. His record will not soon be surpassed. From 1976 through 1979, he was the Number One Elkhound and in 1978 and 1979 was Number One Hound at AKC shows. His winning included 63 all-breed Bests in Show and 177 Group Firsts including two at Westminster Kennel Club. His offspring, Ch. Vin-Melca's The Smuggler and Ch. Vin-Melca's Southern Rain, have continued the family tradition as winners.

Not only the Vin-Melca males have compiled enviable show records. In recent years Pat Craige has campaigned a top winning bitch to Best in Show honors—Ch. Vin-Melca's Last Call, "Gilda", who started her career when still a puppy by being named Winners Bitch at the National Specialty in Denver in 1980 and then going Best of Breed at the Columbine Specialty Show the next day. Bred to Ch. Ronan's Cupcake Prince, Gilda produced a litter of 8 champions.

To an uncommon extent, dog shows have been a way of life for the Craiges and Vin-Melca dogs. Their influence has spread throughout the breed as others have utilized their bloodlines and campaigned with the Vin-Melca kennel name as their banner. But none can duplicate the magic that Pat Craige works when she enters the ring with a Vickssen, Howdy, Vagabond or Nimbus. Ever the expert handler, the picture of Pat and an Elkhound in the ring are forever a part of Elkhound folklore.

Elvin, Karen and Kristin — *Sangrud* — Minneapolis, MN

Karen Elvin and her daughter, Kristin, represent the second and third generation of their family to devote their time to the Norwegian Elkhound. Elkhounds were the family pets of the Blood family and Karen and her three sisters grew up with them. Often, at fun matches, one of the faithful dogs would be entered in three or four classes so that each child could have a "turn" to show the dog. From 1943 on, the family raised a few selected litters from Silver Queen av Zimmies; her last litter was sired by Ch. Paal av Jarlsberg before he was sent to California.

After graduation from college, Karen's interest in the breed persisted and Ch. Lisa av Sangrud became the foundation of the Sangrud Elkhounds. In combination with the interests and expertise of Sue Ann Erickson (Ericsgaard Kennels), a few select litters were bred with an eye to the importance of soundness of structure and health. During the late 1960s, Karen served on the committee that worked to clarify the breed standard, and for several years she was the NEAA's breed columnist in the AKC's official magazine, *Pure-Bred Dogs—AK Gazette*.

74

Ch. Vin-Melca's Hex av Norflamma, owned by Herbert Coplin (Stormevaer).

Ch. Sangrud Kolle's Tomten, bred and owned by Kristin and Karen Elvin (Sangrud).

Ch. Ericsgaard Munin, bred and owned by Sue Ann Erickson.

75

Karen's love of the breed is shared by her daughter Kristin who has competed in Junior Showmanship with the Sangrud Elkhounds, qualifying to attend the competition at Westminster Kennel Club in 1985. Only a few litters are raised by the Elvins. Standards of OFA hip certification and normal eye status are but some of the considerations kept uppermost in planning litters. Strong linebreeding to imported lines combined with the strengths of the old lines from Sangrud, Ericksgaard and the Windy Cove imports have produced soundness of movement, type and temperament of special quality.

In one litter from Ch. Camalot Trykk Windrow Tapper and Sangrud's Tanrydoon Kolle, Ch. Sangrud Kolle's Tapper and Ch. Sangrud Kolle's Tomten are both Group winners. Their sister, Ch. Sangrud's Windrow Tinker, was Winners Bitch and BOS at the 1984 NEAM Specialty under Mr. Olav Campbell.

While showing the dogs is an enjoyable addendum, the breeding of sounder, more typical dogs that will reproduce the best in the breed consistently is the long term goal. Their greatest pleasure comes from having others enjoy the companionship of Elkhounds from Sangrud as much as the Elvin family has enjoyed the dogs for more than 40 years.

Erickson, Sue Ann — *Ericsgaard* — Webster, MN

From the time her first Elkhound convinced Sue that there was no better family dog to be had, the study of the breed has been a top priority for her. Beginning her breeding program at a time when news of such difficulties as hip dysplasia and PRA was just coming to light, Sue sought the knowledge necessary to try to eliminate these problems from the breed, so that the average pet owner need not go through the heartache of dealing with incapacitating handicaps in a pet dog. She studied pedigrees and pursued scientific knowledge most thoroughly, including a comprehensive survey of functional anatomy as related to the structure and movement of the Elkhound. Her films of several national specialties are of excellent quality and are unique studies in the movement of our dogs.

The fine Elkhounds produced by her careful planning and study include the two brothers, Ch. Ericsgaard Munin and Ch. Ericsgaard Mirkel, offspring of Ch. Ericsgaard Fram bred to a daughter, Ch. Ericsgaard Lefle. Intensive line breeding produced consistent results, and while structure and soundness were important, temperament and health were first considerations.

The Ericsgaard Elkhounds were raised with the Erickson children, a common theme with Elkhound fanciers. Elkhound intelligence is not without its problems however; Sue spent considerable time retrieving the puppies that one bitch tried repeatedly to lead away from home. The mama apparently felt it was time to push the youngsters out of the nest and let them make their own way.

In recent years, the Erickson family has moved to a country home only to find that country life does not necessarily mean more freedom or leisure time for raising pups. Two recent additions to the Erickson menagerie have been a pair of Nova Scotia Duck Tolling Retrievers with a greater inclination to stay at home than the worldly Elkhounds.

Forsythe, Milton and Marty — *MilMar* — Houston, TX

The Forsythes have campaigned several top winners under the Vin-Melca kennel name including Ch. Vin-Melca's Buckpasser and Ch. Vin-Melca's the Snuggler. Their own breedings have used the Vin-Melca lines and they have some

Ch. Jackson's Storm av Nitro, owned by Glenn D. Frisby (Buckcreek).

Am. and Can. Ch. Rob-Ron's Trollson's Tarpan, owned by Delores Friend (Vendall).

Ch. Vin-Melca's Mount Vernon, owned by Chas. and Peggy Giles (Pegaway).

winning youngsters sired by Ch. Vin-Melca's Call To Arms including Ch. MilMar's Buttons and Beaus.

Frey, Cecelia and Dennis — Ambridge, PA

In the late 1970s the Freys acquired from Karen and Russel Weir the dog that was to become Am. & Can. Ch. Ivarson av Ruskar, CD. At the age of 16 months he earned his American CD and shortly thereafter repeated that title in Canada at the same time he earned his Canadian championship. The Freys have been active in supporting the formation of the new Norwegian Elkhound Club in the Cleveland, Ohio area. Cecelia is Chairman of the 1988 National Specialty, to be held in Cleveland.

Friend, Dolores — *Venndal* — Toledo, OH

Dolores Friend established her Venndal Kennel in 1970 with purchase of Rob-Ron's Trollson's Tarpan, who became an American and Canadian champion. Her second purchase, Trilla's Tami of Cricklewood, was bred to "Tor" producing Am. & Can. Ch. Venndal Trollyk Torak. The Heart of Ohio Norwegian Elkhound Association was founded in 1975 when Dolores' mother also became deeply interested in the breed and saw a need for breeder and exhibitor communication in the area.

Frisby, Glen D. — *Buckcreek* — Springfield, OH

For the Frisbys, no breed can compare to the Elkhound in versatility, personality, friendliness and love of the hunt. They chose the breed as the one best suited to life with two growing boys. Says Glen, "We tried other breeds but none compared to the Elkhound." After owning Elkhounds as pets for several years, Glen acquired Jackson's Recall as a show-quality bitch and she produced several promising youngsters for their program. The Frisby roll of champions include Ch. Jackson's Storm av Nitro.

Froelich, Fred and Dody — *Vin-Melca Alaska* — Anchorage, AK

For some years the Froelichs were residents of Colorado and were active in kennel club activities there. Their first Elkhounds were trained to CD degrees. Their association with the Vin-Melca Kennels has included the co-ownership of several top winning dogs, and when they moved to Alaska their Vin-Melca dogs (including such notables as Ch. Vin-Melca's Hornblower and Ch. Vin-Melca's Mandate) dominated the Alaskan shows for some time—often winning Best in Show. They often travel to the lower states to assist Pat Craige with exhibiting the dogs at specialty and large all-breed shows. Dody has served as a Director of the NEAA, and as breed columnist in the AKC's official *Pure-Bred Dogs—AK Gazette*. She has been the co-breeder of several Vin-Melca champions, and is a co-owner of the winning Nimbus son, Ch. Vin-Melca's the Smuggler.

Giles, Charles and Peggy — *Pegaway* — Southlake, TX

While living in Kansas in the early 1970s, the Giles started their Elkhound kennel with purchase of Ch. Tanrydoon Imp's Toreadero (Ch. Windy Cove Tascadero ex Windy Cove Mona's Importance) from John and Sharon Henschel. He was followed by purchases from Vin Melca Kennels including Ch. Vin Melca's Hallelujah, Vin-Melca's Honestly, Ch. Vin-Melca's Saucy Sadie and Ch. Vin-

Ch. Vin-Melca's Hornblower, Best in Show winner. Owned by Dody Froehlich.

Ch. Vin-Melca's Mandate, multi all-breed Best in Show winner. Owned by Dody Froehlich.

Ch. Bifrost's Starlight Love, CD, owned by Stanley and Joan Green (Norden).

Melca's Mount Vernon. From Don and Betty Duerksen they obtained Ch. Nordsvaal's Social Whirl. In 1976 the Giles moved to the Dallas-Ft. Worth area of Texas and changed their kennel name from Wymelk to Pegaway.

Green, Stan and Joan — *Norden* — Thousand Oaks, CA
Aiming to produce sound, stable Elkhounds, the Greens have had success both in the show ring and in Obedience. Their Orion of Norden, UDT, was the first Elkhound to obtain a UD and a tracking degree in California. They acquired a nice bitch from Mike and Penny Wilkes who became Ch. Bifrost's Starlight Love, CD, and this group-placement winner produced a fine litter sired by Ch. Tarroma's Hooper. Ch. Bifrost's Lovin Spoonful, CD, was campaigned to both titles by the Greens. Stan has served on the board of the NEAA and Joan judged Sweepstakes for the Northeastern Illinois Norwegian Elkhound Association in 1984.

Gustafson, Sven and Jackie — *Midwest* — Steger, IL
The Gustafsons have produced some of the top Elkhounds in the Illinois area. Their first Elkhound, Lady Gustafson of Chicago, was acquired in the late 1960s and became the dam of their foundation brood bitch, Midwest Tania. In the early '70s the Gustafsons purchased Ch. Crafdal Tryg N Thor Grand Prix who became a multiple Group placement winner and sire of many champions and Obedience titlists. Ch. Stina of Raisen, owned by Sven Gustafson and Mary O'Brien, was a top producing dam of the mid-'70s.

Hall, Beatrice, Laura and Edward — *So Merri* — South Merrimack, NH
Searching for a family dog for her young children, Bea Hall wanted a medium-sized, rugged, good-tempered, healthy dog. The Elkhound filled the bill excellently. Since the acquisition of that first companion, the Halls have raised over forty litters and have had considerable success in the show ring in the New England area. As they grew up, Laura and Ed shared their mother's interest and enthusiasm for the breed. The present day So Merri Elkhounds trace their pedigrees back to that first fine Elkhound, Ch. Bea's Lady Jade. Among their more recent winners are Ch. So Merri Kid Curry, Ch. So Merri Darth Vader and So Merri Reise Elv. Ed has served as president of the Norwegian Elkhound Association of America as well as of the Norwegian Elkhound Minuteman Association, and is an approved judge of Norwegian Elkhounds and several other Hound breeds. Laura serves as NEAA historian.

Hall, Rick and Lana — *Rikkana* — Lakewood, CO
Since starting in Elkhounds in the 1960s, when the Halls lived in Michigan, Rikkana Kennels has produced well over a score of champions. Lana is quite a competitor and her dogs are very well handled in the ring. Over the years Rikkana has combined the lines of Howdy Rowdy and their imported English dog Ch. Ravenstone Teodore with fine success. Teodore, who had a fine show record handled by Margaret Mott, became a top producing sire with many champion get.

Ch. Rikkana's Free Wheeler was a Best in Show and multi-Group winner of the '70s. At the 1984 National Specialty, 12-year-old Ch. Rikkana's Look At Me Now won a top quality Veterans Bitch class to the cheers of the spectators. Other notable dogs bred by Rikkana include Ch. Rikkana's Brother Love and Ch. Rikkana's What A Love.

Ch. Rikkana's Free Wheeler, Best in Show winner. Owned by Lana Hall (Rikkana).

Ch. Ravenstone Teodor, import, owned by Rick and Lana Hall (Rikkana).

Ch. Rikkana's Look At Me Now, owned by Lana Hall (Rikkana).

Ch. Freyja av Greenmountain, owned by Janice Hemphill (Cibola).

Ch. Cibola Brother Silas, bred and owned by Cibola Kennels.

Ch. Crafdal Tryg N Thors Grand Prix, owned by Sven and Jacquie Gustafson (Midwest).

Ch. Harka's Rising Moment, multi Group winner. Bred and owned by Harry and Kay Hawn (Harka).

Hawn, Kay and Harry — *Harka* — San Ramon, CA

Another small kennel that takes the future of the breed seriously is this owned by Kay and Harry Hawn. Though they have not raised large numbers of litters, they have over the years bred more than 30 champions—dogs of good type and happy disposition that will influence the breed positively in years to come. Their Ch. Harka's Sampson has been an influential sire, and their Ch. Harka-Diablo's Gamay Rose has been both an excellent producing dam and a sparkling showgirl. Her offspring by Ch. Camalot Bella's Trykk include Ch. Harka's White Linnen, Ch. Harka's Private Collection, Ch. Harka's Cinnebar and Ch. Harka's Aramis.

Hemphill, Janice — *Cibola* — Castle Rock, CO

The Cibola story began, as many do, with "getting a dog for the family." That dog, Ch. Freyja av Greenmountain, was to become matriarch of the Cibola kennel and the dam of several champions. Showing dogs was not their original goal, but they have certainly come to be a significant part of the Colorado dog show scene. Ch. Cibola Brother Gideon and Ch. Cibola Brother Silas (both sired by Ch. Vin-Melca's Nordic Storm) were both rated in the Top Ten in 1979.

Daughter Casandra has handled many of their homebred dogs to championship. The untimely death of Janice's husband, Henry, left her with the entire burden of the kennel operation, but she and Casandra have carried on the breeding and showing of their nice Elkhounds. Their primary goal has always been in the best interests for the dogs and several of their pointed dogs have been placed in homes with more regard for the dog's happiness than for a show career.

Huber, Nelson — *Nel-Von* — Denver, CO

Nelson Huber is now an approved judge of Norwegian Elkhounds.

His association with the breed has taken him from the East Coast to the high Rocky Mountains. Originally living and showing dogs in the Mid-Atlantic states, he became a professional handler and finished many champions in this way. Raising a few litters along the way, he has shown many dogs of his own breeding to their championships and to Group placement wins. Most beloved of his dogs was Ch. Valdemar's Winter Storm, a grand veteran who continued to win at a very advanced age and was always a crowd pleaser.

After moving to the Denver area, Nelson continued as a professional handler, winning with dogs of several breeds. He handled Connie Britt's Ch. Zachary of Starrane to a Best in Show win. In recent years Ch. Valdemar's Critic's Choice, a dog of his breeding, has been a consistent winner.

Indeglia, Dr. Robert and Katheryn W. — *Tekdal* — Narragansett, RI

The Indeglias acquired their first Norwegian Elkhound in the late 1950s after seeing the breed and meeting several members of the Norwegian Elkhound Association of Minnesota at dog shows in the Minneapolis area, where Bob attended the University of Minnesota Medical School as a resident.

Their first champion was Ch. Tassar av Eriksen, shown to his championship by Larry Downey. "Caesar" was soon joined by Cedarstone's Vidundergut (Ch. Wabeth's Gustav ex Ch. Cedarstone's Zorie), obtained from Thelma Heyworth, and Finn's Tekla av Narvikwood, obtained from Frances Hubbard. Both dogs attained their championships and Tekla provided the basis for their kennel name as well as their first home-raised litter, sired by Ch. Wabeth's Gustav. From this litter came Gus's HiLo av Tekdal, a foundation bitch for Tekdal.

In 1966 Ch. Mikkel of Keyport was purchased from Mrs. Halvor Hoff of Seattle, and was shown in the Midwest to a nice record. "Mike" was mated to both HiLo and Tekla, producing several nice litters. When the Indeglias returned to the East Coast, Tekla was acquired by John and Sharon Henschel.

Reestablishing their kennel in Narraganset, Rhode Island, the Indeglias acquired other breeding stock including Ch. Vin Melca's Countdown. More recently they have campaigned Ch. Tom Terrific of Tekdal and Ch. Tekdal's Joe DiMaggio.

Dr. Indeglia has served the Norwegian Elkhound Association of America in several offices including President, Vice President and as its delegate to the American Kennel Club. He is also an AKC-approved judge of Elkhounds and all other Hound breeds.

Jackson, Johnnie and Virginia — *Jackson's* — Carroll, OH

As with many other enthusiasts, the Jacksons' love of the breed and interest in the show ring developed out of ownership of a pet Elkhound. Their foundation stock included Ch. Nel-Von's Storm Bell and his son, Ch. Jackson's Oden Storm. Storm Bell was also the sire of Ch. Jackson's Hot Shot, the Jacksons' first homebred champion, and Ch. Jackson's Grey Dawn. Another prominent winner bred by the Jacksons was Ch. Jackson's Nitro, who in turn sired Ch. Jackson's Stormy av Nitro (owned by Glenn Frisby). With aim of introducing new blood in their lines the Jacksons acquired Ch. Wabeth's Buck av Jackson and Ch. Wabeth's Windy av Jackson from the Wabeth Kennels in Washington state.

Several of the Jackson dogs have been successfully used as coon hunters.

Jelinek, Lori — *Charilor* — Cicero, IL

Lori began her association with Norwegian Elkhounds in the Obedience ring as the owner of Daniel's Dusti Fawn, UD and Ch. Lordan's Sweet Gypsy Rose, CDX. In the breed ring, litters from her Ch. Midwest Lordan's Sweet Charity have done well. Charity when bred to Ch. Norlund's Jon Steiner av Vinland produced Ch. Lordan's Viken Warrior, Ch. Lordan's Trailblazer, Ch. Lordan's Sweet Princess and Ch. Lordan's Sweet Sasha. Bred to Ch. ThomThom Hextar Love Bird she produced ThomThom Lordan's B-Sweet P and Ch. Lordan's Viking Storm. A repeat of this breeding has produced some promising youngsters.

Lori has been a hard worker for the Northeastern Illinois Norwegian Elkhound Association and has served as Secretary, Vice President and President of the Norwegian Elkhound Association of America.

Jones, Marietta — *Woodsprings* — Shreveport, LA

A busy and creative person, Marietta Jones was instrumental in the publication of the two issues of *Great Gray Dogs*. Her skills as a photographer are well known to dog show exhibitors in the southern states. She served as the photographer for the National Specialty in Massachusetts in 1982, even though a trouble-plagued automobile trip almost prevented her from getting there.

She has bred a few Elkhounds under the Woodsprings prefix, including Ch. Woodsprings Etterman's Utter Von. She also has a strong interest in Elkhound

Ch. Valdemar's Winter Storm, multiple Group and Best in Show winner. Owned by Nelson and Yvonne Huber (Nel-Von).

Ch. Woodsprings Eterman Uter Von, owned by Marietta Jones (Woodsprings).

Ch. Tekdal's Joe Di Maggio, owned by Dr. Robert Indeglia (Tekdal).

history and memorabilia, and collects things from all over the world if they relate to Elkhounds. She even has a fine English automobile hood ornament statuette of one of the Great Gray Dogs.

Keszler, Arnold and Fern — *Forest Hills* — Oregon City, OR

Forest Hills aptly describes the setting for this small but dedicated Elkhound kennel. Starting in 1964 with a pup purchased from Marie and Joe Peterson named Windy Cove Wendy's Comanche (who easily finished to championship), they have bred carefully and selectively over the years. They imported a bitch from Sweden named Tuffmars Pia av Algvallen, who when bred to Ch. Windy Cove Mona's Mr. Imported, a son of Ch. Windy Cove Mona av Oftenasen imported in utero, gave them a fine bitch in Forest Hills Arna. Their goal remains constant—a few good ones, carefully bred and home raised.

Korneliusen, Lee and Diana — *Sirdal* — Bothell, WA

The Korneliusens did a thorough research of many breeds before starting their kennel and chose the Norwegian Elkhound as their ideal. Their kennel name, Sirdal, reflects the geographic origin of Lee's family in Norway and means "South Valley."

Their first dog was Sirdal's Thor av Vikesland, obtained from Tony Wilson, and showing him became a rewarding hobby. Establishing a breeding program also involved careful research. Their first bitch, Sirdal's Sonja av Galaxy, had nearly completed her championship when she was tragically lost. As a replacement they obtained a daughter of Ch. Vin-Melca's Nimbus and Ch. Vin-Melca's Victoria who became Ch. Vin-Melca's Just Plain Jane. Jane has produced several promising litters and the Korneliusens feel that their years of study and planning are paying off in the quality of Jane's offspring.

Von Kugler, Joan and Don — *von Kugler* — San Bruno, CA

Although they have bred just a few, the von Kugler Elkhounds are well known in the California area. Notable among their dogs is Ch. von Kugler's Avenger, sired by Ch. Haar Vel's Rusken av Oftenasen. Avenger's dam, von Kugler's Thorina, is the dam of five champions—an excellent producer. Terry von Kugler, Joan and Don's daughter, has done much of the showing of the dogs and is a skilled young handler.

Lawton, Viki and Bob — *Vikiro* — Dovsman, WI

Vikiro Kennels had its start in New Jersey, where the Lawtons lived in 1976. Their first bitch, obtained from Doris Transue and Edna Mae Bieber, was Bermarba's Elske Tara (by Ch. Vin-Melca's Huck Finn ex Thornbeck Kynde). In 1977, from Mari Misbeek, they obtained Camalot Tryste's Trinket, sired by Ch. Ravenstone Teodore out of Mari's imported Ch. Camalot Ruff's Tryste av Bella. Trinket proved to be a marvelous show dog, enjoying every minute of her ring time, and was owner-handled to many Bests of Breed. She was the Top Winning Norwegian Elkhound Bitch of 1980.

A breeding of Bermarba's Elske Tara to Ch. Camalot Ruff's Trogan av Bella produced three winning males: Ch. Vikiro Tara's Macho Man (BOS Junior Puppy at the 1980 National Specialty in Denver); Ch. Vikiro's Silver Shadow (a BOB and Group placement winner); and Ch. Vikiro Tara's Adventurer, who finished his

Ch. Forest Hills Arna, bred and owned by Arnold and Fern Keszler (Forest Hills).

Sirdals Heads Up (at 8 mos.), owned by Lee and Diana Korneliusen (Sirdal).

Ch. Von Kugler's Avenger, owned by Joan and Don Von Kugler.

Ch. Jo-Cala's One and Only, bred and owned by Jon LaBree, Jr. and A. Stranahan.

Ch. Ivar of Pitch Road, CD, owned by Janet Maier (Polestar).

Elka Sonja II, owned by Carol and Bob Loitfellner (Hoyna).

championship with a Group first. A breeding of Trinket to Ch. Vikiro Tara's Macho Man has also produced three champions to date: Ch. Vikiro's Ravishing Ruby; Ch. Vikiro's Gold N' Sunshine; and Ch. Vikiro's Genuine Jade.

LaBree, Camile and Jon — *Jo Cala* — Hanover Park, IL
With their children as interested in showing dogs as Mom and Dad, the LaBrees have had considerable success with their homebred dogs. They have combined the bloodlines of an imported English bitch, Ch. Barskimming Sonda, and Ch. Rikanna's Independence, and they have produced some nice stock by outcrossing to Ch. Titanic's Freddie Fudpucker. They have several Group placements with their young Ch. Jo-Cala's The Gray Ghost. Jon and Camile have served the Northeastern Illinois Norwegian Elkhound Association as officers and tireless workers. Camile has also served as an officer and director of NEAA and Jon is an AKC-approved judge of Elkhounds. Still they find time to show their crop of young Elkhounds and the Elkhounds' friend, a Whippet.

Loitfellner, Carol and Bob — *Hoyna* — Ingleside, IL
The Hoyna breeding program, based on imported bloodlines out of Norway's foremost hunting and show champions and developed with careful research, has been a successful one despite limited showing. The top priority here is maintaining the traditional Elkhound hardiness and intelligence in their stock.

Lux, Maureen and Rudy — *Tarroma* — Thousand Oaks, CA
The Luxes have built a solid foundation, combining the lines of Windy Cove Kennels and Rikkana Kennels to produce some good winners and producers. From their bitch Ch. Windy Cove Ruffen's Romance, bred to Ch. Windy Cove Tara's Nimbusson, they got Ch. Tarroma's Hooper, who in turn sired some nice offspring including Ch. Tarroma's Silver Sunshine, a Group winning bitch. Their future seems assured with such quality.

Lyas, Beverly — *Tyken* — San Jose, CA
Beverly has been involved with Elkhounds for many years, and has been successful in combining some of the best of the California lines. In the 1970s she acquired (from Lucille Waterman) a son of Ch. Vin-Melca's Howdy Rowdy who became Ch. Tyken's Hustler. Hustler, himself a fine winner, sired more than a score of notable champions on the West Coast.

Maier, Janet — *Polestar* — Monaca, PA
Polestar is a small, private kennel breeding a line noteworthy in both show and Obedience in the U.S. and in Canada. Janet's Ch. Ivar of Pitch Road, CD, sired many breed and Obedience titlists including Am. & Can. Ch. Polestar's Arcturus, CD (owned by Robert L. Maier and Joyce Diamond); Can. Ch. Ivarsson of Ruskar, Am. & Can. CD (owned by Dennis and Cecilia Frye); and Ch. Trojan's Kaia (owned by Sandi Peterson).

Mazarro, Frank, Carol and Laura — *Ledgerock* — Huntington, CT
When they chose an Elkhound puppy from a nice litter bred by Florence Smith, the Mazarros did not realize how extensive a family venture it would become. The team of their daughter Laura with Am. & Can. Ch. Kim Kima's of

Walter Moore with Wabeth dog sled team.   Wabeth Toralf of Greenwood is the lead dog.

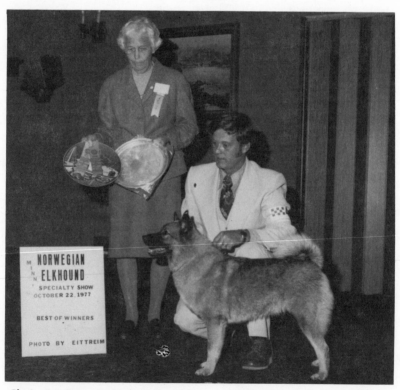

NORWEGIAN
MINN ELKHOUND
SPECIALTY SHOW
OCTOBER 22, 1977

BEST OF WINNERS

PHOTO BY EITTREIM

Ch. Lu Per Canssom Mo's Major Girl, owned by E. Gary and Marlene Oliver, going Best of Winners at NEAM Specialty 1977 under judge Gerd Berbom.

Ch. Vikiro Tara's Adventurer, owned by Bob and Viki Lawton (Vikiro).

Ch. Windy Cove Ruffen's Romance, owned by Rudy and Maureen Lux (Tarroma).

Ch. Tyken's Hustler, sire of 24 champions. Owned by Beverly Lyas and Diane Eastman.

Am. and Can. Ch. Kim Kima's of Stonylea winning BOS at the 1974 NEAA National Specialty under judge Olaf Roig of Norway, handled by young Laura Mazarro, owned by Frank and Carol Mazarro (Ledgerock).

Ch. Fromar's Nordic Pardner, pictured in win of RWD at 1976 NEAA Specialty. Bred by Fromar Kennels (Frank and Rose Martino) and later owned by Carol and Gary Minnich.

Stonylea was to be a delight to many friends and fans during the years they competed. Laura was only 11 years old and Kim only 13 months old when she finished him to championship. Together they went on to many honors including Laura's top of the world win of Best Junior Handler at Westminster K.C. and Kim's win of Best Opposite at the 1974 NEAA National Specialty under Norwegian judge Olaf Roig. Kim won 150 Bests of Breed and had 25 Group placements. The Mazarros have always been concerned with the homes their dogs go to, and champions out of their carefully planned breeding program include Ch. Ledgerock's Mr. Personality and Ch. Kim's Turn Out of Ledgerock.

Martino, Frank and Rose — *Fromar* — Millersville, MD

The Martinos are charter members of the Potomac Valley Norwegian Elkhound Association. Their interest in the breed dates from 1958 when they were acquainted with Jack and Mary Brownson (Galaxy Kennels) who owned Elkhounds that served their family as both hunters and pets. Some time later Rose received, as a Christmas present, the dog that was to become their foundation bitch, Ch. Vin-Melca's Solitaire. "Teri," as she was known, produced eight champions and thus ranks among the breed's top producing bitches. The Martinos limit themselves to two or three dogs and breed most selectively.

Misbeek, Mari — *Camalot* — Santa Barbara, CA

After owning an Elkhound pet during the late 1960s, the Misbeeks decided to devote their time and energy to the best the breed has to offer. In order to better understand the Elghund in its native land, Mari took lessons in the Norwegian language so as to be able to write and speak with Norwegian breeders and judges. After several months of study they imported Camalot's Tuften av Trondelag, bred by Magne Grotan of Norway.

In 1973 they spent a month in Norway to learn and to acquire good breeding stock for their kennel. While there, Mari enjoyed the honor of being allowed to serve as "judge in training" at a major show judged by Olav Campbell. Most impressed with the winner of this show, a bitch named "Bella," they learned that she was a champion and also, that she was the beloved pet of a young boy, Dag Jorn Aalarud. So they returned to America with the promise of puppies from Bella, but not Bella herself.

In June 1974 two puppies from Bella, sired by Norwegian Field and Show Ch. Ruffs, 68/4275, arrived in California. They became Ch. Camalot Ruff's Trogan av Bella and Ch. Camalot Ruff's Tryste av Bella, and both have made significant contributions to the breed through their offspring.

The following spring Bella was again bred to a top Norwegian champion— Trogen (10267/72) and again the puppies came to the United States. One of them, shown for the first time at the 1976 NEAA National Specialty judged by Dr. Jesper Hallingby, Camalot Trulle av Bella, was Winners Bitch and soon finished her championship. A consistent winner, Trulle produced many outstanding offspring including the top Obedience contender, O.T. Ch. Camalot Trulle Ayla, CDX, owned by Marilyn Rotier, and Ch. Camalot Trulle's Spec'l Delite, owned by Craig and Christopher Ausse.

Bella's final contribution to the quality of U.S. Elkhounds came in 1976 from a repeat of the breeding that produced Trulle. The young pups that came from

Norway later became Ch. Camalot Bella's Trykk and Ch. Camalot's Tigger, both of whom have sired fine quality dogs. Remarkable also was the bitch puppy that came from this breeding—she became the first Obedience Trial Champion in Elkhound history, O.T. Ch. Camalot's Bella Tigra, co-owned and trained by Don Rotier.

Trogan, Tryste, Trulle, and Trykk have not only added a great deal to the quality of our breed in the United States, but their offspring have been exported to Israel and Australia as well, spreading their influence still farther.

The Camalot Kennels record stands as an exceptional example of careful study and dedication to quality. Since 1972 they have bred more than 30 breed champions, 15 of which have been Specialty Show winners. With such care and concern this is a record that is sure to grow. Mari has also judged Puppy Sweepstakes at regional Specialty Shows in recent years.

Moore, Walter and Betty — *Wabeth* — Gardiner, WA

For more than 25 years, the Moores' lives have been shared by their Elkhounds, and their dogs have made significant contributions to many other kennels throughout the country. It began when they were attracted to a newspaper picture of Lady Linda of Greenwood, who had just won a Best in Show. Walter and Betty agreed that they could be very interested in a breed that looked like that. Some months later they contacted Linda Scott, owner of the Greenwood Kennels in Seattle, and acquired Sonja of Greenwood. They were not interested in showing her but Mrs. Scott persuaded them to enter her once "just for fun." Sonja won a blue ribbon and they were hooked! She soon completed her championship and was bred to Mrs. Halver Hoff's Norwegian import, Ch. Viking. A second breeding of Sonja to Viking produced the well-known Ch. Wabeth's Gustav, a Best in Show winner and sire of Best in Show winning offspring.

Over the years the Moores have produced many fine champions, among them Ch. Wabeth's Brenda, Ch. Wabeth's Betze, Ch. Wabeth's Brigand, Ch. Vin Melca's Betze Ross, and Ch. Wabeth's Blue Bonnet. But they feel there is more to life with Elkhounds than showing—the dogs have accompanied them on many family outings to the mountains and Walt has used them as sled dogs on many occasions.

Mott, Margaret — *Kamgaard* — Harris, NY

Kamgaard started as a childhood dream when Maggie Mott owned her first Elkhound as an eight-year-old child. Showing, raising and loving Elkhounds has become a way of life for her. More than 50 Kamgaard champions have been bred or owned by her and she considers those who have purchased Kamgaard Elkhounds as "extended family"—a close group of good friends bound by a common interest.

Kamgaard bloodlines are particularly strong on the distaff side. Ch. Kamgaard Bonnie Parker rates as a Top Producer, and Ch. Kamgaard Keepsake and Ch. Kamgaard Kiss Me Kate are also notable for their show records and their offspring. In 1984 Ch. Kamgaard Kit N' Kaboodle was bred to Ch. Kamgaard The Kissing Bandit and then exported to England where she whelped her litter in quarantine. She returned in whelp to a top English stud and thus provided a great exchange of bloodlines.

As a professional handler, Maggie has been instrumental in finishing and campaigning dogs for other Elkhound fanciers. Notable winners she has handled include Ch. Ravenstone Teodor and Ch. Fredrika's Field Marshal, and she has

Ch. Camalot Bella's Trykk, Norwegian import. Bred by Dag Jorn Aalerud, and owned by Mari Misbeek (Camalot).

Ch. Camalot's Trulle av Bella, Norwegian import. Bred by Dag Jorn Aalerud, and owned by Mari and Caren Misbeek.

Ch. Camalot Ruff's Tryste av Bella, Norwegian import. Bred by Dag Jorn Aalerud, and owned by Caren and Mari Misbeek.

shown over 100 Elkhounds to championships. But her strongest interest is in the line she is creating with her breeding program.

In 1983 Maggie had the honor and pleasure of judging the British Elkhound Club's Diamond Jubilee Championship show with an entry of over 300 dogs—a special tribute to her knowledge and skill. In addition to a bustling career as handler and breeder, she has been active in the affairs of the NEAA since 1963, and in those of the Garden State Norwegian Elkhound Club. She also keeps busy with her hobby, photography. Her favorite photo subject? Elkhounds, of course.

Oliver, Gary and Marlene — *Peer Gynt* — Mankato, MN

The Olivers acquired their first Elkhound and much of their early knowledge of the breed from their Mankato neighbors, Chuck and Dot Pryor. As their interest increased, they acquired from Luke Perry the puppy that was to become Ch. Lu Per Canssom Mo's Major Girl ("Jory"), their foundation bitch. Marlene returned from a trip to England with a puppy from the Llychlyn Kennels who grew up to be Ch. Llychlyn Idris. A litter from Ch. Peer Gynt Act I Solveg's Song and Ch. Redhills Tuff Stuff produced a winner in Ch. Peer Gynt Act II Tuff E Nuff, owned by Carol Harmon. Marlene has taken an active part in the affairs of the Norwegian Elkhound Association of America and was elected Recording Secretary in 1986.

Patterson, Molly — *Vinland* — Oklahoma City, OK

Molly Patterson started her Vinland Kennels in 1964. Her first dog, Var Loki av Algon, CD, was the boss of the house for more than 14 years. He traced his roots to old American Elkhound stock like Ch. Sigurd av Roughacres. In 1967 Molly purchased Ch. Nor Elks Lady Lisa, a descendant of Ch. Tortasens Bjonn II. In 1969 she imported Ch. Vesle Frikk from Else and Even Riiser of Hobol, Norway. Frikk had no trouble winning his championship and as a sire passed on his qualities of excellent gait and extraordinary lightness on his feet. One of the fine champions out of the combining of American and Norwegian lines at Vinland has been Ch. Vinland's Genuine Risk.

Perry, Luke and Pat — *Lu Per* — Lakeside, CA

Located on a one-acre estate near San Diego, Lu Per Kennels has raised and shown both Elkhounds and Salukis. Foundation of their breeding program was Ch. Crafdal Tryg N Thors Ron, who enjoyed a successful show career in the early 1970s and sired many champions. His offspring and descendants include Ch. Lu Per Tryg N Thors Winston, Ch. Lu Per Tryg N Thor's Candor, Ch. Lu Per Tryg N Thors Trina and Ch. Lu Per's Wayward Traveler. These dogs have provided the foundation stock for several other kennels including the Sventre Kennels of Shirley Smith and the Peer Gynt Kennels of Gary and Marlene Oliver.

Peters, Sandy and Ron — *Rai-Mai* — Cleveland, TN

Starting small, the Peters have added to their breeding stock carefully. The mainstay of their kennel has been a fine bitch, Ch. Harka's Morning Glory, CD, bred by the Hawns. She has produced some nice winners. One, now Ch. Rai-Mai Buccaneer, was a Sweepstakes winner at the 1982 NEAA National Specialty in Massachusetts and has sired winning stock.

Ch. Kamgaard Keepsake, top Elkhound bitch of 1979. Bred and owned by Margaret K. Mott (Kamgaard).

Ch. Kirkssted Kamgaard Kelly, bred by Bob and Ruth Ness, and owned by Margaret K. Mott (Kamgaard).

Ch. Kamgaard Kit 'N Kaboodle, Hound Group winner exported to England in whelp to young Kamgaard The Kissing Bandit and then imported back to the United States in whelp to a top English stud. Bred and owned by Margaret K. Mott.

Ch. Kamgaard Kiss Me Kate, CD, Specialty BIS winner. Her CD was earned in 3 trials with 2 Top Scoring Hound awards along the way. Owned by Bob and Ruth Ness. Bred and handled by Margaret K. Mott.

97

Ch. Vesle Frikk, by Nor. Ch. Finn ex Deisi. Owned by Molly Patterson (Vinnland).

Am., Mex. and Can. Ch. Crafdal Tryg N Thors Ron, sire of 10 champions. Owned by Luke and Pat Perry (Lu Per).

Ch. Rai-Mai's Buccaneer, pictured at 6 mos. in Sweepstakes win at 1982 NEAA Specialty. Owned by Ronald and Sandra Peters (Rai-Mai).

98

Ch. Asgaard's Sugar 'N Spice, owned by Sharon Poulin (Tonian).

Ch. Frederika's Field Marshal, all-breed Best in Show winner. Co-owned by Edna May Bieber and Jean Hart.

Ch. Oakwood's Jack-O-Lantern, owned by Sylvia J. Sizemore (Oakwood) and James P. Stever.

Peterson, Marie and Joe — *Windy Cove* — Atascadero, CA

When Marie and Joe Peterson set out to find a companion for their three active young sons in 1953, they little realized the extent to which Elkhounds would become their way of life. Living in Washington state at the time, they first acquired an Elkhound bitch from Mrs. Halvor Hoff and then a male from Marge Pugh's Coulee Meadow Kennels. They soon became involved in all-breed and Obedience club work, and their interest in handling and training their own dogs grew apace. Their kennel name, "Windy Cove," reflects the prairie weather of the Spokane area.

Over the next years, their kennel stock increased through the acquisition of the dogs that became Ch. Windy's Tusko of Greenwood, CD, and Ch. Baadkarls Tona of Windy Cove. In three litters, these two dogs produced 16 puppies, of which nine finished to championship. Many of these dogs figure prominently in pedigrees throughout the country. Prominent among them were Ch. Windy Cove Silver Son, owned by Gladys and Guy Cutter, and Ch. Windy Cove Rowdy Ringo, owned by Georgia Cole. Ringo sired Ch. Vin-Melca's Howdy Rowdy and was himself a Best in Show winner.

As their sons grew up, the Elkhound breeding program advanced. Ch. Windy Coves Sweda became a top producer (dam of 10 champions) and lived to 14 years as a beloved pet of the Peterson sons.

In 1965 the Windy Cove family moved to California—a major undertaking considering the many dogs involved, the building of a new home and kennels, plus adjusting to the much warmer climate.

After the move, the efforts to improve their stock continued. From Norway they imported a fine puppy who became Ch. Windy Cove Tass of Oftenasen. Two years later Tass was joined by his litter sister, Windy Cove Mona av Oftenasen. She had been bred in Norway to an exceptional male and delivered her litter shortly after her arrival. She was awarded Best of Opposite Sex at the 1968 NEAA Specialty by Norwegian judge, Olav Campbell. Mona contributed much to Windy Cove bloodlines, as well as to the lines of many other kennels throughout the United States.

The Petersons traveled to Norway several times, continuing to select good dogs to bring back to America to strengthen their pedigrees. The combination of these new bloodlines with the old produced strong, typical hunting-type Elkhounds and the Windy Cove dogs consistently won championships and important show placings for the Petersons and those that had placed faith in their breeding program.

A breeding of their Ch. Blackbrook Lady Tara O Tass to the record-winning Ch. Vin-Melca's Nimbus produced Ch. Windy Cove Tara's Nimbusson, a consistent winner and producer in recent years. Another top producing bitch in their kennels is Ch. Windy Cove Bicen's Cut Crystal who was dam of the 1984 National Specialty winners—Windy Cove Chief Cochise and Ch. Windy Cove Indian Maiden.

After more than 30 years with the breed the Petersons remain dedicated to breeding better dogs. All Windy Cove breeding stock is OFA certified and their concern for health and soundness is reflected in the continued success of their dogs. Even though the Peterson sons are now grown, with families of their own, they live close by and still share an interest in the dogs. Marie became an approved judge of the breed in 1980 and has judged at several important Specialties.

Ch. Windy Cove Tara's Nimbusson, the No. 1 male Elkhound of 1982, and the No. 1 sire in 1983. By Ch. Vin-Melca's Nimbus ex Ch. Blackbrooke Lady Tara O Tass. Bred and owned by Joe and Marie Peterson (Windy Cove).

Ch. Windy Cove Jr. Bicentennial winning Best in Show in follow-up to WD win at the 1977 NEA of Minnesota Specialty under judge Miss Gerd Berbom of Norway. Karen Elvin presents the trophies. Bred and owned by Joe and Marie Peterson (Windy Cove).

Ch. Blackbrooke Lady Tara O Tass, owned by Marie and Joe Peterson (Windy Cove).

Ch. Windy Cove Tass av Oftenasen. Imported as a puppy. Specialty BIS winner and sire of 17 champions. Owned by Marie and Joe Peterson.

Ch. Windy Cove Mona av Oftenasen, litter sister of Ch. Windy Cove Tass av Oftenasen. Dam of 7 champions in one litter. Owned by Joe and Marie Peterson (Windy Cove).

Phelps, Rosemary and Bob — *Windrow* — Baldwin, WI

The Windrow Elkhounds have the advantage of country living on the Phelps' Wisconsin farm plus trips to their northern Minnesota and Wisconsin hunting retreats. Often, the whole family—kids, dogs and all—spend time in the woods where the Phelps' Elkhounds and Labrador Retrievers can hunt to their heart's content.

After an experience with two lovable Elkhounds of dubious background, who were plagued with serious health problems, Rosemary set high standards of health and soundness for her dogs. Their few litters have been of good quality and the purchase of the pup who was to become Ch. Camalot Trykk Windrow Tapper added new strengths. His daughter, Ch. Sangrud's Windrow Tinker, finished her championship under Norwegian judge, Olav Campbell at the 1984 NEAM Specialty, but much prefers to hunt and is the dam of a litter of excellent, correct hunting type. Tinker has been known to find the grouse on hunting expeditions when the Labradors missed!

Poulin, Sharon — *Tonian* — Andover, MA

Although Tonian is a small kennel, owner Sharon Poulin has established a nice record with it in a few short years. Her foundation bitch, Ch. Asgaard's Sugar 'N Spice was Winners Bitch at the NEAA National Specialty in 1980 and received an Award of Merit at the 1982 Specialty. Spice has further proven herself as the dam of several champions. Sharon is a member of the Norwegian Elkhound Minuteman Association.

Pryor, Charles and Dorothy — *Pebble Point* — Arroyo Grande, CA

The Pryors' loving concern for their Elkhounds is evidenced by the fact that whenever they travel away from home, ALL the dogs go along! Their motor home is outfitted to accommodate the dogs and they are often seen with their portable pens set up outside the parking site at shows and vacation spots.

The Pryors got started with the breed while living in Minnesota. Their first champion, Ch. Pebble Point Eryk av Meshka got Dot enthused about conformation showing. Chuck's main interest has been Obedience work and he put CD degrees on several of their dogs while Dot's handling enabled them to gain their championships.

They acquired Lu Per Tryg N Thor's Silver Mist from Luke Perry and she easily made her championship and was bred to Eryk, producing several champions including Ch. Misty Eryka av Pebble Point and Ch. Misty Sonne av Pebble Point. A fine young male acquired from Marie and Joe Peterson also quickly made championship—Ch. Windy Cove Bicen's Tatoo. Bred to Eryka, Tatoo has produced fine offspring including Kristi and Duane Olson's Pebble Point Tarek's Sonda, CDX.

Deciding that the Minnesota winters were too hard to deal with, the Pryors moved to California in 1983, where they again lived in their motor home for eight months with all the dogs until their new house could be built.

Ricks, Tom and Betty — *Oshima* — Chesapeake, VA

On the East Coast, Oshima Elkhounds have made a name for the Ricks in the show ring. They are the owners of Ch. Oshima's Windstorm, Ch. Vin-Melca's

103

Chinook and Ch. Rikanna's What A Love. Tom is a recently elected member of the NEAA Board of Directors.

Roby, Barbara — *Liseldun* — Lyme Center, NH

Nestled in the hills of northern New Hampshire, Barbara Roby's Liseldun Kennels provides 100 acres of rugged landscape to enhance the natural qualities of the Norwegian Elkhound that she values so much. Although she finished her first champion—Ch. Silver Skii of Pomfret—in 1954, it was not until 1969 that she realized her dream of having her own kennel and breeding program. She chose as her foundation Ch. Solveig of Pomfret, purchased as a puppy from Susan Phillips—out of one of the last litters raised at Susan's famous Pomfret Kennels. From Solveig has come a succession of champions including Ch. Rivendell's Brand, Ch. Rivendell's Liv and Ch. Kim's Turn Out of Ledge Rock. Barbara's goal has always been to produce Elkhounds of consistent high quality, suitable for breeding, showing and as family pets. Her success in this is perhaps best seen in such dogs as the Group-winning Ch. Liseldun's Cirion (owned by Susan Maguire) and the nation's first Norwegian Elkhound certified Hearing Ear Dog, Liseldun's Irish Maggie (owned by Ann McClusky).

More recently, breedings to Ch. Camalot Trykk av Bella and Ch. Red Hills' Tuff Stuff have produced such winners as Ch. Liseldun Frieda and Ch. Liseldun Viktor for Barbara. She serves as the NEAA Information Center and is the author of the NEAA breed pamphlet, "*The Norwegian Elkhound*."

Ross, Paul and Nina — *Misty Tara* — Memphis, TN

Although Paul and Nina Ross had owned Elkhounds since the early 1950s, active training and showing of their dogs and the establishment of Misty Tara Kennels began in the '60s. Their Ch. Crafdal Thor Mhors Paulette, UD, was not only one of the all-time Obedience greats, but also was dam of nine champions. Their Ch. Misty Tara Kyrietuf Mho, a Group placement winner, also produced several champion offspring.

In 1977 the Rosses imported two dogs from the Lillabo Kennels in England. Ch. Lillabo Grimm, one of these dogs, has made a particularly significant contribution to American bloodlines through his offspring. His lines, combined with the bloodlines imported from Norway by Mari and George Misbeek (represented in Ch. Camalot Ruff's Trogan and Ch. Camalot's Bella Trykk) have given the Rosses several nice winners in recent years.

As an educator, Dr. Nina Ross has maintained a strong interest in puppy education and Obedience work. Paul has served on the Board of Directors of the parent NEAA, and both Nina and Paul are AKC-approved judges of Elkhounds and several other breeds.

Sanders, Janet E. — *Skjonberg* — Minneapolis, MN

When Jan Sanders decided to get herself a dog, she selected a Norwegian Elkhound—obviously influenced by the strong Norwegian traditions of the Minnesota area in which she grew up. After a long search, the right puppy—Skjon Frossen Jenni Rose—became part of the Sanders household. Through Jenni, Jan learned much about Obedience training and the wonderful Elkhound temperament. Jenni earned her CD degree in short order and in time produced a fine litter of puppies sired by the Norwegian import, Raidar, owned by Ingrid Halverson. Jan

Ch. Solveig of Pomfret, one of the last of the Pomfret champions bred by Susan D. Phillips, owned by Barbara D. Roby (Liseldun).

Ch. Stillhavets Jack Daniels, owned by Buzz and Virginia Sawyer (Norgren) and always shown by their daughter, Kelly, who was 9 years old at the time of this pictured BOB win (on to GR3).

Ch. Norgren's Ravishing Ruby, bred by Buzz and Virginia Sawyer and owned by Windy Cove Kennel (Joe and Marie Peterson).

acquired a puppy from Don and Betty Duerksen who grew up to become Ch. Nordsvaal's Kippen Vinne. Kippen introduced Jan to conformation shows and has produced some fine puppies including Ch. Skjonberg's O Min Dov Nonne, whose sire was Ch. Camalot Tigger—an imported dog that Jan purchased from Mari Misbeek. Tigger completed his championship within a year of his move to Minnesota.

In her work with mentally handicapped and stressed children in the Anoka, Minnesota area schools, Jan has found her dogs to be an invaluable aid; the dogs are often able to "communicate" with a stressed unhappy youngster in a way that adult humans cannot. Always willing to give her time to others, Jan has frequently put on Obedience demonstrations with her dogs and has invited youngsters to her home to help with puppy raising and socializing.

Sawyer, Grenville (Buzz) and Virginia — *Norgren* — Sumner, WA

For the Sawyers, Norgren is a small hobby kennel devoted to the enjoyment of, and the betterment of, the Norwegian Elkhound. Through the years, it has been successful on both counts.

Many fine dogs have come from the limited breeding program here. One is Ch. Norgren's Ravishing Ruby, a top producing bitch owned by the Petersons' Windy Cove Kennels. Careful combining of the best bloodlines available to them has produced dogs of good, leggy Norwegian type such as the Group-placement winner, Ch. Norgren's Pith and Vinegar, who spent some time in the Eastern United States, where he was bred to several bitches. His breeding with Ch. Kamgaard Bonnie Parker produced Ch. Kamgaard Kit N' Kaboodle, who was later "loaned" to England. Thus the influence of Norgren Kennels has been international.

As with many Elkhound-owning families, the Sawyer children often help to train and show the dogs and the Sawyers have fun wherever they travel to show their dogs.

Schleimer, Louis and Etta — *La Habra Hills* — La Habra, CA

Lou's recent passing was a real loss to the Norwegian Elkhound fancy. He and his wife served the NEA of Southern California in many roles and he is remembered as a special friend and a hard-working sportsman. The La Habra Elkhounds were descended from a long line of excellent dogs going back to the early winners in California including Ch. Rolf av Beach Crest. Breedings to Ch. Windy Cove Tass of Oftenasen produced some fine winners including Ch. Lief O Tass of La Habra Hills.

Shew, Harold and Nelda — *Ouachita* — Little Rock, AR

The Ouachita Elkhounds are most often seen in Midwestern competition. However, one of its most prominent dogs, and a dog that traveled farther, was Ch. Vanguard Four Wheel Drive. Harold Shew was instrumental in the publication of the 1970 and 1974 editions of the fine book, *Great Grey Dogs*—volumes that have been enjoyed by Elkhound history buffs everywhere. Harold's interest in education and member information and his administrative skills are currently being put to good use—he was elected president of the Norwegian Elkhound Association of America in 1986.

Silverman, Stan and Cotton — *Statton* — Rehoboth, MA

The Silvermans purchased their first Elkhound, Statton of Poo, CD, in 1972

Ch. Statton's Silver Sej, owned
by Stan and Cotton Silverman
(Statton).

Am. and Can. Ch. Kimur's Howdi Titan,
owned by Harold and Carol Sodeman
(Titanic).

Ch. Elbamoor Vixen V Silversmith,
co-owned by Barbara Haines, Elizabeth Evans and Thomas Toland.

and their enthusiasm for the breed has grown ever since. Their first champion, Ch. Ledgerock's Jahna of Statton, CDX, was purchased from Frank and Carol Mazzaro. A breeding of Jahna to Barbara Roby's Ch. Rivendell's Brand produced Ch. Statton's Silver Sej, who in turn sired Ch. Satuit Sejaria av Statton. New lines were introduced to Statton with the acquisition (from Mari Misbeek) of Camalot Trulle All Ours, CDX, a bitch sired by Ch. Vin-Melca's Nimbus out of Ch. Camalot Trulle av Bella. Bred to Sej, she produced Ch. Statton's Jr. Skol of Stonylea and Ch. Statton's Jesteri av Do-T-Do.

The Statton dogs are always owner-handled. Cotton's first love is the Obedience ring, so most of their dogs are shown both in Obedience and conformation. They are justly proud of Statton's Silver McNeill, a hearing ear dog serving in Pennsylvania. Stan and Cotton have served the Norwegian Elkhound Minuteman Association as officers and board members, and Cotton was chairman of the 1982 National Specialty held in Massachusetts.

Sizemore, Sylvia — *Oakwood* — Portland, OR

The Oakwood Kennels moved from Virginia to Oregon, and while the lack of time has somewhat limited the scale of Sylvia's activities, she nevertheless maintains her interest in Elkhound doings in the Portland area. Among the good Oakwood champions that have helped make a name for this small kennel have been Ch. Oakwood's Jack-O-Lantern (hailed by judge Hallingby at the 1976 NEAA Specialty as being of correct Norwegian type and in condition "that could hunt in Norway") and Ch. Oakwood's Roadrunner.

Smith, Florence — *Stonylea* — Avon, CT

In her eighth decade, Florence Smith attended the NEAA Specialty in Los Angeles and renewed friendships from across the land. In her small home nestled in the Connecticut countryside, the Elkhounds of Stonylea have her undivided attention and love. Ever ready to help the novice, she is an unassuming but knowledgeable lady whose kitchen is open and the coffee pot on to any visitor wishing to talk dogs. For a small kennel, she has produced a remarkable string of fine dogs, many of which became the springboard stock for other kennels. They include such notables as: Am. & Can. Ch. Kim Kima's of Stonylea, Ch. Lara's Britt of Stonylea, Stonylea's Solveg, Stonylea's Bobbi and many others. Of late, Florence shares her home with Ch. Statton Jr. Skol of Stonylea and Ch. Valdemar's Winter Belle.

Smith, Shirley and Mary Freeman — *Sventre* — Houston, TX

Shirley Smith and her mother, Mary Freeman, were among the earliest fanciers involved with the development of Norwegian Elkhound interest in the Texas area. In 1970 they began with Obedience, and then entered conformation competition with their Princess Tanya of the Elkies, CD. Since that time they have bred and owned several American and Mexican champions including Ch. Sventre's Saturday Night Fever.

Smolley, Robert and Jeanne — *Bomark* — Portugese Bend, CA

Bob and Jeanne Smolley have bred and shown Elkhounds in conformation and Obedience since the early 1960s. The foundation bitch of their kennels, purchased from Crafdal Farms, was a daughter of Ch. Trygvie Vikingsson who

Am. and Mex. Ch. Lu Per Tryg 'N Thors Trina, owned by Shirley Smith and Mary Freeman (Sventre).

Ch. Sassy Sonya av Pebble Point, owned by Charles and Dorothy Pryor (Pebble Point).

Ch. Linvicta's Sherman Tank, multi-Group winner. BOB 1981 NEA of Northern California Specialty. Owned by Ken and Judy Strakbein (Linvicta).

Ch. ThomThom Acer Tab Jupiter, bred and owned by Chris and Gayle Thomas (Thom-Thom).

Ch. Bomark Tarquin, owned and bred by Teresa Burrell, Anchorage, Alaska.

Elkhounds with a record set of Alaskan moose antlers. Owned by Mr. and Mrs. Robert Smolley (Bomark). —*Photo, Robert Smolley*

became Ch. Crafdal Trygs Tiara, CD. Bred twice to Ch. Crafdal Thor Mhor (a Norwegian-bred import from Ireland), Tiara produced seven champions.

Bomark Elkhounds have included Ch. Bomark Tryg N Thors Rikka (owned by Bill and Betty Garrison) and two of her offspring—Ch. Bomark Bayou Bengal and Ch. Bomark Bayou Beef. Teresa Burrel of Anchorage, Alaska, an avid dog sledder, acquired Ch. Bomark Tryg N Thors Tatina, who produced two champions.

Another fine producer is Bomark Kal Ericsson. Although his show career was terminated by a broken tail, he has sired quality offspring.

The Smolleys have devoted much effort to the maintenance of the health and quality of life of their Elkhounds. In addition, Jeanne has served as an officer of her regional club, the Norwegian Elkhound Association of Southern California, and as Secretary of the parent NEAA. She was a member of the Standard Revision Committee from 1968 to 1972.

Sodeman, Buzz and Carol — *Titanic* — Saginaw, MI

Titanic Kennels was launched in 1971 with purchase of Kimur's Howdy Titan, a son of Ch. Vin-Melca's Howdy Rowdy. Titan finished to both American and Canadian championship in 1973. His offspring include: Ch. Titanic's Showtime, Ch. Titanic's Black Russian, CD, and Ch. Titanic's Freddie Fudpucker. A daughter of Ch. Haar Vel's Rusken av Oftenasen, Titanic's Liv av Lindeland, proved to be a fine brood bitch and is the dam of Warlord, Showtime, Bounty Hunter and Lusitania, all of the Titanic prefix.

Fredrika's Fancy Stepper, a daughter of English import Ch. Ravenstone Teodor, was owner-handled to her American and Canadian championships with an impressive record of 22 BOS placements. As a brood bitch she produced Ch. Titanic's Black Russian and Ch. Titanic's Freddie Fudpucker. Freddie, especially appreciated for his good leg length and movement, made his mark as a fine sire and a Group-placement winning showman.

Strakbein, Ken and Judy — *Linvicta* — Fair Oaks, CA

Although they have been Elkhound fanciers for more than 20 years, the Strakbeins have bred most selectively—just over a dozen litters and always with aim toward bettering their stock and striving for true hunting type. They were co-owners, with Pat Craige, of Ch. Vin-Melca's Howdy Linvicta, a Group winning dog. More recently, their Ch. Linvicta's Sherman Tank, Ch. Linvicta's Town Clown and Ch. Linvicta's Hit Man have compiled fine show records. Excellent bitches of their own breeding have included Ch. Linvicta's Echo Again, Ch. Linvicta's Backtalk and Ch. Linvicta's Misty Morning. Ken served as Sweepstakes judge at the 1986 NEAA Specialty in Houston.

Thomas, Chris and Gayle — *ThomThom Farm* — DeForest, WI

At ThomThom Farm, located on the outskirts of Madison, Wisconsin, the Elkhounds have 22 acres to play on. Chris and Gayle Thomas are enthusiastic advocates of the breed, much concerned with the health and soundness of their dogs. All stock is OFA certified and the dogs are graded as young puppies for quality and show potential. In developing their breeding program they utilized dogs of the Crafdal and Windy Cove lines, and in recent years have raised a number of litters in cooperation with other breeders in the Illinois/Wisconsin area. One of their top winners has been Ch. ThomThom Acer Tab Jupiter.

Toland, Pat and Tom — *Tolandia* — Central Islip, NY

Pat and Tom Toland became captivated with the Norwegian Elkhound through their Obedience winner, Vivacious Vara of Valhalla, CD—her charm and common sense sold them on the breed. Foundation of their kennel was Ch. Crafdal Tryglik Toshja, obtained from Glenna Crafts. Their breeding program soon produced several champions, foremost of which was Ch. Tolandia Tryg N Thors V-Boy. They showed several fine dogs in co-ownership with Barbara Haines and Elizabeth Evans, notably Ch. Elbamoor Vixen V Silversmith. Tom Toland's death in 1983 was a great loss for the Elkhound world.

Torbet, Nancy — *Eidsvold* — Mundelein, IL

Nancy Torbet's interest in Elkhounds goes back to the time she was 16 years old and owned her first champion, Ch. Thor of Kongsberg. Next, she owned Ch. Boreas av Eidsvold. She imported Noste av Kotojell, sister of the famous Ch. Driv av Kotojell and utilized this excellent bloodline in her breeding. Nancy raises only a few Elkhounds, always the hunting type, but her dogs continue winning their fair share of show awards.

Viken, Patricia and Vicki — *Viken* — Franklin Park, IL

Patricia Viken and her daughter, Vicki, have been strong members of the Northeastern Illinois Norwegian Elkhound Association and Pat has served the club in several official capacities. She has also served as Secretary of the parent Norwegian Elkhound Association of America, and was instrumental in organizing the fine effort of the NEINEA in putting on the 1978 National Specialty. Pat and Vicki have shown several of their dogs to championship, including Ch. Lordan's Viken Warrior, a multiple BOB winner.

Wilkes, Mike and Penny — *Bifrost* — La Jolla, CA

While living in Oregon in the early 1970s the Wilkes purchased a puppy who became Eyorik of Bifrost, CD, and was the high scoring Obedience dog of the Norwegian Elkhound Association of Southern California in 1973 after their move there.

Following the move to La Jolla, the Wilkes acquired a five-weeks-old puppy of Crafdal bloodlines who became Ch. Solv Kriger av Bifrost, a multiple Best of Breed and Group winner. "Loki," as he was called, sired a litter out of Ch. Lu Per's Bifrost Breeze which included Ch. Bifrost's Sea Raider, Ch. Bifrost Sea Fury av Elgshire (owned by the Carters in Texas) and Ch. Bifrost's Sea Love.

In 1975 Ch. Jaegor av Green Mountain came to their kennel from Colorado. He was campaigned and became one of the Top Ten Elkhounds in the rating systems for 1976 and 1977.

As well as devoting time to showing their dogs as owner-handlers, the Wilkes have edited their club's newsletter for several years and have written articles that have won prize recognition from the Dog Writers Association of America. Mike's clever cartoons of Elkhounds in action are well known and warmly appreciated by the fancy.

112

Ch. Ouachita Rowdy Rackensacker, bred
by Marietta Jones and Harold Shew and
owned by Mr. Shew (Ouachita).

Ch. Solv Kriger av Bifrost, owned by Mike
and Penny Wilkes (Bifrost).

113

Ch. Gladjac Royal Oslo, winner, winner of the 1962 NEAA
Specialty held in conjunction with the Chicago Inter-
national show and judged by Johnny Aarflot of Norway.
Oslo went on to win Best in Show all-breeds at the event.
Owned by Mrs. Susan Phillips (Pomfret).

Ch. Arctic Storm of Pomfret winning the second National
NEAA Specialty at San Francisco, 1965, 122 entries, judged by
Miss Gerd Berbom of Norway. Storm, owned by Doris
Gustafson, was handled at the Specialty by his breeder, Mrs.
Susan B. Phillips.

5

The Norwegian Elkhound Association of America

FANCIERS of the Norwegian Elkhound during the early 1930s were perceptive enough to realize that the best qualities of the breed could be fostered and preserved through an association of interested breeders and exhibitors. At the Morris and Essex show in May of 1934, a group including Bayard Boyesen, Edith Cluett and Amory Coolidge met to discuss the establishment of such an organization. These three people were appointed to draw up a Constitution and By Laws for the group and by the time of the Westminster Kennel Club show in February of 1935, the new club was established and included four breeder members and nine associate members. By the end of 1935 the membership had grown to nearly double its original size and the Constitution and By Laws were adopted. The Morris and Essex show was designated as the club's supported Specialty Show and in May, 1935, an entry of 52 Elkhounds was presented for the dean of Norwegian judges, Mr. Johnny Aarflot. In November of 1935, the Norwegian breed standard, as translated by Mr. Aarflot, was adopted by the club and approved by the AKC.

In 1936, the club was admitted as a member club of the American Kennel Club. As the NEAA membership grew, the club was able to support shows in the New England area by giving cash prizes. The organization was nurtured by the dedication and work of several individuals during this period, including original founders and other dedicated individuals such as George Brooks and most especially, Lawrence Litchfield, Jr. who served as Secretary and AKC delegate from 1936 to 1949. He was also elected

Ch. Vin-Melca's Howdy Rowdy winning the 1968 NEAA Specialty, held in conjunction with the Springfield KC show in Massachusetts, judged by Olav Campbell of Norway. Owned by Dr. and Mrs. John Craige (Vin-Melca).

Ch. Vin-Melca's Matinee Idol winning the 198_ NEAA Specialty, held independently at Denv_ and judged by Mrs. Mary Jarman of Englan_ Owned by Patricia V. Craige and Peter Eckroat.

Ch. Vin-Melca's Happy Hour winning the 1974 NEAA National Specialty held at Anaheim, California. Judge, Olaf Roig of Norway. Owner, Patricia V. Craige. Mr. A. Wells Peck presents the trophy. Happy Hour stands as the only bitch to have ever won the Specialty.

president of the organization in 1947, a post he held until 1950. Another staunch supporter of the group during these years was Thomas White, who served until his tragic death in a plane crash in 1951.

As interest in the breed grew during the late thirties and the war years of the 1940s, the club made accommodations and changes to allow for the growth in membership and to maintain a newsletter as communications vehicle among members. Additional educational literature was published under the stewardship of the club and the breed showed a steady, controlled growth in popularity.

As the breed became known across the country, groups of fanciers became established in different parts of the country. Until this time the center of interest in the breed and the nucleus of the NEAA had been the New England states. In 1946 a club was established in Minnesota and was soon recognized by the NEAA as the first regional club of Norwegian Elkhound fanciers. Soon afterward, clubs were formed in California and the Puget Sound area. This period of growth required the NEAA to revise its membership requirements to accommodate the regional clubs and a far flung membership.

During these years from the late 1940s to the early 1970s the club was supported and led by hard-working members such as Thomas White, A. Wells and Catherine Peck, Susan D. Phillips, Doris Phillips and Florence Palmer. The major work of the Association during the late 1960s was the preparation of a breed standard better suited to the needs of American judges. A committee that included Susan Phillips, Mary O. Jenkins, Karen B. Elvin and Jeanne Smolley worked for three years on a careful revision of the breed standard which preserved the essence of the Norwegian standard with expanded interpretation for American breeders and judges. This standard, which received praise from the American Kennel Club and other breed clubs seeking to improve their standards, was adopted by vote of the NEAA membership in 1973. A pamphlet called *Interpretive Comments on the Breed Standard* was prepared and disseminated shortly thereafter by the NEAA to further assist judges in evaluating dogs in the breed ring.

The NEAA sponsored National Specialty Shows beginning in 1962. The first one was held in conjunction with the Chicago International dog show in that year with Herr Johnny Aarflot judging, just as he had with the first supported show at Morris and Essex in 1935. Specialty shows were held every third year until 1976, since which they have been held on a biennial basis. With two exceptions the judges for these events have been selected from the roster of premier judges in Norway. The aim has been to give direction and guidance to American breeders so that a great divergence of type does not exist between the hunting type Elgund in Norway and the American Elkhound.

By 1980 the membership of the NEAA had increased to nearly 350 members throughout the United States and in several foreign countries.

The chief function of the club has continued to be communication between members through its newsletter and the promotion of educational programs and literature and the sponsorship of regional symposiums for breeders and exhibitors chiefly in connection with their biennial specialty shows. The club is strengthened by the network of regional clubs who are admitted as members and who are represented by a regional advisory committee that serves the purpose of channeling members' ideas to the Board of Directors. Thus a small group of dedicated fanciers formed a group whose influence has continued for fifty years and has guided the growth of the breed in the United States.

A sweep for Windy Cove at the 1984 NEAA National Specialty at Anaheim. Judge, Jakob P. Holsing, Norway. BOB, BW and WD was Windy Cove Chief Cochise. BOS was Ch. Windy Cove Indian Maiden. Both dogs bred and owned by Mrs. Joe Peterson.

NORWEGIAN ELKHOUND ASSOCIATION OF AMERICA

NATIONAL SPECIALTY WINNERS

1962 April 7-8, Held in conjunction with the International Kennel Club of Chicago, Illinois
Judge: Herr Johnny Aarflot, Norway—73 entries
BOB: Ch. Gladjac Royal Oslo (Group 1 and BIS also awarded.)
Owner: Susan D. Phillips; Breeder: Armine St. Germaine
BOS, BW, WB: Cedarstone's Zori
Breeder/Owner: Thelma Heyworth
WD: Frosti of Pomfret
Breeder/Owner: Susan D. Phillips

1965 January 16-17, Held in conjunction with Golden Gate Kennel Club of San Francisco, California.
Judge: Miss Gerd Berbom, Norway—122 entries
BOB, WD, BW: Arctic Storm of Pomfret
Owner: Doris Gustafson; Breeder: Susan D. Phillips
BOS, WB: Vin Melca's Rebel Cry
Breeder/Owner: Patricia V. Craige

1968 May 11, Held in conjunction with the Springfield Kennel Club at West Springfield, Massachusetts.
Judge: Olav Campbell, Norway—132 entries
BOB: Ch. Vin-Melca's Howdy Rowdy
Owners: Dr. & Mrs. John Craige; Breeders: Fred & Lois Turner
BOS, BW, WB: Windy Cove Mona av Oftenasen
Owner: Marie Peterson
WD: Crafdal Tryg N Thor's Rollo
Breeder/Owner: Glenna Crafts

1971 October 23, First independent specialty held in Minneapolis, Minnesota.
Judge: Herr Johnny Aarflot, Norway—175 entries
BOB, BW, WD: Vin-Melca's Huck Finn
Breeder/Owner: Patricia V. Craige (Owned following Specialty by Edna Mae Bieber, via prior arrangement)
BOS: Ch. Vin-Melca's Hanky Panky
Owner: John Whitemarsh; Breeder: Patricia V. Craige
WB: Branstock's However
Breeder/Owner: Georgia Cole

1974 April 26-27, Held independently at Anaheim, California
Judges: Olaf Roig & Oivind Asp, Norway—243 entries
BOB: Ch. Vin-Melca's Happy Hour
Owner: Patricia V. Craige
BOS: Ch. Kim Kima's of Stonylea
Owners: Frank & Laura Mazzaro; Breeder: Cynthia Peck
BW, WB: Vin-Melca's Hot Pants
Owners: John & Dawn Haydin
WD: Vin-Melca's Nordic Storm
Owners: Patricia Craige & Ernest Marshall

1976 September 24-25, Held independently at Washington, D.C.
Judge: Dr. Jesper Hallingby, Norway—210 entries
BOB, BW, WD: Loki of Stormy Lea
Owner: E. A. Hillman; Breeders: Brian & Lynn Riley
BOS: Ch. Crafdal TNT Viv Imp Vamp
Owners: Charles & Mary Hammes; Breeder: Glenna Crafts
WB: Camalot Trulle av Bella
Owner: Mrs. George Misbeek; Breeder: Dag Jorn Aalerud

1978 June 23, Held independently at Hillside, Illinois.
Judge: Dr. Arthur E. T. Sneeden, Scotland—256 entries
BOB, BW, WD: Titanic's Porcupine Pie
Owners: Joel & Nan Tessin; Breeder: Buzz Sodeman
BOS: Ch. Titanic's Holly Holy
Owners: Kim & Steve Balder; Breeder: Buzz Sodeman
WB: Scaiern's Pathand av Redhill
Owners: Sheryl Blackwell-Caltagirone & Freeman Claus

1980 June 20, Held independently at Denver, Colorado.
Judge: Mrs. Mary Jarman, England—247 entries
BOB: Ch. Vin-Melca's Matinee Idol
Owners: Patricia V. Craige & Peter Eckroat; Breeder: Robert Maddox
BOS: Ch. Kamgaard Kiss Me Kate
Owners: Robert & Ruth Ness & Margaret Mott; Breeder: Margaret Mott
BW, WD: Vin-Melca's Namesake
Breeder/Owners: Patricia V. Craige & Dodi Froehlich
WB: Asgaard's Sugar N Spice
Owner: Sharon A. Poulin; Breeder: Kimm Slater

1982 May 6-7, Held independently at Attleboro, Massachusetts.
Judge: Baroness Susan Van Boetzelaer, Holland—219 entries
BOB, BW, WD: Karin's Yogi Bear
Owner: Gary Proudfoot; Breeder: Barbara A. Innes
WB: Norlund's Koola av Kirkssted
Owners: Robert & Ruth Ness & Kristine Brandt; Breeder: Kristine Brandt

1984 June 14-15, Held independently at Anaheim, California.
Judge: Jakob Petter Holsing, Norway—273 entries
BOB, BW, WD: Windy Cove Chief Cochise
Breeder/Owner: Mrs. Joe Peterson
BOS: Ch. Windy Cove Indian Maiden
Breeder/Owner: Mrs. Joe Peterson
WB: Vin-Melca's Love Call
Owner: Janet Allen; Breeders: Patricia V. Craige & Dodi Froehlich.

1986 April 17-18, Held independently at Houston, Texas.
Judge: Mrs. Mary Newton, England
BOB: Ch. Kirkssted Olav
Owners: T. and C. Reese and Robert Ness
BOS, BW, WB: Royal Crown's Amaretto
Owner: Katherine Ellis, D.V.M.
WD: Rikkana's Skid Mark
Breeder/Owner: Lana Hall

120

Ch. Kamgaard Bard av Dunharrow, Best in Show winner (1980). Owned by Donald and Judith Reichenbach.

Ch. Vin-Melca's the Gray Raider, Best in Show winner (1980). Owned by German Garcia y Garcia.

Ch. Graahund's Dusky Debutante, Best in Show winner, Canada's top winning bitch of all time. Owned by Donald and Diana Hirtle (Hirtzlheim).

Ch. Torr's Nordic Prince Thor, Best in Show winner. A favorite of the Hirtzlheim Kennels, Reg'd., owned by Donald and Diana Hirtle.

6

The Norwegian Elkhound in Canada

NO COUNTRY in the world has greater potential for being the ideal realm of the Norwegian Elkhound than has our neighbor to the north. It is a land tremendously rich in large and small game—including moose and caribou—along with such marauders as wolves, mountain lions and coyotes. It is a hunter's paradise, a land rich in untapped natural resources, but it must be controlled and protected.

One of the pioneer kennels for Norwegian Elkhounds in Canada was the Vakker-Lund Kennels, owned by Mr. and Mrs. John Terrely of Gravenhust, Ontario. The Terellys showed their Elkhounds all over Canada and at many shows in the United States. They produced not only fine show dogs, but dogs that were good moose, deer and bear hunters.

The show champion and the moose-hunting Elkhound should be one and the same. Once, on a moose hunt, one of the Vakker-Lund dogs got lost. They spent 40 days in the wilderness in search of him. Happily, he was found and returned to the Terellys on Christmas Eve, strong and healthy. What a Christmas that must have been!

It just goes to show what the Elkhound is made of; he can live off the land if he has to, and still look good in the show ring. That's a combination that's hard to beat.

When Mr. and Mrs. Arulf Flaten of Cumberland, Ontario, decided to raise Norwegian Elkhounds, they didn't fool around. From Norway they imported a dog of Suteraas bloodlines that became Can. Ch. Storm. J. Hallingby of Norway selected Sonja av Suteraas for them, bred by Christian and Iskar Svae. The Flatens produced some fine dogs from these imports.

Mr. and Mrs. H. O. Swanson of Ottawa acquired Margot of Greenwood, a daughter of Ch. Lady Kazana of Greenwood, in 1954. Mr. Swanson was then in the Foreign Service of the United States government, and Margot went wherever the Swansons did, adjusting herself very well to the changes of climate and the different homes. In 1966 the Swansons established their Valgtor Kennels. They were the owners of Ch. Norsemen's Unnlepe Kunstner, a handsome dog that won many prizes in Canada.

The first Elkhound owned by Mr. and Mrs. James Spence was an Obedience training dog named Yogi, who scored 199 points in her first competition. What a way to start! The Spences owned the Yokipi Kennels in Richmond, British Columbia.

Another remarkable Obedience win was scored by Ch. Prince Peter, owned by young Marra Stein, then living in Tuxedo, Manitoba. In one show, Peter made something of a record—finishing his championship in conformation and then completing his CD in Obedience—all within a half hour! Marra, now Marra Shoshany, emigrated to Israel and was instrumental in establishing the Norwegian Elkhound there in the 1970s.

The Elkhound breeders in Canada have made tremendous progress in the breeding and promotion of the breed over recent years. Not only have they imported some of the finest stock from Norway and other lands, but they have also produced some fine Elkhounds of their own. These dogs can compete in any show, any place, and as a rule I find very few dogs trimmed or altered. That is a great tribute to the Canadian breeders who insist that Canada produce true hunting type Elkhounds—healthy, strong hunting dogs.

Breeders have expressed interest in getting permission from the Canadian Fish & Wildlife Department for staging a field trial, with aim of demonstrating what the Norwegian Elkhound can do in hunting moose. I suggest that in doing this, they invite one or two hunters from Norway with excellent hunting dogs, for the dogs must know the difference between a moose, deer or bear. That is very important. If the Elkhound is not trained to hunt moose he will hunt and chase anything he can find, and that, of course, would spoil everything.

It is hoped that Canadian breeders will continue to work together—guarding against "puppy mills" and overproduction—and keep its future in the hands of those who have a deep understanding and care for the breed. Following is a quick introduction to some of the kennels who, at the time of this writing, are active with the breed:

124

Dell, Lorna — *Glitnir* — Millarsville, Alberta, Can.

So often Elkhound breeders dream about a place in the country with plenty of room to hike, play and run with the dogs. Such a place is the Glitnir Kennels, located in the beautiful foothills of the Rockies. With many lonesome trails and forgotten old roads, it is a heaven for young and old Elkhounds. Because Glitner is a small kennel with only a few dogs, its dogs get the personal touch—there is more time to play and talk to the puppies and to develop their personalities. Lorna Dell has bred many champions. One of the more famous is Ch. Glitnir Haakon, bred on Norway's Independence Day (May 17) in 1975, and sold to Kathy Wayne.

When the time comes to hunt, the dogs' natural gift is not forgotten; there is plenty of wild game in the foothills of the Rocky Mountains.

Galloway, Don R. — *Vikinghund* — Kamloops, B.C., Can.

For people interested in breeding Norwegian Elkhounds, the main thing is to start with the best material available to you. Sadly, this was not the way in which Don Galloway got started in Elkhounds, but it did not take him long to discover he was on the wrong track. Then, from Norman Vig's Vigeland Kennels he got hold of some imported stock from Norway and began linebreeding. He shipped Ch. Brine 8,000 miles (round trip) to Can. Ch. Torr's Nordic Prince Thor in Halifax—only the best was good enough!

Don is very interested in moose hunting and has talked informally with the Canadian Fish and Wildlife Department re staging a field trial for moose hunting. He also discovered that some biologists use Elkhounds to conduct game counts in Canada. It will take some time, but I believe that moose hunting in Canada will be a sport of the future.

Hirtle, Donald and Diana — *Hirtzlheim* — Waverley, Nova Scotia, Can.

Not many can match the Hirtles in enthusiasm for the Norwegian Elkhound. And in Can. Ch. Torr's Nordic Prince Thor, who they purchased from Mrs. W. R. Torrance of Manitoba, they found all the best qualities for which the breed is noted. He was adopted not only as a member of the family, but also as the kingpin of the kennel. He breezed easily to his Canadian championship and won many Group placings and Best in Show. He's been featured on TV and in newspaper and magazine articles. Diana has traced his pedigree back 16 generations; it includes such famous champions as Ch. Driv av Kotofjell and Ch. Vardetoppens Burre. Diana is a director of the Norwegian Elkhound Club of Canada.

Innes, Barbara A. — *Karin* — Oshawa, Ont., Can.

Mrs. Innes began breeding Norwegian Elkhounds in 1955, and with the help of breeding stock from Crafdal, Holmes, Lillabo and Vin-Melca, her Karin Kennels has produced many handsome winners. Her Can. Ch. Karin's Big Benny was a real standout with many big wins all over Canada. Mrs. Innes has this good advice for serious breeders: "If your competitors at Elkhound shows have something you consider better in quality than your stock, and it is for sale, by all means buy it." With such an excellent outlook, the Karin Kennels should be producing handsome Elkhounds for many more years.

Kennedy, Edine — *Elvlund* — Vermette, Manitoba, Can.

The name Elvlund is a nice Norwegian name—*elv* means river and *lund* is a cluster of trees. Edine Kennedy's first Elkhound was Tage of Vikam, a male from Vakkerlund and Narvikwood lines. In 1968 she purchased two bitches from Monica Torrance, and then acquired a male, Ch. Melreva Rik's Crispie from Estelle Matthews. Then came Wesmor's Vikesund Snowboy from Mrs. R. Morrison and he was bred to Ch. Norja av Elvlund. From this breeding came the outstanding Ch. Tage av Elvlund, whelped in 1973. Tage was an American, Canadian, and Bermudian champion and a Best in Show winner in all three countries—something very few Elkhounds on this continent have achieved. The skillful blending of many lines, together with a thorough study of Elkhound character and the breed's purpose in peoples' lives, has produced many champions for Elvlund.

Matthews, Estelle — *Melreva* — Regina, Sask., Can.

Melreva Kennels was first registered in England by Estelle Matthews, whose interest in the Norwegian Elkhound began in 1958. Her first bitch was Carmunnock Omo, who was bred to Friochan Sande (Kitty Heffer). The Matthews moved from Scotland to Regina in 1966 and Melreva is now registered in Canada. Melreva Knut was sold to Germany, but later came back to the States where he developed an interest in duck hunting. Dr. George Gill, an avid hunter, was surprised to find that this splendid animal was a natural retriever, and with no special training brought back any duck that Doc knocked down. Knut thought it was a great sport. The doctor, who owned numerous other hunting dogs, proclaimed him "the smartest dog I ever hunted with."

McCorkell, Jerry and Grace — *Stormfjell* — Woodslee, Ont., Can.

The McCorkells selected a genuine Norse name for their kennel, Stormfjell— *storm,* with the same meaning it has in English, and *fjell,* meaning mountain. Mountains are something Norway has in abundance, and many Elkhound kennels there have *fjell* in their name.

The saga of the Stormfjell Kennels started in 1969-70 with the acquisition of two dogs. Because of their admiration and love of these two dogs, Jerry and Grace started a limited breeding program in 1973, basing it on imported Norwegian lines. From Arne Furuset's Sokomdal Kennel came Ch. Binna av Sokomdal. Then came Ch. Styri Nor-Mor av Stran, bred by Oddvar Hoelseter Styri. In their pedigrees, along with dogs of the Sokomdal and Styri prefixes are dogs from the Suteraas and Kotofjell Kennels, some of the best breeding stock in Norway. Also in their pedigrees is Norwegian and Swedish Ch. Tass, and some sprinkling from Windy Cove (USA) imports. Having this fine breeding stock as foundation takes on added significance for the McCorkells—they are interested in moose hunting, and for moose hunting they must have the hunting type Elghund.

Torrance, Mr. and Mrs. W. R. — *Torr* — Headingly, Manitoba, Can.

It is a fact that the average kennel in the United States lasts from four to five years, but this has not been the case with Mr. and Mrs. Torrance in Canada. They purchased their first Elkhound in 1955 and he became their first champion—Ch. Bairnley's Life of Norfin, CD. Since that time, they have bred and raised Norwegian Elkhounds steadily. Operating on a limited scale, with quality—not quantity—as their goal, they have produced many champions. Most famous of these is Can. Ch. Torr's Nordic Prince Thor, who was sold to Mr. and Mrs. Donald Hirtle of

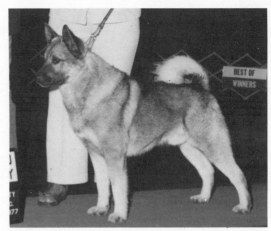

an., Bda. and Am. Ch. Tage av Elvlund, an outstand-
g winner in all three countries. Owned by Mrs.
'ine Kennedy (Elvlund).

Am. and Can. Ch. Boltown Solomon (Eir), a multi-
Group winner in the U.S. and Canada in the 1970s. Sire
of many champions. Bred by C. Cairnes, Ireland.
Owned by Jean and Tony Whiting (Houndhaven).

an. Ch. Binna av Søkomdal, Norwegian import grand-
ughter of Nor. and Swed. Ch. Tass. Bred by Arne
ruseth, Norway. Owned by Jerry and Grace
cCorkell (Stormfjell).

Styri Nor-Mor Av-Stran, Norwegian import, great
grandson of Nor. and Swed. Ch. Tass. Bred by Oddvar
Hoelseter, Norway. Owned by Jerry and Grace
McCorkell (Stormfjell).

Waverley, Nova Scotia, where he had a wonderful home, a glorious show career and a real good time.

Mrs. Torrance has been very active in Obedience instruction for many years and has traveled far and wide to judge Obedience shows in Canada. Torr Kennels has imported some handsome Elkhounds from Norway, especially from Vardetop Kennel.

Vig, Norman — *Vigeland* — Mission, B.C., Can.

Norman Vig has bred Norwegian Elkhounds for years and has a deep understanding of its saga, its hunting ability and its natural personality. Quoting from his letter: "I have been breeding Elkhounds for 17 years now and have been fighting such things as the clipping and trimming of Elkhounds, as well as the removal of whiskers for show purposes. It seemed I was fighting a losing battle alone, until your book brought these matters to the attention of all Elkhound fanciers. I am happy to say a clipped, whiskerless Elkhound is a rarity in the show-rings now in Canada." To which I say, "Amen."

Norman imported his first Elkhound from Norway in 1968, from Ryfjeld Kennel; Ryfjeld's Driva av Vigeland has provided the foundation for many other new kennels as well as for his own. Her first litter, by Ch. Listerland's Finn (out of a Norwegian import), produced Ch. Vigeland's Trygg Sigbjorn. Trygg was a handsome dog and a winning show dog in Canada in the 1970s. He produced outstanding offspring which have been shown all over Canada and in the United States. A more recent import, now Ch. Binna av Vigeland, boasts some of the most outstanding Elghunds of Norway in her pedigree.

Wayne, Kathy — Calgary, Alberta, Can.

Kathy Wayne's champions—Ch. Glitnir Jorgen and Ch. Glitnir Helga—are out of the Glitnir Kennels' heritage. Strong and healthy, and residing in a land with lots of room to play and hunt, no quarry is too small or too big for their interests—from squirrels, rabbits, porcupines, to—of course—bear and moose.

Whiting, Jean and Tony — *Houndhaven* — Rockwood, Ont., Can.

Jean and Tony Whiting emigrated from England, bringing their Elkhound stock with them, and established their kennel in Canada in 1972. They became one of the largest Elkhound kennels in North America. Their foundation bitch was Ch. Kilternan Bergitta, dam of 13 champions—a great Elkhound and a real pillar in the Houndhaven breeding program.

Jean Whiting has made great strides in handling Houndhaven dogs to impressive wins in tough dog show competition in both Canada and the United States. The many notable champions out of Houndhaven include such standouts as Am. & Can. Ch. Boltown Solomon ("Eir"), a multi-Group winner in Canada and the USA and a leading sire, and Am. & Can. Ch. Houndhaven's Borealis, a multi Group-placement winning bitch.

Ch. Vigeland's Trygg Sigbjørn, Top Canadian Elkhound of 1974, sire of many outstanding champions. Bred and owned by Norman A. Vig (Vigeland).

Can. Ch. Vigeland's Tara, bred by Norman Vig and owned by Donald R. Galloway (Vikinghund).

Ch. Fanto of Glitnir, top winning Canadian Elkhound of 1977. Son of Ch. Vigeland's Trygg Sigbjørn. Owned by Lorna Dell (Glitnir).

Ch. Glitnir's Haakon, pictured in BOB win at 11 months, going on to Best Puppy in Group. Bred by Lorna Dell and owned and shown by Kathy Wayne.

129

Eng. Ch. Borellan Kaymaur Thor, Elkhound Dog of the Year, 1971-74. Winner of 30 CCs, to that time a record for the breed, and an outstanding sire. Bred by Mrs. C. Tomlinson. Owned by Mrs. J. Block.

Eng. Ch. Borellan Larsen, a very successful sire. Bred by Mrs. J. Block and owned by Mrs. J. Cowper.

Eng. Ch. Rothenborg Christian, son of Larsen. Best in Show all-breeds, Richmond 1977. Bred and owned by Mrs. J. Cowper.

7

Norwegian Elkhounds in England and Scotland

by Mary Jarman

THE FIRST Norwegian Elkhound registered in the *Kennel Club Stud Book* in England was Foerdig, 7848, whelped in 1874 and owned by Major Godfrey Faussett. The breeder and pedigree of this dog were unknown. From time to time, a variety of specimens were brought to England from Norway by sportsmen on fishing trips and the first imports were recorded in 1878. Three years later, Ch. Admiral 11056 was imported by W. K. Taunton who, in *The Illustrated Book of the Dog* had this to say about his dog, "My own dog Admiral was black, mixed with grey, with white chest, legs and feet. I consider him the finest specimen I have seen; he was obtained for me direct from Norway by a friend who took considerable trouble to secure the best he could obtain. He was exhibited at the last Alexandra Palace Show, where he was awarded a silver medal. He is an active, good tempered dog and very companionable; and the breed only wants to be introduced into this country when I think it would very quickly become a favorite with the public."

In those early days, the Elkhound was variously known in England as the Norrlandsk Spetz, Grahund, Jamthund, Graa Dyrehund, Norwegian Bear Dog, and Norwegian Elk Dog. For many years the breed was shown in the Foreign Dog Class where it sometimes competed with such breeds as the Dogue de Bourdeaux, Siberian Sled Dog, and Esquimaux. Evidently

Ch. Woden, wh. 1915, a top winner of his time. Bred and owned by Mrs. George Powell.

there was considerable variation in color, some being dark gray, others black, light and tan, a few blue gray, and one sable and white. The Iceland Elkhound, Frigga 1928B was white.

Among early Elkhounds registered with pedigree unknown were Kvik, Saleer, Leyswood Wolf, Thorr II and L'Homme de Niege. The last named dog came from Lapland; Scandinavian King was imported from Sweden. Hon. W. Harbord's Sharpe, mated to Blue produced Norse, Blue Bell, and Viking while W. C. Atherton's Thelma, mated to Blue produced Olga, Freda, Dr. Nansen, Wolf IV, and Flink. Leonard W. Beddowe had an imported bitch called Ingered, the dam of Fiord and Lapland Lassie. Dogs such as these and their offspring represented the breed in England prior to 1900.

The larger shows, such as Crystal Palace, had a few Elkhound entries, sufficient to provide bench show interest. About this time, Jaeger more or less set the style for the breed as he was considered by the judges to be the most typical Elkhound. He was imported by Lady Cathcart from Swedish Lapland, where Sir Reginald Cathcart frequently hunted elk and bear with native dogs. Then, as now, the Norwegians were loath to part with their best hunting dogs and asked enormous prices for them. Cathcart said that the best specimens were dark gray with straight legs, cat feet, dense rain-resistant coats, prick ears, fox-like faces, and double curled tails. Although the dogs seemed wild by nature when hunting, they were faithful and devoted to their owners.

Jaeger 1986B (Pil ex Polka and whelped in 1896) bred by S. Hanson was dark gray, 20 inches high, and 50 pounds in weight. He was the fountainhead of the old English strains of Elkhound through his descendants such as Ch. King, Mansos, Clinker, Wolfram, Ch. Woden, Gerda, Ch. Thorval, and Ch. Beltsa. Ch. King 2221D (Jaeger ex Blue Bell) whelped April 11, 1899, bred by Rev. G.M.D. Longinotto and owned by Major A.W. Hicks-Beach, won many prizes at shows.

132

Ch. Woden 559AA (Wolfram ex Thelma) whelped in 1915, was bred and owned by Mrs. George Powell. This dog, considered one of the best of his time, was nicely balanced, medium-sized, good headed with brown eyes and had correct tail carriage. His nephew Jansen, a bigger dog with yellow eyes, was his frequent competitor in bench shows. From Woden and Feiga came Ch. Beltsa, Ch. Thorvah, Astrid, and Thor, who figure in the pedigrees of many present day champions. In fact, Astrid was the granddam of Ch. Mirkel of the Hollow.

Between 1900 and 1918, the breed faded to less than 50 registrations for the period. But, after the war, interest revived and in 1923 the British Elkhound Society was formed with Lady Dorothy Wood (Viscountess of Halifax) as President, and Colonel G.J. Scoville as Secretary. On a visit to Norway, Col. Scoville purchased two Glitre dogs from veterinary surgeon T. Hemsen of Ski: Ch. Rugg av Glitre and Bjonn av Glitre. Bob and Binna av Glitre, both sired by Dyre av Glitre, also were imported as well as Nora av Glitre and W.F. Holmes' Ch. Gaupa av Glitre. Gaupa, often referred to as the matriarch of the breed, was never defeated in British shows. These Glitre dogs, which were quite different from the old English dogs, influenced the breed greatly in Britain, and even in America, for many of their offspring went to the United States. W.F. Holmes' Ch. Rugg av Glitre won 21 certificates in England, Bob won 15, and Int. Ch. Peik II av Glitre won 13. The Norwegian dog, Dyre av Glitre, who won 27 certificates, sired such famous ones as Ch. Skrub, Rugg, Styrs, and Heika, all "av Glitre."

Ch. Wythall, who died at four years, was Rugg's most famous son. Ch. Brenda of Pannal (9 Challenge Certificates) was an outstanding daughter. From imported Ch. Finnegutten and Ch. Gaupa av Glitre came Ch. Patsy of the Holm, later exported to America. Ch. Garrowby Haakon, Gaupa's grandson, should be given great credit as a producer. It is reported that Gaupa inclined toward coarseness. A distinct outcross to the Glitre blood which came from Norway was the line from Sweden through Rulle, Ch. Laila and Ch. Carros. G.H. Harland's Ch. Kit and the Dogsthorpe dogs of W. Stuart-Thompson trace back to these Swedish strains. The imported Ch. Finnegutten from Norway, a son of Ch. Tas av Lifjell, was the first Elkhound to place in the Variety Group in England in 1928.

In this era of importation, there was great variation in type, but there gradually evolved from the medley the English stamp of Elkhound. Certainly the infusion of Norwegian and of Swedish blood contributed to improvement in bone and conformation. W. Stuart-Thompson said, "There is not a single Elkhound in England that does not descend from Senny II or from Gerda, sister to Ch. Woden, even though these two brood matrons stem from two different Elkhound strains. They transmitted the correct type that they inherited."

One of the most prominent kennels of Elkhounds in England during the pre-war years was "Fourwents" owned by F. Joyce Esdaile (later to become Mrs. Winter). In the decade following 1929, she had six champion bitches: Ch. Fourwents Brighde, Ch. Fourwents Fenya, Ch. Fourwents Sonja, Ch. Fourwents Grisla, Ch. Fourwents Minna, and American Ch. Fourwents Binne. There were five champion dogs: Ch. Fourwents Gustav, Ch. Fourwents Dyfrin, Ch. Fourwents Frodi, Ch. Fourwents Bring, and American Ch. Fourwents Paal. In 1938, Miss Esdaile became Secretary of the newly formed Elkhound Club. Shortly before World War II, she imported Ch. Varg av Skromtefjell. Later Fourwents dogs of note included Ch. Fourwents Grinta, Fourwents Gota, Wota of the Holm, Fourwents Garbo, and Fourwents Froyen.

"The Holm" affix belonging to Mr. W. F. Holmes, became world famous. Among his dogs were Elsa of the Holm, Karl of the Holm, Kula of the Holm, Rosa of the Holm, Ch. Gaupa av Glitre, Ulla of the Holm, Fram of the Holm, Ula, Zeno of the Holm, Ch. Stryx av Glitre, Ch. Peik II av Glitre, Ch. Rugg av Glitre, Ch. Krans av Glitre, Ch. Dick of the Holm, and Ch. Delia of the Holm. Mr. Holmes bred litters by the famous Ch. Garroby Haakon and by Ch. Krans. He was president of the Elkhound Club, and through the years he imported many dogs and also exported quite a few. In fact, many American Elkhounds had some "of the Holm" bloodlines. Ch. Patsy of the Holm, Ch. Marko of the Holm, and Ch. Greta of the Holm were among the dogs exported to America.

Another well-known affix of this period was "of the Hollow" used by Mrs. L.F.G. Powys-Lybbe. Famous dogs bearing the name included Ch. Martin, Ch. Mirkel, Ch. Marta, Ch. Anna, Ch. Lisken, Ch. Tora, Ch. Kren, Ch. Bodil, Ch. Gylf; and others. Kren, Gylfi, and Martin were brothers. Ch. Mirkel heads the list of producing sires tabulated by W. F. Holmes.

Other kennels of the period included the Garrowby Kennels of Viscountess Halifax, the Friochan Kennels of Mrs. Kitty Heffer, the Aalesund Kennels of Charles N. Thompson, and the Inverailort Kennels of Mrs. C.H.J. Cameron-Head.

The Post-War Years, 1945–1969

The pattern of Elkhound breeding in England changed considerably after the Second World War. Many of the pre-war kennels had been dispersed and their owners did not recommence breeding. Newcomers to the breed were unable to run large establishments due to difficulties in finding staff, and of course for the first few years, problems of feeding the dogs. However, they carried on as best they could with fewer dogs and coping by themselves without any help.

The Jarlsberg Kennels of Miss Gerd Berbom, a Norwegian girl who lived in England for a while and then returned to Norway, were noted for Lasse of Hyna, Ch. Bamse av Jarlsberg and Ch. Steig av Jarlsberg. Bamse was the first post-war champion brought from Norway in 1946 by Miss Berbom. He sired many winners and was used at stud extensively in the breed before returning to Norway with his owner. Other imports from Norway were Mrs. Powys-Lybbe's Gaupstein Ruggen imported in 1947 and Mrs. Heffer's Glennas Rugg in 1948. Several years later, Mrs. Kincaid-Lennox imported Tortasen's Moman.

The Holm Kennels, owned by W. F. Holmes and known worldwide since 1924, remained the largest kennel of the breed in England throughout this period. It occupied eight acres of ground, with very large runs and ideal conditions for rearing Elkhounds. Ch. Yama and Ch. Yacca of the Holm, two litter sisters, were bred to Mrs. Powyse-Lybbe's Gaupstein Ruggen in 1947. Mrs. Heffer's Ch. Narvik of the Holm also became important in Holms pedigrees. Other champions of the kennel included Ch. Essen of the Holm, sired by Mrs. Kincaid Lennox's Norwegian import, Tortasen's Moman, Ch. Musti and Ch. Lapp of the Holm.

The Fourwents Kennels of Mrs. Winter (formerly Miss F. J. Esdaile) were active immediately after the War. The first champion was Fourwents Rugg af Aalesund, winner of many Challenge Certificates and sire of numerous good progeny in England before he was exported to America where he quickly made his American championship. Another well known champion was the bitch Fourwents Trygg. After her marriage, Mrs. Winter was unable to continue with her kennels for some years but eventually returned to the show ring and made up Ch. Fourwents Gretel of Eskamere. Also from Fourwents blood came the famous English and Irish Ch. Lofoten Anton, owned and bred by Mr. and Mrs. Irons. Anton was the winner of 18 certificates and the sire of Ch. Ravenstone Houmorist and Ch. Henningsvaer Lief.

The Friochan Kennels of Mrs. Kitty Heffer were also very well known and Mrs. Heffer remained for many years a keen and active member of the Elkhound community. The Norwegian import, Ch. Glennas Rugg, was her first post-war champion and he was used on many different bloodlines, producing a great number of successful, winning progeny including his son, Ch. Friochan Dolf. Other Friochan champions included Friochan Valda, Friochan Alvar and Friochan Horsa.

Forty or more Elkhounds were entered at most Championship shows during this time, so the competition was keen. There were two breed clubs in England—the British Elkhound Society and the Elkhound Club, and in Scotland, the Elkhound Association of Scotland.

Norwegian Elkhounds in England After 1970

The years after 1970 saw greater changes than any similar period in the history of Elkhounds in Great Britain. They covered the retirement from active participation in breed affairs of the last of those breeders who had

Eng. Ch. Mageroy Waysider, important winner and sire. Bred by Mrs. M. Newton. Owned by Mrs. S. Haddon.

Eng. Ch. Vikynn of Vandavell, 1977 Reserve BIS winner. Bred and owned by Mr. and Mrs. W. Howes.

Eng. Ch. Malator Helga, a Thor daughter. Bred and owned by Mrs. B. Grace.

been active from the pre-war years and the virtual disappearance of large kennels. Mrs. Kitty Heffer gave up her post as President of the British Elkhound Society in late 1970 after holding it from 1963 on. Previously she had put in 25 years of hard work as Secretary of the Society. Throughout her service she devoted her efforts, heart and soul, to what would benefit Elkhounds and all those concerned with them. Even in retirement she has kept up her contact with the breed and contributes weekly notes to the dog press. Other notable retirements were Mrs. Joyce Winter who ended some 35 years of working with the Elkhound Club and even longer as a breeder and, most remarkable of all, Mr. W. F. Holmes—who called it a day after over 50 years of activity when he himself was over 90 years of age.

The changing pattern of Elkhound ownership, and in particular the larger number living as pets, led to new problems as more became homeless. These needs led, in 1971, to the founding of the informal Elkhound Rescue Fund. The Fund acts to benefit dogs who through no fault of their own, such as the illness or loss of their owners or some other reason, need to be found a new home. Much excellent and careful work has been done in finding suitable homes, the necessary funds being raised by rallies and film shows of various kinds and of course by generous donations.

Economic pressures had a hand in the important decision made in 1972, that it was in the best interests of the breed that the British Elkhound Society and the Elkhound Club should merge. The officers and members of the Committees of both Society and Club worked hard to bring the plans to a successful conclusion and on January 1, 1973, the new British Elkhound Club came into being. It continues to make progress, always working for the good of the breed.

1969 was remarkable for an event of a different kind as Mrs. Haddon and Mrs. Newton imported a Norwegian bitch, Gaupa (Nor. Ch. Finn ex Deisi). She was in whelp to Nor. Ch. Fix, and produced six puppies while in quarantine, four dogs and two bitches. Three were registered in Mrs. Haddon's prefix, "Norsled" and three in Mrs. Newton's prefix, "Mageroy."

One notable occasion in this period was the Crufts Show in 1971 when Mrs. F. J. Winter's Ch. Fourwents Gretel of Eskamere, bred by Mrs. A. Heward, brought honor and glory to the breed by winning the Hound Group. Perhaps the best overall performance in early 1971 was that of Ch. Borellan Kaymaur Thor (Ravenstone Thinvollr Harald ex Ardenwood Trilla), bred by Mrs. C. Tomlinson. Owing to unfortunate circumstances in his early life, he was found in the hands of the Royal Society for the Prevention of Cruelty to Animals and rescued by his breeder. He then joined the kennel of Mrs. J. Block. When he had settled down and was put in condition, he became almost unbeatable and went on to win 30 challenge certificates thus setting a new record for the breed. He was Best in Show, All Breeds at Dumfries Championship Show in 1972, Best Hound and

Reserve Best in Show at Leicester Championship Show 1973. He was Elkhound Dog of the Year for four years from 1971 to 1974 and Leading Stud Dog in 1973 and 1974. He sired quite a number of champions and his get showed a quality which won them many first prizes.

Another from the same kennel, Ch. Borellan Larsen, bred by Mrs. Block and owned by Mrs. J. Cowper, also made his mark on the breed. He was used very successfully at stud and produced some very nice winning stock including his son Ch. Rothenborg Christian, winner of many challenge certificates and Best in Show at Richmond 1977. A litter sister to Larsen became Ch. Borellan Lola of Torden.

Among other big winners was the dog Ch. Mageroy Waysider (Ch. Borellan Ollerton Trigg ex Gaupa, Norwegian import). Bred by Mrs. M. Newton and owned by Mrs. S. Haddon, he sired many winners and promising puppies. How he came by his name makes an interesting story. His dam, Gaupa, had been mated to Trigg but showed no signs of being in whelp until one day, when out for a walk, she gave birth to this one puppy, literally by the wayside!

A bitch of note during this time was Ch. Lillabo Sara (Lillabo Emil ex Lillabo Brighde), bred by Miss E. Langman and owned by Mr. and Mrs. Howes. She won 17 challenge certificates and was often placed in the Hound Group where she was a good advertisement for the breed. She was mated to Ch. Borellan Larsen and produced a champion son and daughter in her first litter.

Ch. Vikynn of Vandavell and Ch. Vinko of Vandavell were top winners in 1977. Vikynn was Reserve Best in Show All Breeds at the 1977 Hound Show. Another top winner was Ch. Rikarlo Ruskin (Wavensmere Gripp ex Joretor Anguar), bred by Mrs. M. Smart and owned by Mrs. Ana Sanches.

The years 1970 to 1980 were remarkable for the increasingly successful Scottish contingent in the show ring, many good Elkhounds having been bred in and campaigned from Scotland. Ch. Invergloy Babs (Ch. Borellay Kaymaur Thor ex Ch. Lillabo Berit), bred and owned by Mrs. J. MacLennan, won 11 challenge certificates and was Elkhound Bitch of the Year in 1974 and winner of the Hound Group and Reserve Best in Show at Manchester in 1974 as well as Best in Show at both the British Elkhound Club and Elkhound Association of Scotland Shows that year. Ch. Norwing Ajax and his litter sister Ch. Norwind Anouk won many challenge certificates. Anouk was owned and shown by her breeder, J. W. Brown, and Ajax was owned by J. Wallace. A third member of the litter, Norwind Alida, also did well in the show ring. They were sired by Norwind Lillabo Mac ex Ch. Barskimming Wanda who in this and other litters proved herself an excellent brood bitch.

At the end of 1976 there were two new Norwegian bloodlines in Scotland. The Koriston Kennel of Mr. and Mrs. F. Anderson housed a

Eng. Ch. Norwind Anouk, bred and owned by J.W. Brown (Scotland).

Eng. Ch. Lillabo Sara, winner of 17 CCs. Dam of champions. Bred by Miss E. Langman and owned by Mr. and Mrs. W. Howes.

Eng. Ch. Rikarlo Ruskin. Bred by Mrs. M. Smart and owned by Mrs. Ann Sanchez.

Ch. Borellan Lola of Torden, litter sister of Ch. Borellan Larsen. Owned by Mrs. J. Jarburn.

smart young Norwegian dog, Vardetoppen's Busse of Koriston, who was imported by Mrs. Cairnes when she returned from Norway. His first crop of puppies showed great promise. Mrs. Isobel Clarkson made history in 1974 when her bitch, Laekness Katrina, whelped two male puppies as the result of artificial insemination with deep frozen semen imported from Norway. The semen came from Oftenasens Raggen, owned by Herr Knut Bevolden. The first attempt to inseminate the bitch failed, but ten months later Katrina proved in whelp and delivered two puppies. Laekness Norsk Andy's Boy was kept by Mrs. Clarkson and his brother, Laekness Norsk Kjell's Buster, went to the Koriston Kennel.

Herr J. Hallingby came from Norway to judge the Elkhound Association of Scotland Championship Show in October 1977. His choice for Best in Show was Mr. and Mrs. Howe's home-bred Ch. Vikynn of Vandavell, climaxing a very successful year in the show ring for Vikynn.

Some of the kennel prefixes active during this time in England and Wales were: Borellan (Mrs. J. Block), Eskamere (Mrs. A. Howard), Kistrand (Miss E. Wilson), Lillabo (Miss E. M. Langman), Mageroy (Mrs. M. Newton), Malator (Mrs. B. Grace), Mindas (Mrs. B. Parkes), Myradal (Mrs. C. Tomlinson), Norsled (Mrs. S. Haddon), Pevyre (Mr. E. Peffer), Ravenstone (Miss A.N.A. Lovell), Rogersome (Mrs. M. Rogers), Rothenborg (Mrs. J. Cowper), Torden (Mrs. J. Harburn), Tortawe (Mr. and Mrs. H. Griffiths), Vandavel (Mr. and Mrs. W. Howes).

In Scotland, active kennels at this time included: Barskimming (Mrs. M. McDonald), Invergloy (Mrs. J. MacLennan), Koriston (Mr. and Mrs. F. Anderson), Laekness (Mrs. Isobel Clarkson), Norwind (Mr. J. W. Brown), Opinan (Dr. A.E.T. Sneeden), Elsken (Mr. K. C. Wallace), Harith (Mrs. E. M. Jamieson), Melfeva (Mr. G. Ferguson).

The opportunities for showing our Elkhounds continue to improve. There are nearly twenty championship shows each year which offer challenge certificates for the Best Dog and Best Bitch in Elkhounds. There are rarely less than 60 or 70 dogs entered at all these shows and the entry often exceeds that number so there is plenty of competition. Prior to the mid 1970s the number of challenge certificates made available by the Kennel Club depended on the average number of registrations at the Kennel Club in the three year period just previous to the year of competition. The average number of registrations during that period (1970-1975) was approximately 300. A new system adopted grants championship certificates available based on the number of entries at championship shows averaged over a three year period. Thus the number of shows that can offer challenge certificates is steadily increasing.

During the 1970s several Norwegian and one Swedish judge have been regularly invited to judge at shows in England and Scotland. These include Olaf Roig, Olav Campbell, Ralf Campbell, K. S. Wilberg, Mrs. U. Segerstrom (Sweden), J. Hallingby, and K. Storholm.

140

In Ireland there is a band of keen and enthusiastic breeders and exhibitors who cross the Irish Sea to compete at shows in England and Scotland. The Norwegian Elkhound Society of Ireland holds a championship show of its own each year. Mrs. Cairnes, who spent some time in Norway, brought back Boltown Vardetoppens Jack who has been used quite extensively at stud and is now owned by Mrs. M. A. Anderson in Donegal. Mrs. Cairnes also imported Vardetoppens Busse of Koriston now owned by Mr. and Mrs. F. Anderson of Scotland. Quite a number of breeders in England and Scotland have availed themselves of this opportunity to use fresh Norwegian bloodlines. Swilley Valley, Boltown and Kavcap are some of the well known prefixes in Ireland.

In 1983 the British Elkhound Club celebrated its Diamond Jubilee— fifty years of organized enthusiastic support for the breed in England, Scotland and Ireland. The British Elkhound Club, formed of the merger of the British Elkhound Society and the British Elkhound Club has maintained the same objectives as its predecessors and despite the high cost of printing has followed the old Society's practice of publishing annual Year Books with a Journal published every two years. These publications form a record of the breed's history and dogs can be traced by pedigree back to the earliest Elkhounds in Britain. Recent imports from Norway and Sweden have again been made and incorporated in present day breeding plans. Also, the breed Standard has been reviewed and amendments made, notably, the addition of descriptions of mouth and gait.

So, nearly sixty years of Elkhound organization has been completed by devoted British breeders. It is hoped that the breed will continue to improve and give great pleasure to present and future generations of enthusiasts.

Two important Holland imports from Norway, Ch. Oftenasens Buster and Ch. Solvi (Oftenasens Raggen Janj). Owned by Mr. Vrij.

Int. Ch. Ivar (Ch. Bikko ex Ornala) and his son, Bamse. Ivar, a very important sire in Holland, was bred by H. Garritsen and is owned by J. Brinks.

8

The Norwegian Elkhound in Other Lands

THE NORWEGIAN ELKHOUND IN HOLLAND

It is never an easy task to help a new breed gain popularity, so in Holland the Elkhound is only slowly increasing in numbers. The Elkhound club of Holland consists of about 350 members and entries at the specialty shows average nearly 100 dogs. This is a fine record in a country where the total breed population numbers perhaps no more than 600.

The first Elkhounds were imported into Holland shortly after World War II in 1946 and 1947. Dr. H. Bonnema was one of the first enthusiastic breeders. He imported dogs first from England and later brought in six dogs from Norway. Another enthusiastic breeder was Miss Duyvendak, who also imported a bitch from England. Upon her return to Holland after the war, Susan Van Boetzelaer brought with her the Elkhound bitch who had been her own house pet.

The list of dogs imported to Holland at that time contains names of dogs which still can be traced in Dutch pedigrees today. It is thanks to these dogs that good quality Elkhounds exist in Holland today. The first dog imported by Dr. Bonnema, Forwents Bjorg (Bamse av Jarlesberg ex Nitra) produced a strain that is still encountered. Bjorg was a fairly big dog, rather dark in color with a very fine disposition. Bjorg and the bitch, Kaisa av Tallo sired by Steig av Jarlsberg, produced many outstanding dogs. Another dog imported from Norway by Dr. Bonnema was Olaf av Tallo. His bloodlines are carried down to present day dogs through his daughter, Ch. Oring's Karen.

Oring's Karen bred to Shorty of Riverland (Skol av Konnerud ex Lulu of Lindvangen) produced an outstanding litter. One of the dogs in this litter, Skol van de Waddenkust, in turn sired many nice litters. It is interesting to note that one of the outstanding sires of the 1970s, Ch. Ivar, goes back to these dogs. His well-known grandson, Odin van Ananiahoeve, is a specialty winner.

Miss Duyvandak bred several litters from her bitch, Fourwents Janda (Ch. Fourwents Rugg av Aalsund ex Fourwents Trigg). From the first litter, sired by Ch. Hei of the Hollow (Gaupesteins Ruggen ex Lynette of the Hollow), came Bamsehjem Bjonnson, a big dog with plenty of bone—a characteristic encountered in many of his relatives including the well known Ch. Bikko.

Susan van Boetzelaer's own dogs go back to three imports of which Lulu of Lindvangen was the first. Lulu was whelped in 1941 and her pedigree contains many of the great old timers of the breed such as Kren of the Hollow, Jerv av Elglia and Friochan Husky. Lulu herself was a small bitch but her offspring were of good size with plenty of bone. She had a wonderful disposition that was passed on to her offspring. Her first litter was sired by the Norwegian dog, Skol av Konneruf (Bjonn av Jarlsberg ex Laila), who unfortunately died when only two years of age. From this litter came the dog, Martini of Riverland who, when bred to another American bitch, Lindy of Lindvangen, produced the brothers Leif of Riverland and Sir Lancelot of Riverland. Both dogs had outstanding dispositions. Today, all Dutch bred dogs trace back to these dogs in some line. It is interesting to note that Lindy herself was not one of the most outstanding bitches but she possessed two qualities that are so often overlooked by breeders and judges and which are the making or undoing of a breed—style and distinctive type. Wherever she went, she attracted attention in a way that was a great advertisement for the breed. She was a fanatic hunter and on one of her rat hunts she contracted leptospirosis, which damaged her kidneys. It was feared that another litter would shorten her life so she had just the one litter, but it is surprising how often her strong characteristics are encountered in today's dogs that are related to her.

During the 1960s and 1970s five dogs imported from Norway have been used to improve the quality of Dutch Elkhounds. One of these, Ola av Grafjall (Trymm ex Tortasen's Ane) was mated to a daughter of Leif of Riverland. Unfortunately this was the only litter he sired. One bitch from this litter was exported to Winnipeg, Canada and became Canadian Ch. Ondine of Riverland. She produced some nice puppies for owner Monica Torrance. Another dog from this litter became the sire of Ch. Bikko who in turn sired Ch. Ivar. As most of the top dogs in Holland today are related to Ivar, it can be seen that Ola played a dominant role in the Dutch strain of Elkhounds.

The *Scandia* Elkhound Club of Holland as a group imported from

Ch. Sir Lancelot of Riverland (1953-68), pictured at 12 years. The only dog of the breed to go Best in Show in Holland, and a very influential sire. —*Veldhuis*

Ch. Goliath von Dulkenstein (Solo of Riverland ex Ch. Freya of Cherubai). Pictured in his win of Best in Group at a Dutch show with about 3,000 dogs. Owned by G.J.C. van Oostern.

—*Photo, Tim Hagendoorn.*

Norway Oftenasen's Buster (Ch. Tass ex Ch. Oftenasens Kaisa) in an effort to bring improvement to the breed. He was stationed with the club treasurer who lived near the center of the country and his stud fees went to the club. Buster lived as the house pet of the club treasurer.

Most unexpectedly an Elkhound bitch came to Holland from Kenya, Africa in 1970. The owner of Freya of Cheubia (Ch. Ben of Cherubai ex Ch. Ravenstone Vinni of Cherubai) was unable to keep the dog he had brought with him from Africa and sought a suitable home for her. The dog was placed with friends of the Van Boetzelaers and proved to be of good type with much style and an appealing disposition. A few weeks later she was entered at the Elkhound specialty show where she won not only her class but was made Best Bitch in show. Freya had three litters, the most outstanding of which was sired by her grandson, Solo of Riverland (Ch. Ivar ex Sarah). Two dogs out of this litter, Goliath van Dulkenstein and Gunnar van Dulkenstein, became champions. Goliath became a consistent winner as he possessed great style and type. Other recent winners have carried Freya as an ancestor several times in their pedigrees. Thus the dog from Africa made a significant contribution to Dutch Elkhounds.

Two enthusiastic Dutch exhibitors visited Norway in the mid 1970s and returned with two litter sisters, Sylvie and Serene. While Sylvie proved impossible to get in whelp, Serene has fortunately had several litters and her grandchildren have become show winners, the most outstanding being Stormwind of Elkwood.

The Scandia Elkhound Club in Holland

In this small country the club organized by fanciers has helped the breed in many ways. Dr. Bonnema founded the club in 1948 with a small group of enthusiastic Elkhound owners who felt that a club was essential. Dr. Bonnema was active in the club for the first ten years and wrote and printed the newsletter several times a year. The articles he wrote were outstanding and membership increased slowly. In the late 1950s the club had some difficult years. Dr. Bonnema was forced to limit his activities due to poor health and membership declined to a small but dedicated group of fanciers. These members helped the club and continued to show their dogs and breed good quality gaining new support for the breed. During this time, the two brothers, Sir Lancelot and Leif of Riverland did much to promote the breed by always placing in the Group when shown and Lancelot was the first Elkhound to win Best in Show in this country. These dogs appealed to many people and their excellent dispositions won many new admirers.

By the mid 1960s the breed had finally gained a firm foothold. Mr. Vry, an active club member and the club treasurer, managed finances so excellently that several specialty shows have been given with Norwegian judges asked to judge.

There are no big kennels in Holland and most litters are bred by people who have their Elkhounds as house pets. Therefore, an important task of the club has been to help members plan the right breedings. About 75% of the litters whelped are the result of these careful selections. At regular shows the entries are usually quite limited. For this reason the shows are of great importance. Club members enjoy the specialty shows and when the entry is nearly 100 dogs, one gets a good idea of overall quality of the breed. Through the club, it is hoped that continued breedings of quality dogs can help to keep the breed from declining and make sure that all Elkhounds in Holland are given the treatment they deserve.

The Hunting Capacity of the Elkhound in Holland

by Baroness Susan Van Boetzelaer

To complete the picture of the Elkhound in Holland, it would be wrong not to mention the exceptional role some of our dogs have played in the hunting field. Although they are not often used in the hunting field we have had a few who were outstanding as retrievers and excellent finders of wounded deer and wild boar. The several owners who used their dogs for deer and boar told me they could tell by the way the dog was barking if he had found a wounded or dead animal. Most of these dogs would only let the owner approach the game they had found.

Another dog I knew very well was an excellent retriever of any game shot. This dog, a bitch, had not been trained but after watching the shooting dogs do this kind of work she became the best retriever her owner had ever had. I can well remember a cold winter day when I had been out watching the shooting dogs and this Elkhound retrieve. The Elkhound was clearly enjoying herself retrieving pheasant, rabbits and hares with the greatest of ease. At the end of the day we were starting home when a pigeon was shot. The retrievers were sent out but couldn't locate it. The Elkhound watched their activity for a while and then suddenly took off. We saw her cross a frozen lake and then disappear out of sight. We decided she must be following a fresh rabbit or hare scent so we turned towards home. We were met at the house by the Elkhound with the pigeon in her mouth. She had found the lost bird and had taken a short cut home.

With my own dogs I have spent countless hours waiting for them to return after taking off after deer or other game. I can remember one occasion when this hunting passion was not too convenient. I was on my way to a dog show in Germany when I stopped in a large woods to give Lance a run. Unfortunately these woods were well populated with deer. My Elkhound, who was one of the most obedient dogs I have ever had, could never resist going after big game. He must have scented the deer in the car, for he vanished into the bushes the moment I opened the car door. There was a lot of creaking in the bushes and some barking, and if I had not stepped aside, I might have been knocked over by a large stag and several doe. I watched them disappear into the woods with Lance close on their heels. One thing I have learned from my dogs is to never search for them as they nearly always follow their own scent back to the spot where they left you. When hunting time does not seem to exist for them; they usually return within an hour or two, although on one occasion I had to wait four hours for one of my bitches to return. This time Lance reappeared within the hour, dripping wet. We arrived at the dog show in time to be judged but Lance was certainly not looking his best.

I have always considered the Elkhound to have a very remarkable scenting capacity. In the years I was able to exercise them on horseback, I was very impressed by the fact that they could also follow the scent of my horse with great ease. There was a very large forest in which I could exercise my horse and dogs safely. It had numerous bridle paths, and as the woods were also used by a great many training stables, the paths were well frequented by other riders. Yet if my dogs would take off and do some hunting on their own they were always able to follow my scent and catch up with me again. Certainly one of the most unforgettable rides I ever had was when one of my dogs held a very large stag at bay. As it was rather late in the afternoon and I did not have a great deal of time, I had only taken one dog with me. I heard him barking in an exceptional way. I found him running around a very large stag. The moment I appeared, the stag broke away but within a very short distance the Elkhound once again managed to hold the deer at bay. It was an overwhelming sight; the stag would constantly charge at the dog, yet he was never fast enough. Although I was duly impressed by the capacity of my dog, I also wanted to get home before dark. I was finally forced to dismount and even then the deer seemed so absorbed by my dog that he did not break away. Luckily I was able to grab my dog and the deer vanished out of sight. However, I did not want to run any more risks. Using my stirrup leathers as a leash, I rode home with my dog leashed for the first time in his life!

It is hard not to go on indefinitely writing about the many unforgettable moments my dogs have given me. They are still a daily source of pleasure in the house or on our walks. However, in our over-populated country the increase in traffic is a constant danger for these active hunting dogs. Yet exercising them on the leash would give neither of us any

148

pleasure. As I grew up with Elkhounds and have known them for nearly 40 years, I feel that I am fairly familiar with their characters and disposition. Yet in these numerous years and the many dogs I have owned or known well, I have never encountered one who was unreliable or was not to be trained. I am glad that in Holland the breed has now earned the admiration it certainly deserves. I sincerely hope that in the future every breeder of Elkhounds will do his utmost to maintain its exceptional characteristics.

Baroness Susan van Boetzelaer pictured at the 1982 NEAA Specialty with Veteran Dog Award of Merit and Scandia KC Special Award winner, Ch. Rikkana's Independence, owned by Jon and Cam LaBree. The Baroness, whose Riverland Kennels was one of the important pioneers in the breeding of Norwegian Elkhounds in the Netherlands, is no stranger to the American fancy. A niece of Lawrence Litchfield, one of the founders of the Norwegian Elkhound Association of America, she has judged the breed in America on several occasions and impressed exhibitors with her appreciation of the purpose and function of the breed. Her original Elkhound, acquired from the Litchfields, was Lulu of Lindvangen. Lulu became one of the foundation dogs of the breed in Holland. Riverland Kennels has exported several dogs to America.

NORWEGIAN ELKHOUNDS IN AUSTRALIA

The history of the Norwegian Elkhound in Australia does not go as far back as in those countries where the breed has enjoyed popularity for many years. Although some Elkhounds may have been imported from England or New Zealand before World War II and in the years just after the war, there are no reliable records to support this fact. The first Elkhound known to have come to Australia from England was the bitch Ravenstone Bjonne, bred by Mrs. Lovell. Her sire was Fourwents Kasper and her dam Ravenstone Rather Lovely. She was imported to Australia by Mr. and Mrs. F. J. Abnett, owners of the now well-known Torgrim Elkhound Kennels. They brought Bjonne with them when they migrated to Australia in 1958. She was then about two years old and although her owners wished to raise a litter from her, they could not locate a mate for her in Australia and she therefore never produced offspring in her lifetime.

In 1963, Len Nicholson of Melbourne imported Friochan Tryg (Friochan Sande ex Ardenwood Breta) from England. On his annual business trips to England, Mr. Nicholson always visited a good friend in Scotland who owned an Elkhound and he became enchanted with the wonderful friendly, alert personality of this dog. When he sought an Elkhound for himself, he was referred to Mrs. Kitty Heffer who was the owner of Friochan Kennels. Tryg arrived in Melbourne just before Christmas in 1963 after a long trip by sea. At that time shipment of dogs by air was not permitted as Australian authorities feared the introduction of rabies, a disease not present in Australia. Tryg was the first Elkhound to be registered in Australia with the Kennel Control Council of Victoria.

In 1965, Mr. Nicholson decided to bring a female to Australia and breed a few litters. He again contacted Mrs. Heffer who offered him the bitch Friochan Brigitte (Friochan Ebor ex Ardenwood Trilla) who was bred by Mrs. C. Tomlinson. Brigitte arrived in Australia early in 1966. The first litter from Tryg and Brigitte was whelped in May of that year and registered under the Nicholson's "Elstern" kennel name. Shortly thereafter, with Mr. Nicholson's assistance, Mr. Lockwood of Melbourne obtained Lillabo Arkel (Lillabo Guntar ex Lollabo Senta). "Kelley" arrived in Australia in May of 1967 and in 1970 a litter sired by him was whelped by Friochan Brigitte. These two litters were of good quality and provided many of the early Australian champions. Altogether 21 puppies were registered under the Elstern prefix and these dogs became the founders of the breed in Australia.

At about the same time in 1966, Mr. and Mrs. Jeff Lumsden, an English couple living in Melbourne and Elkhound fanciers of long standing, decided to import some good Elkhounds for breeding. They purchased Thane of the Mountains from Mr. and Mrs. G. Beasley in England. Thane was a son of the famous Zulu out of Katriona of

Gimle Loki and Gimle Laika, bred and owned by Mr. and Mrs. C. de Goede.

Ch. Invergloy Dirk, imported to Australia from Scotland. Bred by Mrs. J. MacLennan, Scotland. Owned by Mr. and Mrs. C. de Goede.

Ch. Carsuwen Catrina, winner of 10 bitch CC's. Bred by Mr. and Mrs. J. Redstone. Owned by Mr. and Mrs. C. de Goede.

Camalot Trykk Assured Fame, pictured prior to being exported from U.S. to Australia. Breeders, George and Mari Misbeek (Camalot). New owners, Barry and Sue Tucker of Lavington, N.S.W.   —Sequel photo.

Karworth. The Lumsdens also imported a female from New Zealand, Ardena Dreda, bred by Mrs. Nancy Parker. This female was the result of a mating of the Irish import Osvald Ergina to Mrs. Parker's bitch, Vars Vanda. Thane and Dreda produced a litter in 1971 that proved to be of excellent quality, with many of the pups achieving their championship title. One of this litter, Aavald Bjorn, owned by Mr. Tom Ginnan of Canberra, had a strong influence on the breed in Australia through his offspring. Quite tragically, Thane of the Mountains was killed by a car shortly after this first litter was produced and his valuable bloodline was lost to Australian breeders.

Breeders realized that the limited number of breeding dogs available was a handicap, and that new blood was needed if deterioration was to be avoided. The late John Redstone, then Foundation President of the Norwegian Elkhound Club of Australia, decided to import a good quality female from England. He contacted a number of breeders there and ultimately obtained, from Mrs. M. E. Newton of Mageroy Kennels in London, Mageroy Zillah (Ch. Borellan Larsen ex Mageroy Zimena). This dog arrived in Australia in 1973, and after her release from quarantine was mated to Ch. Alesund Thane, who had been purchased by the Redstones from Ron Kemp. Thus, Zillah's first litter was whelped under the Carsuwen prefix in 1974. Several of these pups attained championships and the influence of the Norwegian dogs was apparent in them as their dam, Zillah, was the offspring of the Norwegian dog, Gaupa 1563, who had been imported to England. Gaupa was herself a daughter of Nor. Ch. Finn and a granddaughter of Nor. Ch. Tass, with background from the Kotofjell and Suteraas Kennels.

Ken Herrick, owner of the Norskhund kennel also sought to obtain new dogs of quality and with the help of Mr. Nicholson selected a puppy bred in Scotland by Mrs. J. MacLennen, Invergloy Dirk. Some of the best British and Norwegian bloodlines were represented in his pedigree. Dirk became a champion and has had a profound influence on the breed in Australia as he sired a substantial number of litters. His descendants are to be found in all Australian states and many of them became champions and Group or show winners.

Subsequently, Mr. Herrick imported another male and two females from Mrs. S. A. Haddon in England. These were Norsled Gatsby, Norsled Helga and Norsled Irmelin. Gatsby and Irmelin made a valuable contribution to the genetic pool in Australia and Helga too produced excellent litters under the Helsam kennel name when bred to Ch. Elstern Viscount Sam.

In more recent years, Elkhounds from the United States have also augmented the breeding stock of Australia. In 1982, Camalot Trykk Assured Fame, bred by Mari and George Misbeek of Santa Barbara, California was imported to Australia and with others from the U.S. have given Australian breeders a broader base of selection for their programs. Careful breeding programs and planned matings are the objectives of Australian breeders. It is clear that the younger generations of Australian dogs represent improved quality over the early dogs. This is largely due to the careful selection of those early imports and the careful planning of matings by conscientious breeders. Mr. and Mrs. Brian Edwards of Sydney of Shasnar Kennels have produced fine dogs such as Ch. Sahasnar Kogi, Ch. Shasnar Knut and Ch. Shasnar Palna. In Victoria, the Helsam Kennels of Mrs. Carla Basto and Mrs. Lyn Spry have produced fine dogs such as Ch. Helsam Arkel and Ch. Helsam Freda. Also in Victoria resides Ken Eidem, an immigrant from Norway, and dogs fropm his Geitegaren Kennel have had success at shows in that area. In Tasmania, under the guidance of Miss Ann McMeachan, the Norskhund dogs of Ken Herrick's breeding have continued to be an influence. In The Capital Territory, Mr. and Mrs. Cliff de Goede have produced good Elkhounds under the Gimle prefix.

The Norwegian Elkhound Club of Australia was first started by a small group of enthusiasts exhibiting at a show in Melbourne in 1973. They included Len Nicholson, Ken Herrick, Ron Kemp, Tom Ginnan, Ken Eidem, the late John Redstone and Ms. Barstow, Hope and Strownix. Plans were formulated and on September 21, 1973 the Elkhound Club of Australia was founded. Its first specialty show was held in Canberra in 1977 and thereafter this active organization has endeavored to safeguard the fine qualities of the Elkhound as companion, hunter and guardian.

Unfortunately, the opportunities to hunt with Elkhounds in Australia are limited but their skills as Obedience dogs have been well documented by trainers and owners. As the breed became more popular, Australian hunters began to realize how well they perform in the field and while Australia has no "moose," the dogs' skills with wild boar and even kangaroo are becoming well known.

Australian breeders look to the future with great confidence. The breed is in the hands of concerned caring people in this vast country and with high standards of selection for type and temperament, there is no reason why an Australian-bred Elkhound should not represent the best in the breed anywhere on earth.

NORWEGIAN ELKHOUNDS IN ISRAEL

Despite the difficulties of international relations in the Middle East, fanciers of the Norwegian Elkhound in Israel have gained a foothold and in the true nature of the breed, the dogs have adapted to the hot, dry climate and thrive. Strong supporters of the breed such as Marra Shoshany and Professor Eitan Hochman have imported fine dogs and supported the entry of Norwegian Elkhounds at Israeli dog shows.

The first Elkhound to arrive in Israel in 1975 was Can. & Is. Ch. Wes-Mor Njord's Yuval. He placed first in the Group at a subsequent Spitz Specialty and became a foundation sire for the small Israeli Elkhound population. In 1977, Marra Shoshany imported from Bob and Diane Coleman of Ohio, the bitch that was to become Is. Ch. Normark TNT Promise's Sjera. She was imported in whelp to her half brother, Am. & Can. Ch. Crafdal Tryg 'N Thors Njord. Shortly after her arrival, she whelped the first litter of Norwegian Elkhounds born in Israel.

Three champions came from this litter: Valmara Njord N Sjera's Guin, Valmara Njord N Smera's Nuke and Valmara Njord N Sjera's Cassimasima. The latter, known as "Calli" has many Best of Breed wins and was placed first in the Spitz Group by English judge Percy Whittacker.

Again in 1979 Ms. Shoshany imported a dog from the Colemans. Is. Ch. Normark TNT Nike's Jetsetter was bred to Valmara's Valkyrie (Ch. Wes-Mor Njord's Yuval ex Ch. Normark TNT Promise's Sjera). A dog from this litter, Is. Ch. Valmara's Excellence has become the top winning Spitz Group dog in Israel and has been awarded Best of Breed, Group placements and the coveted Best in Show award from such distinguished international judges as Olav Campbell, Ralf Campbell, Yaniki BarNear and Edward M. Gilbert, Jr. The offspring of this dog exhibit great promise for the future of the breed in Israel.

In 1981, Professor Eitan Hochman imported two dogs from California breeder Mari Misbeek. Camalot Trogan's Exodus has become the sire of several young winners, including Valmara's Steel and Valmara's Tokk, who is owned by the former Miss Universe, Rina Mor.

Shows in Israel are held under the format of the F.C.I. where all dogs are judged individually against the breed standard, receive a written critique and where judges may withhold titles if no worthy specimens are presented. In order to attain a championship a dog must be over 15 months of age and receive three Challenge Certificates from at least two different judges. Interest in preserving the correct hunting type is illustrated by the invitations to specialty judges such as the Campbells. The future of the "Elghund Norvegi" in Israel is in good hands. Concerned breeders will work toward preserving and protecting the breed.

Can. and Israeli Ch. Wes-Mor Njord's Juval, first Elkhound exhibited in Israel. BIS winner at Spitz Specialty, Jerusalem 1976. Owned by Marra Stein.

Valmara Njord n' Sjera's Guin (at 10 months) being judged by Rainer Vuorinen of Finland at the Ashkalon International Dog Show. Owned by Moshe Maoz. Handled by breeder, Marra Stein.

A Norwegian Judge's Picture of Excellence in the Norwegian Elkhound

Boy av Glitre (d), 8318
(Ch. Skrub av Glitre ex Gaupa II av Glitre)
Breeder-Owner: T. Hemsen, "av Glitre" Kennels, Ski, Norway

(Johnny Aarflot was for many years one of the most respected authorities on the Norwegian Elkhound. A breeder (Elglia Kennels in Norway) and a field trial and show judge, he judged the first National Specialty of the Norwegian Elkhound Association of America at Chicago in 1962. This translated excerpt is from an article he wrote for the *Norsk Elghunds 50 Year Jubilee Book*.)

I consider this picture I took of Boy av Glitre as the best illustration of a good Norwegian Elkhound.

The head is excellent—beautiful, and with the serious, alert expression so typical for an Elkhound. The fur forms a nice collar on the well-poised neck. Body and legs are harmoniously proportioned. (An Elkhound's legs will usually seem more frail in a photograph than they really are.) Notice the good straight forelegs, and the correct placement of upper arm and shoulder—important for the beautiful carriage of neck and front. Notice, too, the strong back with a beautiful top line, and the short, well-formed flanks. Boy's hind legs are correctly angulated at the knee and hock joints. Too extreme an angulation is atypical for the Elkhound. He is not a short distance sprinter. His typical gait is a somewhat short canter that he can keep up for hours, even in rugged country.

As the photograph clearly shows, Boy had good close paws. Particularly note the right hind paw. The tail is tightly curled, and is straight on the back. (The lighting in the photograph makes it appear that Boy had a fan tail, but this was not so.) The light harness marking (back of the shoulders) is very typical, as is the dark "saddle" formed by the dark tips of the covering hair on the sides of the chest, and across the front. The light coloring of the legs is also evident. One will often see Elkhounds with the dark color spread all the way down to the paws, and this is not very becoming.

But all of these are just details. What characterizes this picture of Boy above all else is his typiness, and the harmony of his build.

It is most important that we safeguard this original type, and not sacrifice any of it to eliminate less important details. A beautiful coat with good color, a first rate tail, nice dark eyes—all are commendable, but won't help much if the dog lacks the correct harmonious type of body, and the true characteristics of the Elkhound. For example, a short-legged, heavy and overbuilt Elkhound should not rate very high at a show, even if other features are first rate. Nor should a tall-legged, frail dog with a long back be given awards. We repeat—type is the important factor, details are secondary.

157

Norwegian, Swedish, Canadian and American CH. TORTASSEN'S BJONN II
Whelped 1952, by Ch. Bamse ex Ch. Moa. Bred by P.J. Holseng, Norway.
Owned by Mr. and Mrs. A. Wells Peck, Pitch Road Kennels.

9

Official AKC Standard for the Norwegian Elkhound

Approved February 13, 1973

General Description—The Norwegian Elkhound is a hardy gray hunting dog. In appearance, a typical northern dog of medium size and substance, square in profile, close coupled and balanced in proportions. The head is broad with prick ears, and the tail is tightly curled and carried over the back. The distinctive gray coat is dense and smooth-lying. In temperament, the Norwegian Elkhound is bold and energetic, an effective guardian yet normally friendly, with great dignity and independence of character. As a hunter, the Norwegian Elkhound has the courage, agility and stamina to hold moose and other big game at bay by barking and dodging attack, and the endurance to track for long hours in all weather over rough and varied terrain.

In the show ring, presentation in a natural, unaltered condition is essential.

Head—Broad at the ears, wedge-shaped, strong, and dry (without loose skin). Viewed from the side, the forehead and back of the skull are only slightly arched; the stop not large, yet clearly defined. The bridge of the nose is straight, parallel to and about the same length as the skull. The muzzle is thickest at the base and, seen from above or from the side, tapers evenly without being pointed. Lips are tightly closed and teeth meet in a scissors bite.

159

Ears—Set high, firm and erect, yet very mobile. Comparatively small; slightly taller than their width at the base with pointed (not rounded) tips. When the dog is alert, the orifices turn forward and the outer edges are vertical.

Eyes—Very dark brown, medium in size, oval, not protruding.

Neck—Of medium length, muscular, well set up with a slight arch and with no loose skin on the throat.

Body—Square in profile and close coupled. Distance from brisket to ground appears to be half the height at the withers. Distance from forechest to rump equals the height at the withers. Chest deep and moderately broad; brisket level with points of elbows; and ribs well sprung. Loin short and wide with very little tuck-up. The back is straight and strong from its high point at the withers to the root of the tail.

Forequarters—Shoulders sloping with elbows closely set on. Legs well under body and medium in length; substantial, but not coarse, in bone. Seen from the front, the legs appear straight and parallel. Single dewclaws are normally present.

Hindquarters—Moderate angulation at stifle and hock. Thighs are broad and well-muscled. Seen from behind, legs are straight, strong and without dewclaws.

Feet—Paws comparatively small, slightly oval with tightly-closed toes and thick pads. Pasterns are strong and only slightly bent. Feet turn neither in nor out.

Tail—Set high, tightly curled, and carried over the centerline of the back. It is thickly and closely haired, without brush, natural and untrimmed.

Coat—Thick, hard, weather-resisting and smooth-lying; made up of soft, dense, wooly undercoat and coarse, straight covering hairs. Short and even on head, ears, and front of legs; longest on back of neck, buttocks and underside of tail. The coat is not altered by trimming, clipping or artificial treatment. Trimming of whiskers is optional.

Color—Gray, medium preferred, variations in shade determined by the length of black tips and quantity of guard hairs. Undercoat is clear light silver as are legs, stomach, buttocks, and underside of tail. The gray body color is darkest on the saddle, lighter on the chest, mane and distinctive harness mark (a band of longer guard hairs from shoulder to elbow). The muzzle, ears, and tail tip are black. The black of the muzzle shades to lighter gray over the forehead and skull. Yellow or brown shading, white patches, indistinct or irregular markings, "sooty" coloring on the lower legs and light circles around the eyes are undesirable. Any overall color other than gray as described above, such as red, brown, solid black, white or other solid color, disqualifies.

Gait—Normal for an active dog constructed for agility and endurance. At a trot the stride is even and effortless; the back remains level. As the speed of the trot increases, front and rear legs converge equally in straight lines toward a center line beneath the body so that the pads appear to follow in the same tracks (single-track). Front and rear quarters are well balanced in angulation and muscular development.

Size—The height at the withers for dogs is 20½ inches, for bitches 19½ inches. Weight for dogs about 55 pounds; for bitches about 48 pounds.

DISQUALIFICATIONS

Any overall color other than gray as described above, such as red, brown, solid black, white or other solid color.

GOOD HEAD AND EAR SET. Good depth of skull and muzzle, fearless, pleasant expression, correct eye set.

FAULTY HEAD. Low set ears, dark scowling expression.

FAULTY HEAD. Shallow skull, large rounded ears, oriental eye set.

FAULTY HEAD. Ears set too high, head narrow, muzzle pinched and snipey.

10

An In-Depth Consideration of the Standard

by Olav Wallo

FOR MANY YEARS, the official standard for the Norwegian Elkhound in the United States was a translation of the Norwegian standard, as translated by the noted breeder-judge Johnny Aarflot, and approved by the American Kennel Club on November 12, 1935. This standard remained unchanged until July 1969, when one change was made—revising the specification of ideal height for bitches from "about 18 inches" to 19¼ inches.

In 1968, a committee composed of Mary O. Jenkins, Susan D. Phillips, Jeanne Smolley and Karen B. Elvin was delegated by the Norwegian Elkhound Association of America to prepare a standard better suited to the needs of American judges. The new standard was accepted by the NEAA membership and approved by the American Kennel Club in 1973.

Before discussing this standard in detail, one thing should be emphasized above all else—the Elkhound is a hunting breed that must possess the necessary physical qualifications to serve its intended purpose.

Personality—Because of his long and close association with mankind, the Elkhound has an unusual attachment toward his owner and is most friendly, loyal, and dependable. He seems to like nothing better than to be an important and useful member of the family—in fact, he enjoys being the

163

GOOD HEAD. Broad at the ears, muzzle tapers evenly. Line from ear to tip of muzzle shows good fill under eyes.

FAULTY HEAD. Skull rounded, lacks fill under the eyes. Muzzle blocky and not tapered evenly. Eyes protrude.

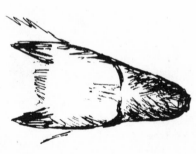

FAULTY HEAD. Narrow skull and muzzle. Long muzzle.

center of attention. Noted for his gentle disposition and even temperament, he seldom starts a fight with other dogs, yet he is bold and aggressive and has plenty of nerve when facing big game. As a guardian of the home and property, this Viking dog shows understanding and intelligence far beyond expectation. Shyness, aggressiveness toward other dogs or people, hyperactivity and nervousness are all unacceptable, not typical of the Elkhound at all, and they should be heavily penalized in the show ring.

General Appearance—The Elkhound is a medium-sized, rugged Northern dog with a square outline, thick, gray, smooth lying but never bristling, coat; pointed, pricked ears; and tightly curled tail carried over the back. There should be balance and harmony in his conformation which will contribute to both his use and his beauty.

Height—The ideal height at the withers for males is 20½ inches (52 cm.) and for females 19½ inches (49 cm.). Variations from these measurements should not exceed one inch. However, undersize should be heavily penalized since small dogs are less effective as hunters and tend to produce small offspring.

Weight—Weight for males should be approximately 55 pounds; for females, 48 pounds. These weights, coupled with correct height, yield a dog suited to the task of hunting big game in rough terrain. Correct proportion should be carefully guarded because a clumsy, heavy-bodied dog is not suited to the work of a hunter. Such a dog will tire too easily and his feet will become sore on rough terrain. He will lack the quickness and agility required of a big game hunter; and, on the trail of the moose, he will pull too hard in the harness. It is desirable to have size without coarseness, good leg length without excessive body bulk. Dogs with short legs and heavy bodies should be severely penalized.

Head—The head is very important for the first impression is created by it. A dog with a poor head, even though he be otherwise good, does not have universal appeal. The description of the Elkhound head by T. Hemsen in *Om Elghunder og Elgjakt i Norge de Siste 50 Ar* is well worth quoting:

"The head of the purebred Elkhound is rather large and very distinctive. It is the head that one first looks at to see if the dog is pure. Elkhound characteristics carry along for generations and when mixed with other breeds, they predominate. For example, a mixture of Elkhound and Shepherd will exhibit mostly Elkhound characteristics. The head, which is typically wedge-shaped, must not be too pinched, tight or dry ahead of the eyes. Viewed from above, the line from nose to ear should be straight; and viewed from the side, the top lines of the skull and the nose should be parallel. The skull is a little higher than the muzzle. It is slightly rounded but from the side fairly straight. Eyebrows define a distinct stop. Underlines of the lips conform to the jaw and do not bend upward at the front. The snoot must be strong and of good size at the tip, so that it does not appear snipish, especially for males. The muzzle length for males of medium size is normally 9 cm. (3½ inches); for females 8 cm. (3⅛ inches). The inside of the lips is dark slate

165

color. The tongue is flesh color. A rounded skull, which is a big fault, seems to be more common recently. It makes the head not typical; the stop is too great and the side lines curve inward with a pinched muzzle ahead of the eyes. If we hope to eliminate the fault we must not breed dogs having that fault, nor award them prizes. The skin of the head shall be dry with no wrinkles."

Emphasis should be placed on a wide full skull, which is one of the basic features of the breed. The bridge of the nose should be straight, not dish-faced or Roman-nosed. The muzzle terminates in nicely finished nostrils, which should be wide open, moist, and dark, but never flesh-colored.

Stop—There should be a definite but slight stop. The line of the stop continues up one-third of the forehead between slightly raised brows. The stop is much more definite than that of other Spitz breeds, thus distinguishing the breed from Siberian Huskies, Finnish Spitz and other breeds and also allowing the line of the backskull to parallel that of the muzzle, a distinctive feature of the Elkhound head.

Mouth—The mouth should be cut back 3 to 3½ inches. The lips, which should be of fairly thin leather, must not extend below the jaw; yet they should cover the teeth when the mouth is closed.

Whiskers—The current AKC standard for the breed, approved in 1973, specifies that "Trimming of whiskers is optional." However, I strongly feel that the whiskers, which are dark and of medium length, should not be cut or trimmed. No judge should ever penalize a dog that has full whiskers. The whiskers are part of the sensory system that enables the dog to assess his environment.

Teeth—Strong, white teeth are essential. A scissors bite (in which the inner surfaces of the upper teeth engage part of the outer surfaces of the lower teeth) is correct. Very seldom does one find an overshot or an undershot mouth in Elkhounds. Missing teeth (except those lost by accident) should be heavily penalized, as full dentition is normal for the breed.

Eyes—One of the most cherished characteristics of a dog is its eyes, for eyes determine the expression, which in the case of the Elkhound should be sparkling, frank, fearless, and friendly. The eyes should be of medium size, very dark brown (nearly black), slightly almond shaped, not round or protruding (if anything, rather deep-set), about two inches apart, with no haws showing and with tight, dark-rimmed lids. The iris fills the whole eye opening so that the white of the eyeball does not show. The eye set is level and straight forward without the slanting, oriental look typical of many Spitz breeds. Light brown or amber eyes should be very heavily penalized.

Ears—The temperament of an Elkhound is reflected by his ears which are very mobile and quick to respond to his feelings. The ears are open

CORRECT HEAD. Muzzle length equals skull length. Eye set level and forward looking. Good depth of muzzle and skull. Good neck arch.

FAULTY HEAD. Skull and muzzle planes not parallel. Eyes set obliquely. Neck arch weak. Muzzle is boxy, not evenly tapered. Weak stop.

FAULTY HEAD. Skull and muzzle too heavy, stop too large. Eyes round, flews evident. Light eye rings spoil expression.

FAULTY HEAD. Shallow skull and muzzle, narrow wolfish squint.

167

forward when the dog is alert or excited, are dropped to the side when he is depressed or sick, and are laid back tight against the neck when he is pleased, affectionate, or in full run. Ears laid back in this position might give the erroneous impression of a mean disposition. Dogs should not be expected to have ears in continuous upright position in the show ring. If the judge is able to assess the ear set and expression, the dog should not be penalized for mobility and positioning of his ears as described. The outer edges of the ears should be vertical, but one occasionally finds ears pointing outward. This may be due to low ear set or to a dog that is sluggish. Ears are usually erect in puppies at five to ten weeks of age. The ears are medium sized when compared to those of other Spitz breeds. Elkhound ears should be pointed, not rounded like that of a German Shepherd Dog. Height of the ear should exceed the width at the base by approximately an inch. The ear, which should open to the front, should be neither too fine nor too coarse in the texture of the leather. Ears when the dog is alert are carried fairly high on the skull. They should be carried slightly forward and they should not lean out like mule ears. The ear box is small. Hair on the ears is short and fine compared to other Northern breeds. Elkhounds have an exceptionally keen sense of hearing and as a breed are not prone to much deafness with age.

Neck—A neck of medium length, muscular, flexible and well arched is desirable. It should be dry and clean at the throat and the arch of the neck should taper smoothly but strongly into the shoulders. Skin on the nape of the neck is somewhat loose but the throat is without excessive dewlap. A fat dog often stores fat in the dewlap. An important characteristic of the neck is the ruff or collar, which is the profuse, long coat of the neck. The appearance of power is magnified by this collar. An upright neck, known in Norway as "*a good rising,*" is much more stylish than a short neck carried horizontally or a weak short neck that lacks a smooth junction with the shoulders.

Shoulders—It seems that "*good rising*" as well as the relative length of the neck, body, and stride are all based on the length and slope of the shoulder blades. Short, upright blades are associated with a short, telescoped neck, longer back and choppy stride. In contrast, long sloping shoulder blades accompany a long neck, short back, and smooth stride. Elkhound shoulders, however, are not as sloping as those of bird dogs. The blades should be of wide bone with good substance. They should be fairly close together at the withers with good muscling in this area and laid close to the body. Loose shoulders are a bad fault caused mostly by insufficient rib spring and underdevelopment of the forechest in terms of ribs and muscles. Muscles should be smooth, long and strong rather than short and bulging. Appropriate here are these observations made by Olav Roig, a

168

past General Secretary of the Norsk Kennel Club and one of the foremost experts on osteology:

"The conception of the function of a dog's shoulder blade (scapula) has undergone quite an evolution over the years. The function of the scapula was first described by the German cynologist, Captain Max v. Stephanitz, at the beginning of this century. Stephanitz believed that the scapula was firmly fixed to the rib cage of the dog, and launched his well-known theory of the 90% front leg angulation. Based on the assumption that the scapula did not move, Stephanitz theorized that the optimum angle on the vertical line should be 45°. Accordingly, with the scapula and the humerus forming an angle of 90°, the greatest stride of the front leg should be achieved when all its joints were stretched to 180°. Thus, dogs whose front legs could make the longest stride were believed to have the most efficient gait.

In the 1930s two major flaws in von Stephanitz's theory were brought to the attention of dog fanciers. It was pointed out, as veterinarians have always known, that the scapula of the dog is *not* joined to the rib cage, nor is it at all connected with the rest of the skeleton as in man. It was shown that when the dog moves there is also a substantial movement of the scapula. It was further pointed out that if the von Stephanitz theory were true, the foot of the front leg would not touch the ground when the front leg was stretched forward. Since the 1930s it has been acknowldged that the movement of the front leg takes place mainly in the shoulder region as the scapula hinges on the central muscle area, and that the movement of joints of the front legs merely supplement the movement of the scapula.

With the era of ultra slow-motion film it was discovered that in addition to the movement of the scapula hinged on the central muscle area, the scapula also moves backward and forward along the rib cage. As the front leg is stretched forward and the foot reaches the ground, the scapula lies well forward on the rib cage. Then the dog literally hauls its body forward with the aid of its shoulder muscles. The scapula is then in a position considerably further back at the end of the stride of the front leg.

Detailed studies have proved that the distance that the scapula moves varies substantially from one dog to another within the same breed. However, dogs with a very efficient gait show the forward and backward movement of the scapula so clearly that, provided the observer is aware of what to look for, it may be observed with the naked eye under normal conditions."

Body—The body should be compact, square, and short loined; but not so short that it is rigid and stiff. Nor should it be so bulky as to hinder the dog's agility. The rib cage is well developed and the loin short yet flexible.

Chest—A broad, and at the same time deep, chest is desirable. For a medium-sized dog the width across the points of shoulder should be 9 to 10 inches. The chest should not be so wide that it causes a waddling gait. Neither should it be shallow and weak causing a paddling front motion. The girth of the chest of a mature Elkhound in good condition, measured just behind the front legs, is usually 29 to 31 inches. When viewed from the front, the shoulders appear somewhat flat and the brisket appears oval and keel-shaped, but not narrowed to a point. The breastbone should carry well

169

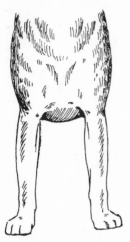

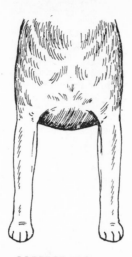

FAULTY FRONT. Narrow, pinched elbows, toes out.

CORRECT FRONT. Straight, toes forward.

FAULTY FRONT. Too wide, elbows out, toes in.

FAULTY REAR. Short legs, bowed rear.

CORRECT REAR. Good leg length, legs straight and parallel.

WEAK REAR. Cowhocks.

through between the upper arms to create a pleasing front line from chin to toes when viewed in profile.

Ribs—The body should be well ribbed to furnish sufficient space for lungs, heart and other vital organs. The curvature of the chest box is heart-shaped in cross section. The rib bones themselves are flat and there is good rib length through the last ribs.

Loin—One of the most important specifications of the breed is that the loin should be short. Three to four inches is a short loin measured from hip to the last rib. There should be little tuck up indicating a deep strongly muscled loin with very slight arch.

Topline—The back should be short and strong with a *"good rising"* to the neck arch and a gradual slope from withers to tail. The height at the withers is generally less than one inch greater than the height at the hips. The croup drops off only slightly from the line of the back giving a good tail set. Too flat a croup may give the appearance of a high tail set but in reality, it reduces rear drive and creates inefficient rear motion.

Underline—Seen in profile the underline is nearly horizontal. Elbows are level with the briskit and there is very little tuck up.

Forelegs—The bone of the forelegs should be straight, sturdy, and of good substance; flat rather than rounded and coarse. Forelegs are set back at the elbows which should be directly under the top point of the shoulder blades, i.e. definitely not "Terrier-fronted." Elbows should not be pinched so as to cause the feet to toe out. On the other hand, a dog with excessive chest width usually toes in and moves with a waddling gait, where the dog throws the feet in a paddling motion.

T. Hemsen wrote: "The legs must not be too thin, but in a natural way they must harmonize with the dog's structure. The front legs should stand a good distance apart viewed from the front, and must be straight from the shoulder to the ground, for the elbows must not be loose or pinched. From the side, the front legs must also be straight with little bending in the pasterns."

Both elbow and knee joints as well as hocks should be strong. The tendons attached to these joints should extend over considerable length to provide efficient leverage. Front pasterns, which should be short and of good substance should be very nearly upright. Too straight pasterns may cause knuckling over in sudden stops or quick turns; pasterns that are too sloping are weak and unable to hold up under hunting stress.

Hind Legs—Again quoting Dr. Hemsen: "The rear legs must also stand well apart when viewed from behind and must be parallel. If they are too close together, it is because the pelvis is too narrow or the stance is crooked. From the side the rear legs should have a little but distinct angulation in hocks and knee. in order that the dog can react with lightning movement. The lower leg must always stand approximately vertical, *but not farther back than the root of the tail.*

In general the hind legs must be muscular, wide and thick with only a little angulation in the stifle and hock. Too straight stifles produce stilted action. Excessive angulation reduces agility, predisposes to cowhocks and inefficient action. The distance from hock to foot can be too short as well as excessively long; its proportion should be pleasing and efficient mechanically for the work that is to be done. There should be no dewclaws on the hind legs."

Feet—Elkhound feet must be comparatively small, somewhat oblong, compact, and with thick, tough pads. They are not cat feet; neither are they hare feet. The toes, which should point forward and be close together, should be well arched with protective hair between them. Open splayed feet with thin pads have a tendency to ball up with ice in thawing winter weather. They will not stand the rough going in rugged country. The nails should be dark gray and of medium length, and strong enough to grip the ground when the dog is in motion and changing direction.

Tail—Like other Northern dogs, the Elkhound carries his tail set high over the back. But, the Elkhound tail differs from other breeds in being tightly curled and carried over the center line of the back. In some instances it curls one and a half times; occasionally one finds it so tightly curled that it looks like a knot, which is undesirable. *A loose, fan shaped tail without sufficient curl is not typical, is undesirable and should be penalized.* The tail should be approximately 10 to 13 inches in length. Short tails are faulty. Hair on the tail should be thick but without brush or the plume of long sparse hair.

Dr. Hemsen wrote:

"The tail, when correctly rolled and carried, is one of the Elkhound's most typical characteristics, and will contribute strongly to the dog's appearance. The tail indicates the dog's temperament. If the tail falls backward, it shows weakness and poor nerves. Emphasis should be placed on this fault. A judge shall also try to judge a dog's inner qualities, if possible, with regard to breeding good hunting dogs. The tail's uprolling starts at the tip. The outermost joint gets so tightly rolled in grown dogs that it makes a crook which cannot be straightened. It may also be so tightly curled that the tip is squeezed out to one side, usually to the left and with a little tuft of black hair to indicate that the dog is right- or left-tailed. Both are regarded equally. I have often heard it said that a right-tailed dog was not purebred, and no good as a hunting dog. I mention this because I want to squelch this old belief. The tail should have the tightest curl that it can have and not go off center on the back. If the tail is loosely rolled, the tail ring is large and unharmonious—fan-like. The tail should have a circular cross section and be relatively short and about the same circumference throughout its length. It should lie so firmly on the pelvis that the hair on the tail is parted at the place where it lies on the pelvis; and the hair on the pelvis is also parted. A good

172

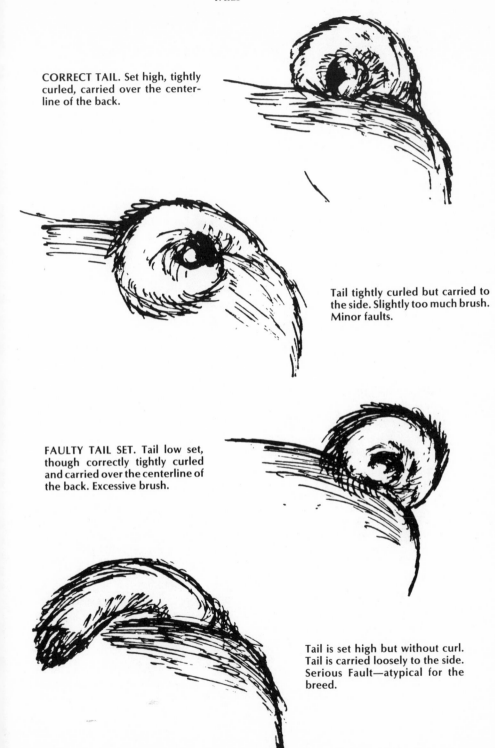

CORRECT TAIL. Set high, tightly curled, carried over the centerline of the back.

Tail tightly curled but carried to the side. Slightly too much brush. Minor faults.

FAULTY TAIL SET. Tail low set, though correctly tightly curled and carried over the centerline of the back. Excessive brush.

Tail is set high but without curl. Tail is carried loosely to the side. Serious Fault—atypical for the breed.

tight tail goes forward from the base or root making the dog appear short and full of fire. A tail that leans slightly backward from the root gives the appearance of not lying well on the back and it easily falls down; furthermore, the dog will seem longer backed."

Coat—The coat of the Elkhound is very important. Its nature is such as to furnish insulation against heat and cold; consequently the dog does not suffer either in winter or summer. The coat is also water-resistant. Because it is thick and smooth-lying, snow does not penetrate it. If the coat is dense, glossy, and hard, burrs, seeds and brambles will not adhere to it and mud will be shed quickly when dry.

The Elkhound coat, which is double, is composed of the longer and harsher cover hairs that are black at the tips, and a lighter woolly undercoat. The hair is longest on the neck, chest, buttocks, backs of the forelegs and underside of the tail. The body of the coat is thick and even in length. In texture, it should not be too soft or silky. Nor is it wiry or open. A bristling, excessively coarse coat, harsh and prickly to the touch, should be penalized as should an excessively soft, open coat.

As a rule, the Elkhound has little or no "doggy odor." A male generally sheds once per year and a bitch twice. Because the dog goes definitely "out of coat" when it sheds, it may be undesirable to show it at that time. There is an old saying that if an Elkhound looks good while shedding, he is a worthy individual.

Color—The most desirable color is silver gray, but not lighter than cream. It should not be a platinum or bluish white; neither too dark or excessively light although light fawn is permissible, especially in young dogs. Brown, rust, or yellow tints should not be tolerated. There should be even coloring, beautifully blended with the long silver black-tipped covering hairs and the light creamy undercoat.

Dr. Hemsen wrote that yellow or brown can be inherited or it can be due to shedding. In the former case where the yellow is uniform to the bottom of the hair, it is a major fault. In the latter, dogs should not be penalized as the condition is normal and passing. During the time just prior to shedding, the coat "dies" and the undercoat becomes yellow, while the new hair underneath grows in clean and gray. A major fault occurs when the ultra-dark dog possesses a sparse brown undercoat, especially on the back.

According to Hemsen, most dogs with normal coloring have dark masks, black ears and black streaks from the eyes to the roots of the ears. The gray of the forehead, which is a lighter color than on the body, must be even, not spoiled by "spectacles," light cheeks, or light gray around the eyes. The black mask of the muzzle grades evenly into the lighter forehead color. The lower jaw should be black throughout its entire length. The ears should be dark or black. On some dogs they are light part way up from the

174

ear root. *An all black head and face, which is not typical, is classed as a MAJOR FAULT,* whereas a light-colored head is only a minor fault. Long dark stiff feelers are found on the muzzle and eyebrows and should not be trimmed off.

Old dogs often have light hairs on the muzzle due to age. Although pronounced white markings should not appear, a little white on the chest or on the toes is not a serious fault. On the other hand, large white blazes, socks and chin stripes are faulty. White tail tips, which seem to be very hereditary, are extremely undesirable.

The mane should be medium gray and the nape of the neck is lighter than the back. Dark gray over the shoulder blades blends into a characteristic lighter band around the body immediately behind the forelegs. This so-called "harness mark" is a vertical stripe approximately two inches wide from withers to elbow points, consisting of longer lighter cover hairs without dark tips. These hairs are longer and stiffer than the rest of the cover coat and blend with the longer hairs over the shoulder for a lighter mark over the shoulders where a harness would lie.

There is a dark gray saddle and lighter shading over the rear quarters. The outside curl of the tail is light and the inside dark. Also of light color are the chest, stomach, britches and area around the anus.

Black soot, or other dark markings on the feet or legs below the knees is a minor fault, which might indicate a throwback to the Black Elghund or Bearhund of Norway. The light silver of the feet and legs should taper gradually into the darker gray of the body.

Gait—Gait is the means by which structure is assessed. It must be remembered that the Elkhound is a hunting dog first and foremost and too few judges and breeders emphasize the importance of a soundly constructed dog. Usually a dog that stands correctly on strong springy legs, high on his toes—not sluggish or floppy—will have the agility and smoothness of gait to make him an efficient hunter.

The standard describes gait as it is viewed in the show ring to help breeders and judges assess the structure of the dog with greater accuracy. The Elkhound is not meant to fly like the wind as his sight hound cousins do. His gait is versatile, efficient, without wasted motion and without flash and flap. The best moving dogs call little attention to themselves as they move, seeming to do it without effort. Short choppy strides are not characteristic. Neither are a high kick and prance. Gait should be "Normal for an active dog constructed for AGILITY and ENDURANCE."

The Elkhound is not a man-made dog, formed or squeezed into a preconceived pattern. He is a time-tested big game hunter, not too big nor too small; not low slung or sway backed. He must have a light easy effortless gait that reflects his function.

Frequently a dog with a narrow chest does not have room between the front legs for normal movement of his hind legs. He may move one or both hind legs out of the track of the front legs, thus causing a sideways or sidewinding gait.

If a dog is bowlegged or the hocks turn out, the hind legs will cross over and track between the front legs. When the hocks turn in (cow hocks) the feet turn outside the track of the front legs. Each results in lost motion and thrust.

Viewed from the front, the legs should move in straight lines, converging under the center line of the body with good (but not excessive or even maximum) forward reach. They should not weave in or out at the elbow. There should be no paddling. The Elkhound's front and hind quarters are not designed for great speed or extremely extended reach. With the Elkhound, it is endurance rather than speed that counts.

In full stride the Elkhound uses the power gallop, not only with full thrust by his hind legs, but also with power from his front legs. When he gallops fast, his hind legs move outside his front legs. On the hunt, he often uses a shorter stride somewhat like a rocking gallop (in Norway called "the Dilt"), which seems to be the easiest locomotion for the Elkhound and a gait that he can continue for hours.

The Elkhound must not lose flexibility because of a false demand that he be short, compact, square and boxy. Neither should he lose his agility through emphasis on over-angulation and flashy gait. Either extreme is equally detrimental to the breed's purpose. More emphasis on correct gait in the show ring should keep us on the right track, breeding for the agile, efficient, capable hunting dog.

11

Judging the
Norwegian Elkhound

by Mary O. Jenkins

> Mary Jenkins served as chairman of the NEAA Committee
> that worked from 1968 through 1973 drafting the current
> AKC breed standard for the Norwegian Elkhound. Mrs.
> Jenkins has been an approved judge of the breed for over 15
> years. She was but the second woman approved as a breeder-
> judge, Edna Mae Bieber being the first. She has traveled in
> Norway and has accompanied Norwegian judges in the show
> rings and in the field on an Elg hunt, viewing the Elkhound at
> work in its natural habitat.

THE current AKC standard for the Norwegian Elkhound is a
good one. It is written in positive terms to describe the ideal of the breed.
Those reading, studying or applying the standard (particularly in the show
ring), should first and foremost keep in mind that since the standard
describes the ideal specimen of the breed, any part of a dog that does not
measure up to the "ideal" must be penalized in relation to the degree of
variance from that ideal.

The words, "*bold and energetic*" could well be considered the most
important in the standard. Since form follows function, we must be aware
that the Norwegian Elkhound is a hunter! His function requires that he
hold a 1500-pound animal at bay for a minimum of one and a half hours to
pass a hunting test which must be accomplished before he can become a
champion in his native country.

Although the Norwegian Elkhound is a bold and energetic hunter, he must also be an intelligent, devoted companion and guardian. He is not a member of a hound pack, but usually hunts with another dog or two from another household. He can be assertive, but not aggressive with other dogs and fighting between Elkhounds on the hunt or in the show ring is atypical behavior.

A judge evaluating the physical appearance of an Elkhound in the show ring should put the statements of the standard in the perspective provided by the Spitz breed grouping used in Europe. The Elkhound's head is similar to other Northern breeds. In this context, his ears are somewhat small, pointed and carried erect. I have never seen a dog with ears too small. The eyes are extremely dark brown, and the black muzzle is equal in length to the skull. The planes of skull and muzzle are parallel distinguishing him from many other Northern breeds. The "dry" close skin on the head and throat are important to appearance. Turkey wattles can take much from the typey appearance of an otherwise handsome dog.

Shortness of loin is the key to the Elkhound's correct, compact body structure. A short rib cage and long loin may make a dog appear to be square in build but the longer loin will not have the quick flexibility necessary to the hunt that the short loined dog will have.

Proper length of leg is an important functional characteristic of the breed. There should be "plenty of air" under the dog, yet he should not appear "leggy" in the sense of the sight hounds. Length of leg should *appear* equal to the depth of the body with the brisket coming down to the elbow. However, in reality, the legs are more than half the height measurement. The natural coat length on the brisket and underline can affect the profile impression of leg length so this should be carefully observed and assessed. The dog should appear to be strong, agile and sturdy without being bulky or coarse. Bone structure is strong but not clumsy.

A particularly distinctive characteristic of the breed is the high set, tightly curled tail which should be carried over the center line of the back, so tight in the ideal specimen that the coat should be parted where the tail rests on the center topline. I have yet to see an Elkhound with a tail too tightly curled, but have seen a number with a tail that is too short or too long, thus curling loosely without resting on the back at all. Often, a correct tail is so tightly curled that it cannot be completely straightened. Incidentally, when evaluating puppies, be aware that the tail begins to curl as early as six weeks of age and should be well curled at six months. The curl may continue to tighten as the dog gets older. A loose, husky-like tail should be penalized. The Elkhound's tail is a good barometer of his temperament. The dog may drop or uncurl the tail when frightened or uneasy but a dog whose tail is continually down or tucked between the rear legs is not bold and energetic.

Color is an important factor in the Elkhound. In the country of origin, the breed is called the "Gra Elghund" which translates to "Gray Moose Dog." There are three other breeds Scandinavia used for moose hunting— all of the Spitz type. The others, though somewhat similar in type are distinctly different in color. Prior to 1875 they were all shown as Moose Dogs and were sometimes interbred. Variance in color makes a dog suspect of carrying genes of the other breeds, as does an excessive amount of white on forechest, legs or other areas of the body. The clear gray with black muzzle, ears and tail tip and the clean light legs and breeches are the hallmark of the Elkhound.

The Elkhound is a medium sized dog. Height is given as 20½″ for males and 19½″ for bitches. Undersize should be greatly penalized, as the small animal could not function effectively as a hunter. An animal reasonably over the ideal, on the other hand, could function well. Thus, an Elkhound as much as 22″, if otherwise of excellent type, well balanced, etc., would be acceptable; whereas, a dog *under* the ideal of the same quality would be heavily penalized because it could not function properly in the rough, varied terrain against the large moose.

The coat of the Elkhound should be thick, hard, close-lying, with an especially dense woolly light gray undercoat. Artificial preparation including scissoring, thinning or trimming of any sort or application of texturizing preparations is definitely to be penalized.

In my opinion, the overall quality of the Norwegian Elkhound in the United States has improved beyond measure in the past 15 years. There are dogs who easily achieved the title of Champion 20 years ago which would hardly be recognized as the same breed today, not because the essential requirements of the standard have changed but because breeders have made excellent use of the few really good dogs we had at that time and combined them with other fine dogs brought in from Norway, England and Ireland. Breeders are to be commended for a job well done.

Bamse, Norwegian Hunting Qualifier, with felled moose.
Owned by Kari Knudsen, Braskereidfoss, Norway.

12

The Hunting Norwegian Elkhound

THE name Norwegian Elkhound is somewhat misleading in that the dog does not hunt elk (wapiti), nor is he technically a Hound. In Norway the Norsk Elghund, as he is called, is used primarily as a hunting dog for big game. Since *elg* refers to a member of the moose family and *hund* is the common European word for dog, the term "moose dog" would seem more appropriate. Sometimes he is referred to as the *graa dyrehund,* which may be translated as the gray big-game dog. No game is too big or too small for this dog of the Vikings. He is equally adept at hunting moose, bear, mountain lion, wolf, fox, rabbit, and even upland birds.

When one appreciates that the Norwegian elk is essentially the same as our large American moose, and when one realizes that as many as 40,000 *elg* are shot in the Scandinavian countries per year, mostly with the help of Elkhounds, then will the Elkhound assume his true significance as a sporting dog.

To find moose in Norway's endless forests without a dog would be well nigh hopeless.

To understand and appreciate this clever dog, it would be advisable to see him in action in his native *fjells* and forests. There he is in his glory!

The hunting season, which starts late in September, lasts only five to ten days. It is absolutely necessary that the dog be in top condition to stand the strenuous run from sunrise to sunset each day of the short season. Having selected a likely place to hunt, you take your dog there. What a picture he makes as he stands like a statue, high on his toes, head up, ears pricked forward and nostrils taking scent through the clear mountain air! His brown eyes peer into the dense forest. His silver coat shines. Every muscle is tense and ready to spring.

Then he is off on the hunt. His movements are quick and noiseless. You start moving in a fairly straight line, always against the wind. Your dog must cover all the territory on both sides of your path, which means in and out through the brush, stumps, stones, and windfalls. It means a steady run, not fast, because the area must be hunted thoroughly, but a half run, half fast walk referred to as *dilt*. Although you may not see the dog for a while, he will be constantly crossing and recrossing your path—sort of reporting to you. Ultimately, he will find a moose track or will catch the direct scent of the animal itself, and then may disappear for a long period.

You stand on a high point and listen for the baying (*los*) to commence which will indicate that your dog has his quarry at bay. His rhythmic notes in the distance stir and thrill you. As you run toward the sounds, you wonder about the moose. Perhaps it is a wise old bull—or it may be a scared young one. Will the moose stay and fight? Or will he run? After a while you stop, open-mouthed, heart pounding, hand behind the ear listening. The stand is closer now. Soon you are on the run again. The knapsack on your back is bouncing up and down. The coffee kettle is rattling. But you do not notice these things. You are thinking of your pal out there, all alone with no one to help him. He is such a small thing against such a big brute.

Think of all the deathtraps into which a smart moose could lure the dog; for instance, thick underbrush where a dog cannot spring aside when the moose strikes with his knife-sharp hoofs, hard as rocks. You can imagine, too, how those massive horns can tear things to shreds.

Another deathtrap is the shallow fjord, where the moose has the dog at a definite disadvantage. While the moose with his long legs wades out into the water, the dog must swim, his progress slower. Under these conditions the moose can turn quickly, seize the dog on his wide antlers, and toss him in the air or trample him to death.

Your thoughts wander to a third trap, the narrow ledge on a mountain precipice, vertical walls on one side and the endless deep on the other, where the sure-footed moose will balance step by step and the low-creeping Elkhound will follow closely. Here is a chance for the moose to put an end to the dog with a sudden stop and a swift kick.

After hours that seem like days, you catch a glimpse through the pines of the two opponents facing each other on the stand, the Elkhound appearing even smaller in comparison with his huge adversary. No wonder the moose is called the "King of the Forest!" When he comes crashing through the woods, higher than a horse, head outstretched, his heavy antlers ripping big branches right and left and knocking over small trees like bowling pins, he is tremendous! Even seasoned hunters tremble when he unexpectedly comes thundering through the brush. He is hot-tempered

Surri, 9738/76, with moose quarry. Note the flags marking the hunter's ownership of the moose tied to the tree. Owned by Ragner Kristoferson, Filtvet, Norway.

Ragner Kristoferson and his horse, Lokke Lisa, bringing home the moose.

and ugly when wounded or trapped, majestic and noble when he raises his great head with lofty horns for his last look over his kingdom.

No other hunting may be compared with moose hunting. You and your dog are pitted against the forest, the mountain, and the river. The sport requires teamwork between man and dog. Both must be in top physical condition to endure. For this work the dog should possess a keen nose, great courage, a powerful, agile body, well developed chest, and short back. One can readily understand why these points are emphasized in the Elkhound Standard.

The most remarkable part of moose hunting in Norway is that even the top ranking show Elkhounds are expected to participate in the sport. If they cannot hunt, they are considered worthless as far as breeding is concerned, and cannot become champions.

Moose hunting, which is far from easy, requires outstanding qualities in the dog. He must have at least four special traits: first, he must have a good nose; second, steady nerves; third, a deep, long-range voice; and fourth, he must be smart. The dog must take scent of the big game from a long distance and be able to differentiate between moose, bear, and other animals.

If the Elkhound is nervous, high-strung, and hot tempered, he should not be used for moose hunting. It would be a waste of time to spend months training such a dog. The natural-born hunter gives the best results.

When the dog has a moose at bay in the distance and his voice is high pitched and squeaky, the hunter cannot hear the baying and will not know where the stand is. Consequently, many an otherwise good Elkhound is of little use as a *loshund,* though he may prove satisfactory as a *bandhund.* The former ranges freely on his own to locate game and hold it at bay. The latter operates in a harness with a twenty-foot leash, which is attached to the hunter's belt. When trailing a moose, the *bandhund* must avoid obstacles such as windfalls and low-hanging branches that would greatly hinder the hunter. This dog trails the moose until he approaches fairly close to his quarry. Then the hunter ties the Elkhound to a tree and proceeds to find and kill the moose.

The experienced hunter is greatly concerned with the dog's performance on the hunt. Some qualities the dog inherits, but others he must be smart enough to learn. On the trail, he must know if the track is too old, or if the moose has traveled at a rapid pace, in which case it probably would be in some distant valley at the time. As a rule, the Elkhound will not try to take scent in the low areas between the ridges, because he knows that the air currents do not often follow the contour of the land. Instead, he will be observed on the hills taking scent. Sometimes he even stands on his hind legs so as to reach higher in the breeze.

It is a critical moment when he has found the moose. A good dog will take his time on the approach. He must then decide whether the moose is

Driv av Kotofjell with a bear killed on a hunt.

old or young, or if it is a cow with a calf. When it is an old one and not too scared, the approach is more direct. The dog tries a small "woof." If nothing happens, he increases the volume and moves in closer. Soon he makes a pass at the big bull and then a fight may follow.

In the case of a young moose, the dog should proceed with caution so as to avoid scaring it into headlong flight. Should the moose not stand, the dog must follow silently, for if he bays the moose will run faster and farther. A mute dog may get another chance to hold the quarry when it stops. The dog should not pursue, however, when the game goes at too fast a pace.

The Elkhound is especially useful in locating a wounded moose. This requires keen scenting ability, courage, and perseverance. It is the law in Norway that hunters must wait approximately two hours after wounding a moose before proceeding to track him down and kill him.

Although bears are not as numerous as they formerly were in the Scandinavian countries, they still are hunted with dogs. As in moose hunting, the bear is trailed by Elkhounds and held at bay by barking and by nipping at its heels. Sometimes the bear is kept at bay for hours by one dog or two dogs.

185

For hunting black cock, *tiur, capercaille,* and other upland birds that flush into trees, the Elkhound is quite proficient. But pointing and retrieving birds are not his forte.

It is our hope that the group referred to as sports hunters will increase from year to year. These men know that it is a privilege and honor to hunt in field and forest on a beautiful autumn day just for the sport of hunting. They do not count the result in dollars, but in happy memories that go on and on. Never to be forgotten are the evenings spent in some secluded cabin where the Elkhounds stretch out on the floor in the flickering glow of the fireplace, where glasses are lifted in toasts to happy field trial and show winners, where stories of the hunt are told and retold, and where friends unite in a fellowship that warms each hunter's heart and soul.

Norwegian Elkhound retrieving cock pheasant.

13

The Elg (Moose)

by Olav Campbell, Norway

THE Moose is our noblest wild big game. He is the King of the Forest. No one who has seen a full-grown bull moose standing with his head lifted high, and the sun shining on the majestic horns, will ever forget the sight.

On a quiet walk in the woods of an early morning, one will often find the moose feeding in the marshes, or standing at a small lake, eating water lilies.

The moose varies much in size and weight. The bull moose can weigh (dressed weight) from 200 to over 300 kilograms, which roughly translates into 400 to over 600 pounds. His body and neck are short and powerful, and the legs are long and sturdy. The head is quite long, with a big, wide nose.

Only the bull has horns, and they are of considerable variation in size and form. Some have shovel horns, others have open racks like the elk.

The hunters, of course, prefer the shovel horns. If the rack is of good size, they are most impressive. The bull moose begins to grow horns at the age of one, and as a rule he has only one point in the first year. By the fall, he is shedding the single point. The horns are shed every late fall and winter, but toward spring, a new rack starts growing.

At first the horns are of soft substance, but they become hard as rock when full grown. The moose gets one point added to the rack (elk horn) every year, and the horn gets stronger and more impressive as the years go by. When the bull gets old, the rack retreats and gets smaller each year, so it

Elgstolens Buster and Elgstolens Jerv, owned by Erik V. Enberg, Oslo.

is hard to judge the bull's age by the horn. Checking his teeth is the surest way to determine his age.

The horns are used as weapons, particularly during the breeding season in the fall when the bulls fight a terrific battle in competition for the cow. Some hunters claim that the bull with the open rack is always the winner.

In a fight against other animals, the bull uses his front hoofs. He leaps forward and at the same time slams his hoofs down like sledge hammers, with his full weight behind them. It is a fearsome weapon and many an Elkhound has been killed on a moose hunt.

In the fall, when the bull moose is on the run in constant search of cows in season, he often digs shallow holes in the ground, and lets his urine in them. There is always a very strong odor from these holes. The meeting place for the bull and the cow has thus been established.

With all the fighting, the bull loses lots of weight each fall, and after a bit becomes thin. The moose meat at this time will often have a bitter taste.

When it is calfing time for the cow, she selects a place where she has good protection against the wind and weather, plus a good view of the surrounding territory. As a rule, the calf is born in May or June, but he can be born as early as April and as late as August.

The pregnancy for the cow is 9 months. She usually has her first calf in her third year. There is generally only one calf, but later twins or triplets can be born. After a short time, the newly-born calf will be able to follow his mother in her wanderings. If some other creatures come too close to the cow's territory when the calf is young, the mother will attack the intruder. At birth, the calf has a red-brown color, which will turn gray in fall or winter. He grows very fast, but if his mother is shot accidentally in the fall, he will have a hard time surviving the tough winter.

The calf will follow his mother for a year. But if she becomes pregnant again, and is within calfing time, she will then chase the yearling away.

The most common territory for the moose is the pine and fir country, but he often wanders to higher ground in the summer, sometimes even going above the timberline. Here he feeds on willow and mountain ash along creeks and small lakes. His main food is brush, twigs, and leaves of aspen and birch.

Famous show and hunting champion Driv av Kotofjell in hunting harness.

14

Elghund Field Trial in Norway

by Dr. Jesper Hallingby, Norway

T HE *Elghund* was originally a hunting dog, and is still very much so in its native Norway. While some are farm dogs, and some watchdogs or pets, the majority are used for hunting.

In contrast to America, dogs are still permitted to take part in big game hunting in Norway. In fact, not only are they permitted, but laws are constantly being proposed that would *require* every hunting team to have dogs, to use in finding wounded animals.

Elg hunting in Norway is thus done mainly with dogs—either free-ranging (*loshund*), or on leash. The loose dog tries to find the *elg* on its own, either by open scent or by tracking it down. When it finds the *elg,* the dog barks and tries to keep the prey at bay until the hunter arrives and kills it. The leashed dog, on the other hand, is led by the hunter. The dog tries to find the *elg* in the same way as the *loshund,* by scent or tracking. When the *elg* is located, the hunter approaches (always against the wind) until he is near enough to the animal to see and shoot it.

Which of the two hunting methods is used depends upon the local circumstances. The loose dog is used where there are large, dense forests. But in terrain where the forestation is more sparse, with big open bogs or mountain area, the leashed dog is employed.

To find the best hunting dogs, so that they may be used for breeding, annual field trials have been established at terrains all over the country.

191

There is no question that an enthusiasm for hunting and many of the other inner qualities that make for a good hunting dog are hereditary, as much as are the readily seen exterior qualities. However, it is more difficult to breed the hunting qualities. It is hoped that study of the results of the field trials will prove a helpful guide for such breeding.

The field trials provide other benefits, too. For one, there is the financial aspect. An award at a hunting test immediately increases the value of a dog for sale, or as a breeding dog.

But for most field trial participants, it is the sheer sport of the tests that counts most—the urge to compete and show what one has. The opportunity of "hunting" for several days in such ideal terrains—with large *elg* stock and most attractive surroundings—is highly prized. And along with an expert judgment on one's dog, it provides a most enjoyable get-together with other eager hunters and dog lovers.

As far as we know, such tests for *Elghunds* are held only in Norway, Sweden and Finland. The rules for the tests vary in each country.

We were rather slow to start field trial competition with our *Elghunds* in Norway—much later than with tests for Beagles and bird dogs. The reason was that it is difficult to find terrains large enough and suitable for *Elghund* field trials. An attempt to test a couple of dogs was made in 1916-1917. Then it was not until 1948 that we, with the initiative furnished by Erik Enberg. Sven Mjaerum, Reidar Stromme and myself, started the so-called field trial for *Elghunds* in the Vang forests. Mjaerum and Enberg placed their hunting terrain at our disposal. Here we gained the experience needed to formulate the Field Trial Rules that have since been in effect.

G. A. Treschow and Harald Lovenskiold let us use their large forest properties at Fritzoe Verk and Nordmarken for tests and the terrains in Nannestadm, Orje, Hoff in Vestfold and Faaberg have been used with good results. Tests have also been conducted in the Verdalsbruket forests in North Trondelag.

We have now come so far with the field trials that the Norsk Kennel Klub has decided that a hunting test award be required before an *Elghund* may become a champion. Recently, we have also established a hunting championship, requiring two First Prizes at hunting tests in two different years. It is also an established principle that the tests should be as close to regular hunting as possible. The only difference is that in the tests that the dog has to be baying and holding the *elg* at bay a specified time before he is called in and leashed.

A field trial is performed in this manner:

The night before the test, the participants meet with dogs and judges at the headquarters. The conductor of the test has a meeting with the judges, and the needed number of terrains are drawn up on the map. The aim is to make the terrains as alike in every way as possible, including the number of *elg* inhabiting them.

192

Each judge is assigned a separate terrain, which is under his control throughout the test. The dogs are tested for two days, and are entitled to at least six hours of testing each day. They are tested by a different judge, in a different terrain, each day. This obviously helps assure a fairer judgment.

Early in the first test day, breakfast is served. Then the trainer with the test dogs and the judge leave for their specific terrain, in the direction that the judge—taking the wind into consideration—deems best.

If an unleashed dog *(loshund)* **is being tested,** the judge orders the dog to be let loose right away. The judge will immediately note the starting move *(utslaget)* of the dog. It is very important the dog start well and show that it is definitely setting out to find *elg.*

When the dog tracks down the *elg,* and starts for it, the judge and the trainer watch developments at a distance. If the *elg* runs and the dog follows, the men have to try to keep up with them. When standing baying *(staa-los)* occurs, the men take position against the wind so as to be able to hear without scaring the *elg.* When the dog has been baying continually for an hour and a half or more, the baying period needed to qualify for a First Prize, the judge will normally carefully position himself close enough so that he can be sure that it really is an *elg,* and to study the behavior of the dog in front of the *elg.* Then the trainer tries to call the dog in order to leash it. In most cases it is difficult because the dog feels encouraged by the presence of its master, and—particularly if the *elg* gets scared—becomes still more eager and insistent. However, if the dog is easily recalled, it is a plus for him in the judge's book. Sooner or later the dog will be back, and can be tried again at tracking and then on another *elg.* It counts much in its favor if the dog is cool and collected at the start *(rolig uttak)* so that it does not scare the *elg,* but instead actually calms it down.

The interest of the dog in other game or animals must not be so intense as to disturb the hunting. Its enthusiasm for hunting must be great enough that it will not give up, but will work all day—if necessary—to find *elg.* And the dog must be eager enough to hold the *elg* at bay, lest it take off at great speed and disappear completely.

The dog's barking may vary very much. Some take it easy—others keep going loud and clear all the time. However, it is the conduct of the dog that by and large really influences the behavior of the *elg.* The sound of the barking identifies whether the dog is dealing with a calm animal or not. The judge has to consider all of this in determining whether the *Elghund* is to be recommended for First, Second, or Third Prize—or no award at all.

In the tracking field trial, the dog is in harness all day. Out in the terrain, the trainer keeps against the wind as much as possible until the dog finds tracks fresh enough to be of interest, or until it gets the scent of *elg.* In tracking, the dog should guide the trainer speedily and surely to the *elg,*

"Oh boy, we don't know what it is, but we like it!"

without letting anything distract him. The dog should clearly indicate when it is close to the animal, soundlessly approach, and be absolutely quiet and silent all the time. The dog should not react to shots, and should possess an eagerness for hunting strong enough to keep him working all day to find *elg* without interest for other game or domestic animals. The award system is the same as for the unleashed (*loshund*) dogs.

Following the test, all documents are forwarded to the Norsk Kennel Klub to be studied and evaluated by the Field Trial Committee, which then presents its recommendtions. The final decision is up to the Board of the Kennel Club.

I would like to point out a few things in connection with the test results up to now. It is often heard at dog shows that "show dogs" cannot be used for hunting. To qualify for the field trial test, an *Elghund must have first received an award at a show.* So while the test does not furnish a measure between "show dogs" and "non-show dogs," its results do prove that "show dogs" can hunt and hunt well. The remarkable fact is that of all the dogs tested up to now, and awarded First Prize, *more than 2/3 had also received First Prizes at shows.* A beautiful exterior does not prevent the dog from becoming a good hunter.

The exterior standard for *Elghunds* has been worked out with an eye to the fact that it is a hunting dog. It is therefore important that this standard be maintained in the judging at the shows, and that the dog is not permitted to become too big and heavy. In countries where the dog is not employed for hunting, there is an unfortunate tendency in this direction.

Another result of the tests has been to prove that the old discrimination against the bitches (*tisper*) is, to put it mildly, absolutely unfounded. The tests prove untrue the claim that bitches are unsuitable as unleashed (*loshund*) dogs.

Furthermore, it is noticeable that the temperament of the *Elghund* is completely different today from what it was a few years ago. It was an old theory that an *Elghund* had to be ill-tempered if used as a hunting dog. So they were at that time. Today, most of them are good-natured and friendly, and easily handled in the show rings or the woods during field trials, wherever competing. Nor has this caused any sacrifice of their hunting qualities.

A field trial is, in a sense, a graduation. There will always be an element of chance involved. The dog may be unlucky and encounter very difficult animals, the weather may be bad, or the dog may simply be indisposed the day the tests are held. On the other hand, the dog may well outdo any previous effort. The important thing is that the owner be sportsman enough to take victory or defeat in the right spirit. If he does, he will find the hunting test days to be among the most eventful of the Fall for him.

For quick reference, here is an extract of the hunting test rules of the Norsk Kennel Klub:

The judge must have a special book during the test. He notes down the weather, the condition of the terrain, the temperature and a calculation of the *elg* population in the field. He also observes the dog during the test, when unleashed or leashed, the exact baying time, its behavior in the terrain and to the *elg* and behavior before, during, and after the baying. The judge must carefully note exact time and place where another dog is heard in order to, if necessary, supplement the impression of the fellow judge. If the judge hears baying coming into his test sector which might be coming from the test dog of another participant, the judge must, if possible, leash his test dog if it has not already found the *elg*. All in all, the judge must make notes of everything of interest during the test. Based on his observations the judge answers the following points:

a. The hunting eagerness of the dog.
b. Interest in finding *elg*.
c. Contact and cooperation with the trainer—obedience.
d. Quiet and calm when he approaches the *elg*.
e. Ability to stop the *elg*.
f. Bark and usage of it.
g. Determination in holding the *elg*.
h. Tracking.
i. Interest in other game and domestic animals.
j. Recommendation for prize degree.

To be awarded First Prize—Unleashed (*Loshund*)—the following is required:
1. He must show extremely good hunting eagerness, with an ease in running and searching for the *elg* in the forest, without losing contact with the trainer.
2. The dog must have a good loud voice and use it sensibly.
3. He must have a sensible calm approach toward the *elg* and good ability to stop the *elg* from moving away.
4. He must hold the *elg* at bay at least 1½ hours. He must also be tried in contact with other *elg*.
   If the *elg* decides to move, the dog must aim to stop him. But the *Elghund* must be silent—no barking. He must be ready to track and trail the *elg*, even in his own tracks.

Hunting tests for leashed dogs:

A leashed dog shall have harness and must never be let loose during the test. The dog's job is to locate the *elg* in the terrain as fast as possible and lead the hunter to it. The dog must show that it works consciously to find *elg*. The dog must be completely silent and never bark or whine. It must not pull so strongly in the leash that it groans or coughs and must be able to move soundlessly across the grounds. Normally it should not follow the *elg* track slavishly but work with head high in order to scent the *elg*. The dog should utilize the terrain and the wind sensibly. If the dog is in doubt about the location of the *elg* the trainer may lead the dog back with the wind before proceeding anew. The dog shall clearly mark when the *elg* is near. If the dog works on *elg* track, it should not be blamed if it leaves the track and closes in on other *elgs* which are nearer, and it is a plus for the dog if it prefers a bull *elg*. It is not a drawback if the dog passes a cow in order to head directly for a bull. The dog should be able to follow the track of a wounded *elg* (blood track) without being distracted by other tracks or animals. The dog should not be blamed if it covers shorter distances to fowl or other animals if it does not work on *elg,* but exaggerated interest in other animals is not permissible. It is a plus for the dog if it exclusively concentrates on *elg*. When shooting occurs the dog should not pull hard in such a way that it makes it difficult to fire more shots. It should not react in such a way that it will not work any more after shots are fired.

For First Prize for leashed dogs, the following is required:

Dog showing superior ability to locate *elg* fast and surely, and faultlessly takes the hunter to the animal.

A general rule for all dogs is that they must not be scared of shots, and must not show such interest in other game and cattle that it disturbs the *elg* hunt.

Preparing to bring home the moose.

197

15

A Norwegian Field
Trial Report

Following is an account of a typical Norwegian field trial, as reported on pages 137 and 138 in *Om Elghunder og Elkjakt i Norge de Siste 50 Ar*. The work of the now famous hunter, Elgstolens Jerv, is described.

"FIELD TRIAL FOR ELKHOUNDS (LOOSE) IN N. VANGS
   DISTRICT, SEPTEMBER 26, 1949

Leader: Sven Mjearum
Judges: Olaf Afkjaernand and Sigurd Hole
Dog's Name: Elgstolens Jerv, 5 years
Owner and Handler: E. V. Enberg, Oslo
Weather Conditions   Wind: Southwest
                      Morning Temperature: 11° C.
                      Noon Temperature: 18° C.
                      Light haze until 9 A.M.
                      Trial terrain height from 575 to 900 meters.

"We went from Lavlia by automobile to Bringebu eight miles away. Jerv was on leash going west from Bringebu toward the Furnes district. At 7:09 A.M. about 500 yards from Furnes, he was turned loose. From the very start the dog showed an intense desire to hunt. He worked incessantly, trying to find moose. We continued northward along the border of Furnes until we were above the timberline. During this period Jerv reported back to his handler twice, at 7:33 A.M. and at 8:05 A.M..

198

"He was hunting in an unfavorable wind. Occasionally old tracks of moose were observed, but no fresh tracks were seen.

"From the Furnes district we hiked along the timberline in the general direction of Aamodt about 2700 feet above sea level. Jerv searched the territory very well.

"Approximately in the middle of our field trial course, we met another field party of four men and two dogs. Half of them joined us. At 10 A.M. Jerv was called in and leashed. When he was turned loose again 23 minutes later, he did not follow the other dog, but started promptly searching for moose tracks.

"At 10:40 A.M. he finally found what he was after; and then the fun started. The stand *(Losen)* was located in a small valley near Kvernbekken, south of Raufjellet. Jerv held the moose at bay until 11:19 A.M. We all were nearby then, but the underbrush was so dense that we could see only the moose's hindquarters. Soon the moose broke into a run, going south toward the river. Jerv followed, trying all the while to stop him and to hold him. The dog was always close behind the moose, which according to his tracks was a young animal, possibly one or two years old. Around us the country was hilly with dense woods, which made it difficult to hear. We stood quiet, listening, until 12:30 P.M. I couldn't say for certain that it was Jerv's voice that I heard at 12:28 P.M.

"Then we took a lunch-break, at the same time looking and listening for Jerv. Finally at 13:37 P.M. he came in, wet and grimy with swamp muck in his hair. Although he seemed tired, he alertly sniffed the air from the southwest.

"At 15:03 P.M., we turned him loose. The terrain was heavy with marsh and underbrush. He continued his search all afternoon. At from ten to twenty-five minute intervals he reported back and then was off again. But he failed to find any fresh tracks and was called in at 18 P.M.

"SUMMARY: The whole day Jerv showed an earnest desire to hunt and maintained good contact with his handler. He started out easily and controlled well when he held the moose. He had a good loud voice. With more practice this dog will show even better results. I recommend Jerv for First Prize."

(Signed) *Sigurd Hole.*

Conrad av Coulee, a 6-months-old Norwegian Elkhound puppy, with a bobcat at bay. Owned by Mrs. Dean Pugh.

Mrs. E.B. Kulbeck of Montana with three Elkhounds and one day's catch of four bobcats.

16

Health Tips for Hunters

by Stephen M. Hewett

SEVERAL FRIENDS who do not hunt have asked me, "What is it like to hunt with a Norwegian Elghund?" The answer: "It's beautiful!" However, the "How To" is not as important as "How to Care" for a hunting Elghund in the fields or woods for the first time.

The most important procedure is a visit to the veterinarian for a physical for the dog. Once the dog's good general health has been determined, prepare a schedule for getting both you and your dog in shape. Silly, eh? Being tired and out of shape is exactly when injuries are likely to occur to both you and your dog. Thirty to 45 minute workouts during the week, plus three to four hour workouts each day on weekends has proved about right for getting Reiker Viking av Ulnar and his master into proper condition for opening day.

Before going into the field, groom your dog carefully from nose to tail, paying attention to pad condition and nail length. If the nails are excessively long, trim to about ⅛ inch from the end of the quick. Nails cut too close will not leave enough nail to dig into the earth for good traction and may cause too much exposure of the front of the pad, resulting in sore pads or nicks. Some hunters use a specially prepared pad compound to toughen up the pads. This is not good. Pad thickness and toughness should come from natural exercise in the field and be the result of preseason conditioning.

Next, check muscles for tension and tone. And check eyes and lids. This inspection ritual is a great time for enjoying the company of your dog

Ch. Crafdal Trygs Tiara, CD, "pointing" a pheasant. Owned by Mrs. Robert Smolley.

Hunting the badger. Glenna's Paal and Sorvangens Kjekk (marked with S on his side). Dogs are marked with letters on their outer coat until shedding because collars are not used.

and for signalling that "Hey! It's time to go hunting." It is paramount to good health and for making the experience enjoyable for your dog.

After returning from the field, groom again. Wear and tear or injuries to the pads can be noticed immediately. Look between the toes for abrasions caused by grinding sand or dirt. Eye irritations, caused by dust, pollen or small seeds, can be noted and the necessary precautions or treatments taken as recommended by the veterinarian. The muscles will show immediate changes in tension and tone. By pressing carefully, you can tell from his reactions if he is sore or hiding an injury otherwise unnoticed.

Field hunting should improve the condition of your Elghund's coat. As the dog travels through the fields rubbing against weeds, grasses and brushes, dead hairs will be removed and natural oils in the coat will be increased. Tough burrs not naturally worked free by the movement of the guard hairs can be brushed or combed out. Even mud, as it dries, will brush out almost completely. Look for ticks and take the steps to remove them.

It is helpful to take good dry absorbent towels for bedding in the traveling crate as well as for drying the dog after a hunt in snow, rain, or in fields wet from early morning dew. If the coat is in proper condition the outer inch or so will be wet. But the inner guard hairs and the inner fur will be dry and continue to insulate during cold weather hunting. If the inner guard hairs and fur are not dry, consult the veterinarian as the coat may need attention.

Always take extra water. You may need to clean a wound as well as provide clean drinking water. Please don't forget a first aid kit, to treat any injuries.

Extra food or biscuits help to maintain energy and reward your dog for a job well done. This is important especially for dogs who hunt in colder climates. It is generally recommended that hunting dogs have two feedings daily with a higher protein content during the hunting season.

I recommend cooking all wild game your dog is allowed to eat. This helps eliminate possible fevers, worms, and other complications.

It is a good idea to rest periodically during a hunting trip. This is a good time to enjoy the outdoors and to field examine your dog to note any wear and tear before it becomes more serious. This paid off one trip when I discovered an inflamed inter-digital cyst. It was disappointing not to use the dog when I needed him, but after the cyst completely healed we went out again and the game was still there!

Basically, good old-fashioned common sense will dictate good care for your first hunt and lay the foundation for many enjoyable hours in the field. Additionally, you will have better service from your dog. He will give ten times the effort and be in good physical shape to do it all day.

Can. O.T. Ch. DuCharme's Dukke a
Framlo, Am. and Can. UD. No. 1 Obedi
ence Elkhound in the U.S. for 1974, '75
'76 and No. 1 in the Hound Group i
Canada in '75 and '76. The first of he
breed to place in a major Obedienc
tournament, "Dukke" placed 8th in the
Top Dog Class of the 1976 Obedienc
World Series. Owned by Don and Marily
Rotier and trained by Don.

The first two AKC O.T. Champions of the
breed. Seated in front: Am. and Can.
O.T. Ch. Camalot Bella Tigra, co-owned
by Don Rotier and Mari Misbeek, and
trained by Don. Imported from Norway
at the age of 9 weeks, Tigra accomplished
her two UDs in one year of competition.
Behind her here is O.T. Ch. Camalot
Trulle Ayla, owned by Marilyn Rotier
and trained by Don Rotier.

17

The Obedience Elkhound

by Donald Rotier

Donald and Marilyn Rotier's devotion to their dogs and the sport of Obedience competition has served our breed nobly. The time and effort involved in preparing a dog for Obedience competition at the top levels is monumental and few people have been willing to do it with an Elkhound.

The combination of careful training supplied by Don and the TLC supplied by Marilyn produces dogs that can compete at the highest levels of Obedience achievement. For many years, their DuCharme's Dukke av Framlo, Am. & Can. UD, was the No. 1 Elkhound in Obedience in the United States and in Canada. Dukke's successor, Camalot Bella's Tigra, Am. & Can. UD, not only bested her record but went on to become the first Norwegian Elkhound to win an Obedience Trial Champion title. Tigra was retired from competition after being hit by a car and being severely injured. Like a true Norwegian, however, she healed herself and became mentor to Camalot's Trulle Ayla, Am. & Can. UD, who became the second and only other Elkhound to achieve the Obedience Trial Champion title.

The degree of Obedience training of the Rotiers' dogs was evidenced when at one social function their matriarch bitch, Baya, was told not to touch the potato chips and dip on the coffee table. During the course of the party, Baya noticed that a chip had fallen on the floor, so she carefully picked it up in her mouth and placed it back on the plate!

The Rotier Elkhounds (Gravenner Kennels, St. Paul, MN) are excellent examples of how a dog's life can be enriched and expanded by the activities involved in training and showing dogs. They have traveled far and wide and have made friends for the breed wherever they've gone. They are part of the family and enjoy their status as such. Their behavior is a credit to the breed wherever they appear and their stable temperaments have allowed them to be taken to many events to represent the breed proudly.

Obedience Competition

Obedience competition is a sport which gains much of its popularity from the fact that it can be enjoyed at all levels of ability. A key factor in this is the scoring system that allows individual competitors to set their own goals and measure their accomplishments against these goals. Not all handler/dog teams have the ability to win against the top competition, but since the scoring system enables each participant to evaluate his performance against self-imposed goals, it's easier to applaud the winners without feeling like a loser. The level of achievement you and your dog can reach is a combination of ambition and ability. If you are working to the extent of your dog's capability, you can be proud of your dog's performance. However, don't degrade a beautiful breed and excuse a low score because "he is working OK for an Elkhound."

The American Kennel Club (AKC) and the Canadian Kennel Club (CKC) have established a level of performance which is considered a minimum for the dog to earn an Obedience degree. This requires a minimum of 170 points out of a possible 200, and more than 50% of the available points in each exercise. After achieving at least this level of performance in three trials, the dog will be awarded the appropriate Obedience degree. The typical handler/dog team loses considerably less than the allowed 30 points, and most teams can regularly achieve scores of 190. This score can be equated to breaking 100 in golf, and is quite obtainable. But it cannot be achieved by a casual training program. For some breeds, Elkhounds included, the effort can be extensive. "Breaking par" in Obedience occurs at a score of 195. Dogs regularly working at this level and above are the competition dogs of the Obedience world. Entry into the United States Obedience Classic or the Obedience World Series requires the demonstrated ability to earn 195 scores.

Booklets covering the rules and regulations of Obedience Trials may be obtained from the American Kennel Club, 51 Madison Avenue, New York, N.Y. 10010. In Canada, write to the Canadian Kennel Club, 2150 Bloor St. West, Toronto, Ontario, M6S 4V7. Both of these organizations can supply the names of local dog clubs that conduct training classes in Obedience and which hold Obedience Trials.

The Utility Dog (UD) degree is the highest and by far the most difficult for a dog to earn in Obedience. A dog reaching this level of training has spent so many hours working with its handler that it begins to think at a level well above that of the average dog. Training a UD dog is a rewarding, though sometimes frustrating, experience. Living with this educated animal is a joy.

206

Ch. Leif of Dragondell, CDX, TD, pictured in harness on the day he became first champion of the breed to win the Tracking title—September, 1961. Leif was owned by the Hon. William H. Timbers, a retired chief U.S. district judge. Judge Timbers has served dogdom as a president of the NEAA, and as Board Chairman of the American Kennel Club.

Ch. Just Torvald That's All, UD, the first champion Elkhound to achieve the UD degree. Whelped in 1954, he achieved his championship and UD within 2½ years. Owned and trained by Louis H. and Kathleen Prince.

AN OBEDIENCE-TRAINED dog is easier to live with because he understands that his owner is his leader, and that pleasing his owner is pleasurable for him as well. Some breeds seem to recognize this from birth; they are constantly trying to please and they react to any praise with exuberance. Alas, the Norwegian Elkhound is not one of these breeds. However, with extra care and effort, the Elkhound *can* be trained to compete successfully against the traditional Obedience breeds. This chapter is intended to encourage the training of Norwegian Elkhounds, to provide some insight into the problems of training the breed, and to honor dog/handler teams that have demonstrated that the breed is capable of outstanding performance in this sport.

The Elkhound has been long bred with the independence needed to work out of sight of his handler, tracking and then holding the moose at bay. His reward has been in the self-satisfaction of doing a good job and making independent decisions, separated from his handler for hours. True, this reward is accented by sharing the joy of the hunt with his handler, but that is not what keeps the dog working hard all day; he works because he enjoys it.

In training the traditional Obedience breeds, the primary problem is teaching the exercises. In training the Elkhound, the primary problem is convincing him that doing the exercise is worth his time and indeed that he is having fun doing it. Here we see that motivation is a key element in education.

The education of your Elkhound should begin with the selection of a school that has demonstrated success with a variety of breeds. Methods which work well with a Sheltie may be ignored by your Elkhound. The praise level that creates drive and animation in a Golden Retriever could lull your Elkhound to sleep. Breeds, and individual dogs within a breed, differ in temperaments. Talk to Obedience competitors in your area and try to locate an instructor who understands these differences.

In training the typical Elkhound you can expect to go through three stages of development: first, *disinterested and independent*; then, *eager and attentive*; and then *competitive*.

The training process starts with a dog that does not particularly want to learn and is not greatly motivated by praise from his handler. Some Elkhounds will be less independent and more responsive to praise, and they'll be easier to motivate. But many Elkhound trainers enter trials and earn Obedience degrees without ever progressing their dogs beyond the "disinterested and independent" stage.

Before a dog can achieve a competitive performance level he must first want to work and have sufficient interest to pay attention to his handler.

209

In 1971 the Higbee family of California were in the unique position of showing two Elkhounds in Utility competition. At left, Crafdal Tryglik Trovson, UD, was the No. 1 Obedience Elkhound of that year. Handled by Holden Higbee. At right, Crafdal Tryglik Trova, UD, handled to title by Holden's 13-year-old daughter, Holly, who had trained "Viki" from puppyhood.

An outstanding Obedience trio owned by Dan and Lori Jelinek (Lordan Kennels). From l. to r.: Dixitara of Lordan, CD; Daniel's Dustifawn, CDX; and Ch. Lordan's Sweet Gypsy Rose. Rose, pictured here at 9 months, was the nation's No. 1 Obedience Elkhound of 1975 and 1976.

Ch. Crafdal Thor Mhors Paulette, UDT, the first Utility Dog Tracker in the breed. "Mhora" earned her UD in 1971 and her TD in 1978 at the age of 10½. Owners Paul and Nina Ross are active in conformation and Obedience, and both are AKC judges.

Owners of the traditional Obedience breeds start at the *"eager and attentive"* stage and can concentrate on developing competitiveness, precision and stability in their dogs. The pace of most training programs assumes a reasonably responsive dog at the start. It is therefore not surprising that many Elkhounds enter competition before they have been conditioned to the stage where they enjoy working. The process of conditioning is a slow one. It can easily take six months to a year of training in which much of the emphasis is on instilling motivation. My dog "Tigra" was well into Utility training and was over a year old before she "joined the team" and began working because she enjoyed the feeling of accomplishment. In her case, the motivational transition started after six months of training, but after two years it was still progressing.

The foundation exercise for Obedience is teaching the dog to heel on lead. Because the handler has physical control over the dog at all times during this exercise, communication is easier and quicker. While a detailed discussion of training is beyond the intention of this chapter, a brief look at this foundation exercise will illustrate some training principles. The Elkhound's independence defeats inductive training techniques until he has been conditioned to enjoy training. We therefore rely on force training to establish a firm handler control over the dog and to convince him that the training session will be more pleasant if he pays attention and works.

Mother and daughter Utility champions. Left, Ch. Crafdal Tryglik Vilja, UD, and right, her daughter, Ch. Crafdal Thor Mhors Torvi, UD, both owned by Charles and Jane Libberton. Torvi was America's No. 1 Obedience Elkhound in 1973.

Two Utility Elkhounds owned by Fred and Joyce Scharringhausen and trained by Joyce. Left, Ranell's Star, UD and Can. CD, the No. 2 Obedience Elkhound of 1974. Right, Ranell's April Mandy, UD.

It is essential that praise be given at the same time as a correction and that this praise convince the dog that he is pleasing you and that he is having fun doing it. With many individuals of the breed, praise will not yield a response. When this is the case, keep in mind that it's difficult to remain in a bad mood when everyone around you is having a good time. Your dog hears your praise and your happy attitude will eventually convince him that training is fun. If you get a positive response, adjust your praise only as required to keep the dog under control. Remember that your first job is to create an eager and attentive attitude.

The accompanying chart lists heeling errors to watch for and correct, in addition to controlling any clowning that was not precipitated by praise. Note the "Eager/Attentive" column indicates a dog that is trying and beginning to pay attention. Unless the errors are really major, don't correct for errors of this type. It is easy to correct a forging Elkhound later; it is very difficult to break a lagging habit. Motivation is a fragile thing, so plan your training and corrections to avoid mistakes.

TYPICAL HEELING ERRORS

Exercise Feature	Disinterested/Independent	Eager/Attentive
Sit at side	• Easily distracted	• Watching handler • Touching handler
Start	• Small lag before dog moves	• Slight handler motion causes dog to move
Normal heeling	• Tendency to lag • Tendency to heel wide • No animation	• Tendency to forge with rapid self correction back to heel position
The "halt"	• Sits slow • Forges ahead of handler and sits crosswise in front of handler	• May anticipate halt • Sits rear-in and crowds handler • If forge develops, corrects self
Fast time	• Small lag at start • No attempt to decrease lag—may increase • Loses interest for long "fast time"	• Changes gait to gallop • Playful • Forges • Starts "fast time" on judge's command
Slow time	• Tendency to forge • Easily distracted	• Heeling not smooth • Anticipating "normal time" or halt
Left turn	• Drifts wide	• Crowds handler
Right turn	• Lag or wide	• No major problem
About turn	• Overshoots turn • Lag or wide coming out of turn	• Crowds handler during turn

213

At left, probably the most titled Eklhound in AKC history—
Am. and Can. Ch. Wabeth's Brigand, Am. and Can. UDT,
Can. TDX. At right, Wabeth's Victor, UDT, Can. CD and TDX.
Owned by Barbara Van Der Cook.

Ch. Margaard's Bamse, UD and Can. CDX, trained to honors as the No. 1 Obedience Elkhound
of 1972 by Ann Nowakowski. Ann also trained Ch. Bermarba's Savage Sam, UD and Can. CDX to
position of No. 2 Obedience Elkhound of 1976.

Some guidelines:

—Don't train when angry. Your sincere praise is essential. Have "fun" no matter how bad things look.

—Your corrections must communicate to the dog what you want him to do. If the dog becomes confused by a correction, don't add to his confusion by continuing to use the same correction.

—The dog must feel successful during portions of the exercise. Break the exercise into small parts and combine parts the dog likes to do with the *one* problem area you are trying to solve.

—Don't correct anticipations. This is a sign that the dog is trying and that you are succeeding.

A word of caution: Don't confuse a fearful reaction to lead corrections as an eagerness to please. This dog will also crowd and try very hard. Ease up on your corrections since this dog is "softer" in temperament and can't take the pressure. Also, there is a fine line between clowning and being very eager. Eagerness includes attention to the handler. Clowning is independence and should be allowed only in small quantities as a release of pressure.

Success in off-lead heeling centers on building the dog's confidence and convincing him that he is really accomplishing something by doing it correctly. On-lead work has shown your dog how to heel and repetition has established a performance pattern, but only desire will carry this performance over into off-lead work.

Do not consider off-lead heeling work until you are getting definite responses in the "Eager/Attentive" category. Off-lead heeling is an inductively trained exercise and is not going to be successful until the dog has been conditioned to having some desire to work. The introduction of off-lead heeling is feasible for a Sheltie or a Golden Retriever after as little as six weeks of training but it can easily take the typical Elkhound three months to reach this readiness. Delaying off-lead work does not cause problems. Starting too early allows the dog to exercise his independence in a training situation before the desire to work has been instilled and can result in a motivational relapse.

When the decision to introduce off-lead heeling is made, you should be aware of which parts of the heeling exercise the dog enjoys, and which parts are still troublesome. Key elements in introducing this exercise are:

- Find a non-distracting environment—your Elkhound is still not as attentive as he should be.

215

Ch. Ledgerock's Jahna av Stratton, CDX and Can. CD, owned by Stan and Cotton Silverman, Statton Kennels.

Orion av Norden, CDX, TD, first Elkhound to earn the TD degree in California. Bred, owned and handled by Joan Green (Norden).

- "Warm up" with on-lead heeling.

- Try only those portions of the exercise that the dog has done well on-lead.

- You have no effective way of correcting errors. All you can do is praise the dog when he is trying and use body language to encourage his performance.

- Keep the session short. His attention span is still quite limited.

To be effective, a physical correction must always be given *before* the dog has a chance to think about the error. Similarly, the reinforcing praise must immediately be present as long as motivation continues to be a problem. The practice of using a "grab tab" on the collar or immediately putting the lead back on to correct an off-lead heeling problem violates the above principle. The attempted correction is too late and your motion toward the dog will be viewed as a prelude to punishment. Since an easy way to avoid this punishment is to get away from the handler, you will find that these attempted corrections result in a condition where a small lag becomes a big lag. The dog, rather than correcting the small lag himself, hangs back further in anticipation of punishment. In general, trying to convert in mid-exercise from an inductive to a compulsive training method does not work unless you really want the dog to view the force as punishment.

Training your Elkhound is initially more difficult than training the traditional Obedience breeds only because of the additional conditioning needed to build enthusiasm for the work. If you lay a good foundation you'll find that the advanced exercises do not present any unique problems. Since the breed has never had to retrieve a moose, he is not a natural retriever. But then, neither are Dobes or German Shepherds. A good "force break" retrieve program, such as the one described by William Koehler in his book *The Koehler Method of Open Training for Ring, Home and Field* (Howell Books) works well with Elkhounds. Properly timed praise is again essential.

Happiness—multiplied by three.

18

Selecting Your Norwegian Elkhound

by Karen B. Elvin

WHEN you purchase a dog, you hope it will be a companion to your family for a dozen years or more. Therefore, this purchase should receive careful thought and consideration. Here are a few guidelines that will help assure you of obtaining a happy, healthy pet that will suit the needs of your family and be worthy of the ancient heritage of the Norwegian Elkhound as a family companion of great versatility and utility.

The mature Norwegian Elkhound is a sturdily built dog with a dense, lovely gray coat, weighing about 50 pounds and standing about 21 inches at the shoulder. Females are only slightly smaller than males. Typical Elkhounds are stable in temperament, and show sensible judgment regarding family situations, guests and intruders; they are normally friendly but still serve as effective guardians of house and home. As hunters, they are courageous and possess great agility and stamina, having been known to hold big game like moose and bear at bay for long hours. They have the endurance to track game for long hours under adverse conditions of weather and landscape. They are independent dogs with typical Scandinavian stubbornness as an element of their happy personalities.

Not all families are suited to the ownership of an Elkhound. While the breed is very adaptable to varieties of climate and living quarters,

Puppy and friend—Roxanna's Tina, owned by Ed-
mond C. Rabut.   —*Photo, Walter Chandoha*

A friend for the family—Larsa Sirrka of Krynn, CD.

Elkhounds—like any medium-sized breed—need adequate exercise and they are most happy when allowed to be a part of the family activities. A fenced yard or means of confining your Elkhound when he cannot be with you will protect him from the hazards of our motorized way of life. If you are not prepared to make your Elkhound an acceptable part of your family through early, consistent training, and to confine him for his own safety, then perhaps another, smaller breed of dog with a less independent personality would be more suitable.

How to Shop for Your Elkhound

Once you have decided that the Elkhound might be the breed for you, do some research to insure that you will obtain a sound, healthy, happy puppy that will grow into a good representative of the breed. Get recommendations from a veterinarian or, if possible, from the nearest Norwegian Elkhound club.* They can put you in touch with people who specialize in raising Norwegian Elkhounds. The breeder who raises good quality dogs is truly interested in finding good homes for them. The best puppies will come from people who raise only one litter at a time, devoting their energy to making that bunch of pups the best they can produce. Places where numerous litters are raised like farm livestock do not offer much hope of providing you with a healthy, well socialized puppy since time and the profit motive often mean that care is of minimal quality. A puppy raised in a kitchen or family room where constant loving attention is provided is your best bet. Let the breeder help you select the puppy that seems best suited to your family's needs.

A reputable breeder is interested in producing sound, healthy dogs. He (or she) devotes much time and thought to determining which dogs to use to produce the best possible offspring. His concern is with structure, pedigree, size and disposition—especially disposition, since the correct temperament in the parent dogs is essential to producing puppies that will have good temperament. He endeavors to produce dogs that meet the accepted American Kennel Club standard for Norwegian Elkhounds (see Chapter 8). The breeder will, out of most litters, hope to have one or two show-ring prospects. The rest of the puppies might also be fine, healthy, beautiful dogs, any one of which will make an excellent family pet; we refer to them as "pet quality" puppies. These "pet quality" pups are as well bred and as well raised as their "show quality" brothers and sisters and will give you an opportunity to acquire a fine dog at a fair price. The only difference between them and their "show quality" littermates is that they appear less likely to grow up to be the "Miss America" of the Elkhound world. In the hands of a conscientious breeder, pets and champions come from the same

*For names and addresses of current secretaries of Norwegian Elkhound clubs, write to: The American Kennel Club, 51 Madison Avenue, New York, N.Y. 10010.

litter; in fact with most breeders, champions are pets first, show dogs second.

The original cost of such a puppy is small when divided by the number of years you will enjoy its companionship. It is just about the best investment you will ever make. When you buy from a reputable, dedicated breeder, you will have as dividends his keen interest in the breed, his help and suggestions with training, and his continued concern about the welfare of the dog throughout its life. With the puppy you may also acquire the friendship of the breeder for life. "I only want a pet" is no excuse for buying a seemingly cheap puppy from a person who is exploiting the popularity of a breed—whose only concern is a fast profit. Large commercial kennels and retail outlets cannot be concerned with, nor are they often even aware of, hereditary faults, health defects and poor temperaments. They do not have the facilities or personnel to give each puppy the individual care and attention necessary to develop puppy personalities to full potential. From these sources you can pay a high price for an unknown quantity.

What are YOUR Requirements?

Determine the age, sex and degree of perfection that are suited to the needs and interests of your own family. Little puppies are cute and fun, but often for families with small children or working adults, an older puppy or dog will be a better choice. Don't turn down an older dog just because of his age. Such dogs usually adjust nicely to new homes and may be much less trouble than a chewing puppy that isn't house-trained.

Advise the breeder if you think you will ever want to show or breed your dog. Not *every* pup is a future champion. No one can guarantee that a pup will grow up to be a perfect specimen, but a knowledgeable breeder can spot potential. The extra cost for a puppy with the possible potential to become a show dog and be worthy of reproducing its kind may be worthwhile to you if you are interested in pursuing the dog show sport. If this is not of concern to you, the "pet puppy" will be just what you need. They will not be likely to do well in the show ring and should NOT be used for breeding since they will not contribute to the improvement of the breed. However, "pet puppies" do not have defects of health or temperament. Many families discover that enrolling their "pet pup" in an Obedience training school is the introduction to the sport of Obedience competition— a worthwhile hobby for so many families today.

Male or Female? This age-old debate must be settled on the basis of your interests and expectations for the dog. Remember that both sexes can (and should be) altered surgically if you do not want to produce puppies. Neutered animals can be shown at American Kennel Club Obedience trials but cannot be shown in conformation competition. Conscientious breeders can advise you objectively with regard to the differences between the sexes as pets. Males tend to be a bit bigger but remember that each dog has its own personality and there are no substantial personality differences between males and females. Both make good pets and their roaming instincts can be managed nicely by training and neutering.

When you buy a puppy, study its parents if they are available. Usually at least the mother is present for you to meet. Remember that the work of raising puppies oftentimes makes a mother dog lose her hair and look run down. This is temporary. Excuse her appearance, but *do* take note of her personality. She should be friendly and outgoing and willing to let you see the puppies. Some mother dogs are more protective than others and this is understandable. If this is the case, meet her away from the puppies. Puppies inherit their temperaments from their parents just as they inherit eye color, size and coat color. There are smart dogs, dull dogs, good dogs and bad dogs in every breed, but careful selection by the breeder makes puppy personality and appearance more predictable.

Questions You Should Ask

A concerned breeder of Norwegian Elkhounds should spend time, money, thought and effort to assure that you, the buyer, get the soundest, healthiest puppy possible. Before you make a purchase, consult with your own veterinarian, and get satisfactory answers to the following questions from the breeders you visit:

1. Does the breeder have a knowledge of the various hereditary conditions that can affect dogs, including Elkhounds? What measures have been taken to insure that the breeder does not use for breeding animals that exhibit or are likely to pass on these conditions? For instance, has their breeding stock been examined for hereditary eye diseases? Have sire and dam been x-rayed for hip dysplasia and shown to have normal hips? X-rays should be read by a veterinary radiologist or certified "Normal" by the Orthopedic Foundation for Animals. (Information about the Orthopedic Foundation for Animals and Hip Dysplasia can be obtained from the O.F.A., Inc., University of Missouri-Columbia, Columbia, MO 65211—(314) 442-0418.)
2. Does the breeder use for breeding only dogs that have sound and stable temperaments, dogs that are bold, energetic and intelligent? Excuses for poor temperament are legion. Most of them are just excuses. Dogs of stable temperament do not become permanently frightened or crazy from unpleasant experiences. Do not accept excuses; accept only stable temperament. Puppies should not show continual fear, dullness or aggression.
3. Does the breeder have knowledge of the stages of social development of the dog? Has each puppy been given regular periods of human companionship away from its littermates? Will the puppy be at least

seven weeks of age before being allowed to leave its dam and littermates? Behavioral studies have proved that contact with the litter and socializing with humans is essential to developing puppy personalities to their full potential. Breeders should know this.

4. Has a program of immunization against infectious disease been established? What kind of shots have been given and when? When is the next one due? That the price of the pup is "cheaper because they haven't had their shots" should never be an inducement. Get the name of the veterinarian that has been working with the breeder to provide health care for the litter.

5. Have the puppies been checked for worms and other parasites and treated if necessary?

6. Is the breeder familiar with the breed standard for Norwegian Elkhounds? Can he discuss the good points and faults of his dogs? Does the selection of breeding stock compensate for these faults to insure improvement in the next generation?

7. Puppies under six months of age should not be termed definitely as of "show or breeding quality" but may be referred to as "promising" or "better than average." What criteria does the breeder have for stating that a very young puppy has potential? If you want a show dog, buy an adult, a known quantity, and be prepared to pay accordingly. Beware of "co-ownership" deals.

8. Will the breeder provide you with the AKC registration certificate or the blue litter registration form, or a written contract stating that one of these will be forthcoming? In the latter case, the AKC registered name and number of the sire and dam, and the date of birth of the litter should be on the contract. There should be no additional charge for AKC papers. If the dog is sold as a pet, the breeder is reasonable in withholding the registration certificate by contract until such time as the dog is neutered. A contract should be provided in addition to the AKC papers. The registration form is not a bill of sale.

9. Will the breeder provide you with at least a four-generation pedigree? It is reasonable to assume that a concerned breeder knows at least this much about his breeding stock. A pedigree is not a substitute for the AKC registration certificate.

10. Will the breeder provide you with help and information about the feeding, health care and training of your puppy?

If the answers you get to these questions are informative and positive, you can be comfortable about purchasing a puppy.

What About Price?

Keep in mind that the original purchase price is only a small percentage of your costs to feed and care for your dog over the years you expect to have him live with you. As you can see, the proper raising of a healthy, happy pup takes time and effort on the part of a conscientious breeder and is an expensive proposition if done properly. If the price quoted to you seems high, consider that the breeder has invested in good nutrition, good veterinary care, kennel equipment, stud fees and personal time in the hope of producing better examples of the breed he (or she) loves so that others can enjoy them as companions. If the price is high and you can see that the time and effort has not been invested, don't buy. If the price quoted seems cheap to you, question where corners have been cut on quality and health care. A reputable breeder will encourage customers to ask questions about the breed and how the dogs are raised. Quality doesn't cost: it pays.

Look Before You Buy

Before you accept ANY dog, use this check list:

1. The premises and the dogs should be CLEAN. See that the dog's coat is clean, thick and rich. A dull, sparse coat can indicate poor health and nutrition.
2. Eyes and nose should be clean and clear. A runny nose and watery eyes are symptoms of several infectious diseases.
3. Is the pup bold and energetic? A shy, cowering pup will not improve with age. Try not to fall for a dull, listless pup out of pity.
4. Check the mouth and teeth. Teeth should be white, gums a healthy pink. Inflamed or pale gums can indicate disease. Discolored teeth can mean the pup was sick during the teething stage.
5. Ears should be smooth and pinkish-gray inside, free from inflammation, discharge or bad odors.
6. Legs should be sturdy and strong. Deformed bones indicate poor nutrition.
7. Check the tummy and groin areas for hernias. Navel hernias are not uncommon and appear as a soft lump in the middle of the abdomen. While rarely life-threatening, they may require surgery.
8. Check the pup's skin. Patches of bare, discolored skin on the face, inner legs or belly may mean mange, ringworm, eczema or fleas.
9. Check the pup's hearing. How does he respond to noise? If he seems inattentive, a further test away from the other pups may be warranted to be sure he is not deaf.

While many of these symptoms can be cleared up, it is much better to start off with a healthy puppy and concerned breeders would agree. Save yourself unnecessary expense and the heartache of watching a sick puppy die.

A newborn puppy at Elgshire Kennels.   —*Carter photo*.

19

A Breeder's Message to New Puppy Owners

As OWNER of a new Norwegian Elkhound puppy, you have a chance to mold a lifetime companion for your family from the happy ball of fur that has come into your household. A little time spent organizing the environment for your puppy and preventing unwanted behavior will pay big dividends as he grows into a handsome adult Elkhound. Because we as the breeders of your pup care about his welfare and the quality and reputation of the Norwegian Elkhound breed, we stand ready to help you should any problems arise. You have joined the fraternity of Elkhound lovers that joins those of us who have a common bond in our Great Gray Dogs. Welcome.

The following information may help answer some of your questions and provide some guidelines for care of your puppy.

"Papers" is a common term used to denote the dog's pedigree and American Kennel Club registration certificate. The pedigree is your dog's family tree showing his ancestors for at least three generations. This paper has no official significance but is of value to you if you ever plan to breed your dog. It will help you when you consult with experienced breeders about a suitable mate for your dog. The American Kennel Club registration slip allows you to register your puppy with the AKC. Some breeders register each puppy individually, in which case your dog will already have an official name. You can call him whatever name you choose, however. Some breeders provide you with a "blue slip," which is a litter registration form. In this case, you may choose the pup's official name and have him registered with the AKC. In either case, you should fill out the form completely to have the dog's registration transferred to your name as provided for in your puppy purchase contract.

Feeding your puppy properly is a simple task. Select a good quality name brand dog food that features as its main ingredients meat, poultry or meat products. Dogs are carnivores and a food that is predominantly cereal will not nourish your pup as well as a meat-based food. Read the list of ingredients and talk with your veterinarian when choosing a food. Feed your pup at regular meal times. This will help you to housebreak him more easily and enable you to monitor his growth and appetite regularly. It also gives you a psychological edge when it comes to training your dog since you are the "provider." Cottage cheese, cooked egg, meat, vegetables and fruits added in small amounts are enjoyed by most Elkhounds and are valuable additions to a dry food diet. Weigh your puppy regularly—at least every two weeks—to be sure he is neither too fat nor too thin and to make sure his growth is steady and within normal limits. Elkhounds tend to gain weight easily, so monitor food intake carefully to prevent obesity—a serious threat to your dog's health.

Establish a good working relationship with a veterinarian in whom you have confidence. This professional can best advise you regarding immunizations and health problems. Keep your puppy up to date on all shots and check regularly for parasite problems following your veterinarian's advice.

If your dog is to serve solely as a family pet and will not be used for showing or breeding, it should be neutered. The serious work of raising the next generation of puppies can be undertaken by professional breeders who devote the necessary time and study to the breed. Both males and females should be neutered at an appropriate age to prevent unwanted puppies and excessive territorial behavior and mate seeking. While neutered dogs cannot be shown in breed competition, they can be exhibited at AKC Obedience trials—a fast growing sport that may interest your family.

Early training should be started as soon as your pup arrives. We suggest following a short daily routine to accustom the puppy to handling and to the restraint of the leash. Use the dog crate for housebreaking and controlling destructive behavior. Groom him regularly so that he becomes used to the brush, having his feet handled and toenails trimmed, and start to teach the basic commands of "Sit," "Down," "Stay," and "Come." There are many excellent books available to help you with this training and many trainers now offer "Puppy Kindergarten" classes for young dogs.

As your puppy grows, you may observe the following:

EARS: Elkhound puppy ears are usually standing up between two and four months of age. Some are up earlier; a very few are not up until later.

228

3 days old.   —*Hirtle photo.*

3-week-old puppies, Forest Hills Kennels.

"Out of my way!" 4-weeks-old puppies of the Jarinor Kennels.

Learning to play with Dad.

—Hirtle photo.

Rarely, very large soft ears do not stand erect at all. Occasionally, ears that were up at two or three months may flop when the puppy teeths at four or five months. This usually corrects itself shortly. Avoid play habits that may injure the ears.

TAIL: As your pup grows older, the curl in its tail becomes more firmly set. It is usually tightly curled by six or seven months of age, but may unroll or be carried down when he is tired, relaxed or ill. Some tails never do acquire the tight, typical Elkhound curl. This does not affect the dog's personality, but it is a fault that should not be passed on to another generation since the Elkhound's tail is one of the breed's most cherished characteristics.

COAT: The Elkhound puppy coat is not shed until the dogs is around a year of age. Until the adult coat comes in, the coat may go through several stages of color change that are normal and should cause no concern. There can be great variation in the number of longer "guard" hairs in a puppy coat depending on heredity, time of year, and nutrition. Many pups look quite woolly and may be more buff colored than the typical shaded gray of an adult dog, but this will change when the adult coat grows in. For good coat and skin health, a good quality oil supplement designed for dogs is a valuable addition to the diet. Elkhounds seem to require a little more fat in their diet than some breeds in order to maintain a luxuriant coat and healthy skin.

SHEDDING: When an Elkhound starts to shed, large tufts of hair can be pulled from the sides and legs quite easily. This is normal and the dog will not fall apart completely! The shedding process can be speeded and controlled by regular combing with a good steel comb or rake to remove as much of the loose hair as possible. A thorough bath with a good quality dog shampoo will loosen the hairs and speed the shedding process. A good vacuum cleaner for the home is a necessity for Elkhound owners. Regular brushing will help stimulate the new coat to grow in and soon the dog will look splendid again. The shedding process normally occurs spring and fall in males and neutered females. Unspayed females usually shed four months after being in season or after raising a litter of puppies. An Elkhound has an amazing amount of hair to shed, but if shedding is continual or results in skin irritation or lesions, consult your veterinarian.

Remember that your puppy is a youngster and therefore needs plenty of rest and understanding guidance. A little time spent in understanding his needs, the characteristics of the breed and organizing his environment to prevent unwanted behavior will make your association with your Elkhound more enjoyable as long as you share each other's lives. May your Norwegian Elkhound mean as much to your family as ours have to us.

—From a Breeder Who Cares.

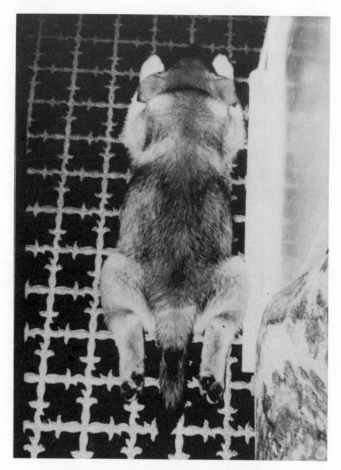

The typical Elghund "frog" resting position.

Elkhound bitch with nine puppies. Owned by the Misses Aarbitz of Nes-i-hole, Norway.

Observations on Feeding
by Olav Wallo

The Elghund is not a big eater. In fact, it worries many owners who expect that a good sized dog needs more food. Of course, over 90% of our dogs are overfed. In olden days, in Gamle Bamse Gram times, Norway had too many people and not enough food. The hunter and his dog had to share what little food there was in the knapsacks. Share and share alike. This may explain why the Elghund can get along with less food for his size.

I asked a famous breeder in Norway what he fed his hunting and show dogs. His answer was, "Meat, potatoes and a generous portion of cod-liver oil." When I imported some of my first Elghunds from Norway, I fed them horse meat (trimmed), dry dog food, and mixed this with a little water. But after some time they developed big sores. The dogs were licking and biting the sores. The veterinarian and I tried everything, but nothing helped. The sores got bigger and more numerous. Finally the veterinarian suggested the dogs were not fit for this climate. I did not agree, because the climate in Norway is quite similar to the weather in Minnesota. It seemed a hopeless case.

But one evening on a hike with all seven Elghunds, they got into a terrible fight. It was not a small scrimmage. They were really fighting. When I finally got them separated I found a two-pound can of bacon fat. That was the thing they were fighting over. I knew then they were starving for fat. Next day I brought home a big chunk of suet. After it was boiled, the dogs seemed as though they could not get enough of the fat. In two weeks the sores cleared up. From then on I always added bacon fat to their food.

233

The foundation for the feeding of dogs is a good dry dog food mixed with some meat, eggs, or fish, and often a can of baked-type beans added. Dogs like a variation. Of course, I never feed my dogs only dry dog food. I don't trust the stuff.

I have, in my kennel, never had hip dysplasia, nor nyctalopia (night blindness). Every two years the veterinarian checks the Elghunds over and gives them rabies and distemper shots. He states the dogs are disgustingly healthy.

A Creative Environment for Norwegian Elkhound Puppies
by Penny Wilkes
(Drawings by Michael Wilkes)

The influences in the early life of a Norwegian Elkhound puppy have a definite effect on his behavior as an adult dog. Although inheritance may predispose him to particularly behavioral traits, the environment plays a more vital role in his development and motivation. Therefore, a creative environment which includes exposure to unique stimuli is very important in order to prevent boredom as well as develop mental and physical abilities.

Norwegian Elkhound puppies are naturally alert, bold and investigative at an early age. They should be exposed to novel shapes, sounds and smells. If they learn to adjust to such things when young without fear, they will have the ability to adapt well to stressful conditions later in life which may test their stamina—such as the many distractions and traumas at a dog show.

After about the fourth week, puppies have found their "sea legs" and can ambulate freely to investigate their surroundings. Instead of sitting and sleeping all day, they are eager to explore and play with whatever is available in their milieu. They are fascinated with objects that move and interesting spaces that can be explored.

234

If puppies do not have a constructive way to occupy their time, they will seek their own diversions to avoid boredom. Such activities may evolve into undesirable behavior when the dog is older, such as nuisance barking, destructive chewing and feces-eating.

A creative environment for growing puppies will stimulate them and encourage their interaction with one another and their playthings. A puppy pen, or existing run, with imagination, can become an exciting place full of challenges to develop a puppy's full potential. It is possible to create an area which has many tantalizing stimulants to attract and amuse the Elkhound.

Large, boulder-type rocks can be used for climbing and cardboard boxes in various shapes and sizes are perfect for playhouses with holes in different sequences on the sides and top to stimulate curiosity. Pups will enjoy them thoroughly; they can drag them around, chew them and sleep within their confines! Gently sloping inclines are confidence builders and private spaces may be created underneath which are good for snuggling and sleeping. Large chimney flues, when placed end to end, create tunnels to explore and also serve as rest areas. The creative possibilities are limitless!

Edibles become destructible toys. Carrots, potatoes, celery stalks and other raw vegetables provide good stimulation for teeth and gums and relieve tension during the teething period. Citrus fruits make wonderful play balls for rolling and batting and create a new taste sensation in the process.

Target orientation training may also begin at this time. This can be accomplished by suspending rubber chew rings and dumbbells at the ends of light ropes so they can hang about six inches off the ground and are free to swing in all directions. As soon as the puppies become aware of them, they will spend hours batting, chewing, pulling and amusing themselves until they fall back, exhausted!

Many forms of antisocial behavior result from lack of environmental stimulation during puppyhood. Boredom is one of the most destructive elements throughout a dog's life and is easily overcome with some of the above techniques. Intelligent, well-adjusted dogs who have grown up in a creative environment will be more responsive, eager to learn, and will also be great companions!

Junior Handlers grow up to be full-fledged fanciers. The tot "practising" her handling above grew up to be Kristin Elvin, pictured at left with Ch. Sangrud Kolle's Tapper, bred and owned by Kristin and her mother, Karen Elvin.

4-H members active in dog care, Obedience and Junior Showmanship. Left to right, Guy, Holly and Heidi Coleman, children of Bob and Diane Coleman (Normark). Diane is a 4-H K-9 club advisor and trainer.

20

The Versatility of the Norwegian Elkhound

FIRST and foremost the Norwegian Elkhound is a hunting dog. This is what has made and shaped him through the years. But, as the stories in this chapter will attest, he has proven himself in many other roles, roles for which his sturdiness and solidity of temperament have made him particularly adaptable.

THE ELKHOUND AS A HEARING EAR DOG

by Ann McCluskey

"My ears have a cold nose!"

Yes, you read that correctly! What does it mean? It means there's a new kind of working dog around the neighborhood these days, and she's performing a valuable service to her "best friend," who in this case is a deaf or hearing impaired person.

The program is so new that many people are not aware it exists. Seeing Eye Dogs have been around for so long everyone takes them for granted, but a Hearing Ear Dog is virtually unknown. As a result, they encounter quite a mixed reaction—from surprise at seeing a dog in a supermarket to a loud "Get that dog out of here!" Pardon the pun, but, it falls on deaf ears. We are too delighted in our new-found ears and the sense of sound they give us to worry about negative reactions.

Perhaps you wonder what this is doing in a book about Norwegian Elkhounds. Simple. Not only do I happen to be the proud owner of a

237

Hearing Ear Dog, but she is, you guessed it, a Norwegian Elkhound. Furthermore, she was the first Elkhound to be trained for this work in her particular school, and the entire staff was so delighted in her personality traits, characteristic of the Elkhound breed, that they were happy to have accepted and trained a second Elkhound right after Irish Maggie graduated. This second Elkhound, Sonya, is now placed with a deaf couple in North Huntington, Pennsylvania.

I am profoundly deaf, happily married for 23 years, and the mother of two grown sons. My hearing loss has spanned over 37 years. First noticeable at the age of seven, I suffered progressive nerve deafness, which has left me with a 95% loss for most of my adult life. I was encouraged to wear a hearing aid to make use of the residual hearing left, which was also a help in maintaining good speech over the years. Today if anyone detects something odd about my speech, it's usually because I'm thought to be foreign-born. Little do people know that it's a combination of all the lip reading I've done in various parts of the world, a bit of Virginia drawl with a New York and New Hampshire accent thrown in—a confusing combination. Over the years, I have remained an active community participant—all the usual parent roles plus social life with my husband, always in the hearing world. Other family members answered the phone or door, but as the years went by, I wondered who'd do all that for me when my teenagers left home. As an interested adult, I also had the opportunity to become more involved in the deaf world, joining organizations or committees that were working for or with the deaf. It opened up a whole new world for me.

It was in 1976 that I first heard of Hearing Ear Dogs, and wrote to a school in Colorado requesting information. The reply I got wasn't too encouraging, but the program was in its infancy, and perhaps I didn't ask the right questions. I filed the thought away for "someday."

In 1978, my family settled in New Hampshire, and after 20 years of military travel, I wanted it all—big house, garden, nice lawn, and of course a nice big dog romping on that lawn. The only dog I'd ever had was a little 14 ball of Heinz 57. This time I wanted something special. I researched various breeds I liked and decided the Norwegian Elkhound had all the traits, personality, size and disposition that would suit me. The day we went to pick up Maggie from Liseldun Kennels, I remember Barbara Roby taking a minute to walk outside alone with that puppy, perhaps to say a private goodbye. I thought, "She needn't do that, I'll take good care of her." If only Barbara and I had both known that day the path that puppy would be following, we'd have both given her an extra hug and kiss to set her on her way.

Maggie came home with us at nine weeks of age and promptly put us through all the trials of puppyhood. (MUST they chew so much??) We set out to teach her good manners and sociability. Everytime the doorbell

Author Ann McCluskey and Liseldun's Irish Maggie, November 1982.

rang, we'd get all excited, hoping to show her it was fun, but that's as far as we went. We didn't know how to train her any further.

Then I had a chance to attend a demonstration put on by a school, showing how Hearing Ear Dogs are trained and what they do. I was so impressed that I applied for the program with the request that Maggie be trained. Accepting a deaf person's own dog for training is rare, for acceptance depends on whether the dog tests well, adapts to kennel life, and in general can be taught sound work. Maggie breezed through all of it and graduated in a record 2½ months. At the age of 14 months, she became a working dog, my constant companion and my ears. That was over a year ago, and still each day is a new delight as she responds to sounds, helps me put on demonstrations at a local civic group meeting, goes to work with me, or is always ready to share my world of silence by lying at my feet ready to jump up with a kiss or wag of her tail. She's worth an hour of conversation every time!

The Training of a Hearing Ear Dog

Teaching a dog to be a Hearing Ear Dog is a long process. The Hearing Ear Dog program at Jefferson, Massachusetts has been on-going for about six years. There is a hard-working staff of six who do all the testing, training, and placement of dogs while keeping the social end going with fund raising, demonstrations, giving sign language classes, and most important, giving their time and attention to the deaf people being trained with their new dogs. The puppies enter the kennels at eight months of age, and usually remain from three to five months, learning basic Obedience, sociability, and sound work. For the latter, they must learn to distinguish between sounds, sound location, and how to alert the trainer to those sounds. The school does not hesitate to flunk out a puppy who isn't working out. Sound work is not easy—it takes a lot of hard work and a special kind of dog.

When deaf people hear of the program and apply, the staff makes use of interviews, application information and other factors in determining which dog will be best for that person. Things to be considered are: babies in the home, allergies, size of the home and even other handicaps. (Two dogs have been placed with deaf persons in wheelchairs.) As possible matches are made, sponsorships are being sought from civic groups such as Kiwanis or Lions Clubs. At present, the training costs about $1800 with the cost to the deaf recipient of the dog only $150.

The final step in acquiring the new dog is a two-week training period on the Hearing Ear Farm. The new team of dog and owner needs to be introduced and must learn to work well together. Daily training sessions transfer the sound work over. Trips are made to town, and the staff gives lessons, advice, and the help that will carry the pair along as they go home and settle in to a real situation. It takes lots of time, much practice and lots of love. I think it took almost a year for Maggie and me to gain full confidence. Soundwork is fun and rewarding, but it doesn't happen without trial and error.

On graduation day, the dog earns the right to wear a yellow web harness and leash. An ID card is provided with a photo of the team, for identification to managers and employees of public establishments. The reaction to Maggie in public is sometimes amusing, but it is also enthusiastic once I explain why she's with me. While I'm challenged on occasion, that isn't my biggest problem. The public is the problem as they do strange things when encountering a dog under these circumstances. Once in a store aisle at K-Mart, a lady got down on her hands and knees and barked at Maggie. Another time, I patted a window sill at work to encourage Maggie to stand up for a look outside. A lady passing by tried to keep me from falling out and was quite embarrassed to see that I wasn't blind after all. Little children are the worst offenders as their moms seem to think they are bored and need to tease Maggie in the bank or supermarket when I'm not looking. To put it bluntly, Maggie's training has taught her to be better behaved than the public is at times.

Maggie leads a lively life, and being full of Elkhound spirit, she keeps me hopping. Her soundwork is improving all the time, for I've added some new sounds since her training school days. She wakes me up to the alarm clock, alerts me to the stove timer or tea kettle, tells me when someone knocks or rings. She answers to MY first name by jumping up on me and leading me to the person speaking. She picks up my dropped car keys, takes me to the front door when either of two smoke alarms goes off, and she'll shake hands with me if she hears a siren when I'm driving. (With all of this, people still ask me if she can "roll over" or "sit up"!) Her basic Obedience is Intermediate level, but how many of you can make your dog sit and stay in a room full of people, or heel through heavy industrial traffic, or ride an elevator with a grin? I swear she is laughing—she's having a ball, though she'll never graduate to Advanced Obedience work.

It continues to be a growing process, building on love and trust. Another Hearing Ear Dog school insisted that the dog cannot be a pet, that there must be a working relationship only. I say, "Baloney!". We're enjoying ourselves too much. The other night she even told me when a pan on the stove began to boil and make the lid rattle. That was a complete surprise for which she got lots of praise and fuss. She tells me where the birds and squirrels are—things I never knew before.

But, when you live with a 24-hour extension of yourself, you learn to take it all in stride. You clean up vomit in the office, or piles in unexpected places (the middle of the street during rush hour, when it was her first week at work and she was scared). You hang on for dear life while walking her by a man using a jackhammer, reassuring her and trying to look naturally relaxed to those passing by. You hush her in a busy supermarket when she decides the old man in the next aisle moves funny and decides to bark at him. Best of all, you remain perfectly calm in the middle of your speech to a Rotary group when you see them chuckling. Having just explained how well she does in basic Obedience, you turn to find your well-behaved dog standing on her hind legs, paws on the president's chest, snapping at a fly. It's all for love of Maggie!

Yes, my ears have a cold nose, but a big warm heart to go with it. Man's faithful companion by the fireplace has taken a new twist. Look out world . . . here comes MAGGIE.

241

THE ELKHOUND AS A HERDING DOG

by Pennijean Heib

I don't think many people realize that besides being an excellent hunting dog, the Elkhound is also a fine farm herd dog. I wasn't aware of this either when I got my first Elkhound, "Guy"; but he soon made it very clear—in that self-satisfied Elkhound manner—that he was a dog of many talents.

Because walking out on our 85-acre ranch every morning and evening in search of a dozen disappearing horses wasn't my idea of fun, I decided to train a dog to do the dirty work. My first choice was a 90-pound Malamute/Shepherd named "Brutus." The reason I chose a Northern-type dog was, of course, our frigid Minnesota weather. But Brutus proved to be incredibly inept around horses. I would patiently take him out in the pasture, find the horses, exhaust myself herding them into the barnyard, and he would promptly chase them out again at a full gallop, which is not the way to herd horses at all. I finally gave up on that idea and decided to try to teach him to herd them *out* of the barn when they were finished eating. He didn't catch on at all. He would chase them out so fast they would stumble and slide on the concrete and he kept chasing them for the next half mile until they were so scared that I thought they would never come back. Finally one day he got really mixed up and, barking wildly, blocked the stall door with me trapped inside with a terrified horse. So, I decided it was time to give up. We found Brutus a new home as he had become too fond of chasing the horses for sport and he was not very adept at ducking their hooves when they tried to avenge themselves.

After failing so miserably, I decided to forget the herd dog idea and get a hunting dog as there was a lot of game around the ranch and both my husband and I liked to hunt. So, we acquired our first Elkhound—Guy.

As soon as he was old enough to follow me out into the fields, Guy showed me that he could hunt nearly anything that moved. As he got older, he decided to show me a few things about herding horses. At first he just tagged along with me. Then I noticed that he seemed to know, much better than I, where the horses were hiding. Gradually, I began to rely more and more on *his* ears and nose. I began finding the horses in half the time it formerly took. Guy would get very excited when the horses started trotting back to the barn. It didn't take him long to start gathering them up and barking and trotting after them. He seemed to have a built-in herding instinct. He knew he had to keep them in a group and not push them too fast. Don't ever believe what you see on TV about cowboys herding horses at a full gallop, whooping and yelling. I don't know of a better way to get

An Elkhound watching the cows on a Norwegian farm.

them busting through fences and spreading out all over creation. Horses have to be herded at a respectable trot and Guy seemed to know this. Soon he would go out with me, find the horses and take them back to the yard on the command "Roof,Roof!" (I'll bet you won't find that one in the training books!)

After he had accomplished the herding IN so easily, I decided to try him on herding the horses OUT. However, remembering my earlier experience with Brutus, I was hesitant. If I had asked Guy, he would have said it was easier than burying a bone. I simply opened the stall door, said "Roof,Roof!" and backed away to see what would happen. He wasn't so dumb as to go into the stall with the horse and risk getting stepped on—he just treated the horse like a moose and baited him out, barking and jumping to and fro. The horse would put his head down and start chasing this impudent little dog toward the door; one quick Elkhound sidestep and Guy would be behind him, taking a nip at the horse's heels to insure his speedy exit. Sometimes a horse would try to nail that little gray pest with a large hard hoof, but by the time the foot shot out, the Elkhound had either bounced over to the other side or, if there wasn't time, he flattened out so

243

that all you could see was a gray splotch on the floor with ears and a tail sticking up out of it. He also knew his job was not to chase the horses across the pasture, but simply to herd them out of the barn, so he would chase one out about twenty feet and dash back in for the next one. He was always very unhappy when we ran out of horses (he never learned to count) but he was always content to wait for next time. We never had to worry about him chasing the horses around for fun inbetween times.

I'm sure he liked herding horses because it is so much like hunting moose. Barking and baiting the horse, dodging the hooves, following the animals but not scaring them with too much barking, and using his nose and ears to find HIS horses. He never did learn to go after the horses by himself, although I think secretly he wanted me to come along so he could show off.

Another thing that convinced me that my Elkhounds thought the horses were moose was puppy Sonja's first time out in the pasture. We were walking along the pasture when we came up over the hill and she spied a whole herd of "moose" grazing down below. She immediately froze to give herself time to figure out what to do. Next, she crept around them stealthily until she was down wind. She came up out of her crouch and advanced on the closest one and started barking and jumping around him, keeping him "at bay." The horse to her complete disgust wouldn't play the game at all. He casually looked up from his grazing at this four-month-old pup, realized it wasn't the official herder Guy, and gave her a look expressing "What's the matter with you?". Then he returned to his grazing. She gave him a puzzled look, shrugged it off and we continued on our way.

Most horsemen don't try to use dogs for herding because horses are so tricky and dangerous for dogs to handle. For one thing, most herding dogs are bred and trained to herd cattle or sheep instead of horses. These animals are much more domesticated than horses as far as their willingness to be herded goes and they tend to kick forward unlike a horse who kicks backward with a vengeance. When we moved into the city, a Collie and an Australian Cattle Dog tried to take over the horse herding duties that Guy had left. The results were unfortunately tragic. Both dogs were killed by the horses within a few months. They simply lacked the agility to get out of the way of the swift hooves. They had never practiced on "moose."

A 9-weeks-old Sangrud puppy.

A COMPANION FOR ALL SEASONS

by Philis Anderson

How do you tell your husband that you are about to become the proud owner of a new bouncy, chewy, unhousebroken puppy when you already have one dog, two cats, five horses, four cows, eight ducks and twenty-three chickens? I did it with a pancake.

Let me explain. When I ride my horses in the deep woods of northern Minnesota that surround our home in Grand Marais, I enjoy the company of a dog to forewarn me and the horse of any unwanted intruders such as bear and moose. Chris, my little American Eskimo Spitz, has aged rapidly in the last few years and his build and physique are not made for hard trail riding with horses. At times I have had to dismount, pick Chris up and carry him in the saddle with me to give him a rest. His usefulness as a lookout is limited.

When I was growing up in Minneapolis my family raised and showed Norwegian Elkhounds—the rugged, sturdy breed whose history extends back to Viking days. I had always wanted an Elkhound, remembering my childhood when our Elkhound companions were intelligent, family-loving dogs that brought us much pleasure. The ideal home for an "American" Elkhound would be right in my back yard, I thought. So, when my sister, Karen, announced the arrival of a beautiful litter of Elkhound puppies, I jumped at the chance to own one. Karen has raised and bred Elkhounds to the best of her ability for the last 35 years. She has put time and effort into breeding sound, healthy, beautiful dogs. She chose to give me the best male puppy from the current litter. I was thrilled, but how would I break the wonderful news to my husband? I knew he would not be thrilled.

Teddibjorn was born on Mother's Day and I would be his new owner before the summer was over. I told my boys about the puppy but as time went on, we could not bring ourselves to tell Dad. The quiet anticipation became hand signals shaped like doggie heads between me and the children when Father wasn't looking. Questions about how big Teddi was now were quietly passed from child to child. Finally in early July, Karen phoned to say that she would bring Teddi to the dog show in Duluth about mid-month. We would meet her there to pick him up. We had still not told Dad about the "puppy surprise." Many times we came close to blurting it out but somehow, the words stuck in our throats. I began to panic! Finally, Saturday morning, the day before our drive to Duluth to get Teddi, I stood frying pancakes in the kitchen. Matt, our creative 16-year-old son, took over the pancake flipping and made a pancake in the shape of a dog to remind me of our predicament. I looked at the pancake and a light went on! "That's it! We'll feed the pancake to Daddy and see if he can guess what it is." From that point on, I thought we could carry out the rest of the task of telling Dad about the Puppy.

Father came in from the garden and sat at the table. I passed the pancakes to him and explained that he had to eat the special pancake and guess what it was. He took the pancake, looked at it and said, "It looks like Snoopy." I said, "No, it's Teddi."

"Teddi? Teddi who?" I proceeded to tell him. When I finished, he began in a loud voice, "We don't need any more dogs, we already have too many animals, we already have a dog . . . etc."

Next morning Kent, our youngest son and I drove to Duluth to meet Teddibjorn. A more beautiful puppy we couldn't have hoped for. He slept peacefully in Kent's arms on the return trip. Teddi adjusted to his new home very quickly. My husband's adjustment was slower.

Teddi became my constant companion. He was with me most of the time as I went to the cow and horse barns, walked to the mail box and tended to the chickens and garden chores. He waited patiently while I milked the cows, often resting his chin on my knee and looking into my eyes. While he was still a little puppy, he treated our horses as if they were moose. He tried to keep them at bay just like a good Elkhound should. Now he understands that they are part of the "family," but his hunting skills also make good herding skills.

In late August when Teddi was three months old, I went to a chamber music camp—something I enjoy in my role as a professional musician and oboe player. I thought Teddi would be better off coming with me than staying at home. He won everyone's heart with his super personality. He was such a good puppy. He went to orchestra rehearsals with me every day.

246

He would find a comfortable spot near my chair and fall asleep in spite of the loud music. I took him swimming several times, carrying him out into the water and gently guiding him toward shore. Since Elkhounds are not by nature water dogs, he paddled quickly toward shore but he was willing to try again. Later that fall, his swimming lessons came in handy when he fell into a water-filled drainage ditch on a stormy pitch dark night. He paddled around in the ice cold water until I came with a flashlight and waded in to help him out. Wrapped in warm blankets, drinking our cocoa, I thought of those summertime swimming lessons and wondered if they helped save his life that dark cold night.

At the end of our week at camp, we had an Award Ceremony. Teddi received the "Best Camper" award—surely the first time a dog won an award at a music camp.

Just for fun, we entered Teddi at the Duluth Kennel Club dog show that fall. I worked with him, teaching him to trot beside me and stand still for the judge. He caught on quickly as he had with all the other training we had done. When show time came, he went into the ring as if he had been doing it all his life, and took the "blue" in his puppy class!

During the winter, I observed that Teddi is very attentive to birds flying over our house and yard. I thought this was peculiar since Elkhounds are supposed to be moose hunters, not bird dogs. When I researched this, I discovered that the Finns who migrated to Norway in the late 1600s used Elkhounds to hunt game birds. Even today, far removed as he is from that time, an Elkhound will instinctively observe flying and roosting birds and from his throat comes the lovely bubbling bell-like sound that is the Elkhound "Bird Call."

Teddi is still growing. That roly-poly dark gray "Pancake Puppy" has matured into a beautiful young silver and gray Elkhound filled with personality and love to share with his family. He accompanies me on my trail rides and his voice and actions warn us of hazards ahead. His good sense, gentle manner and versatility have endeared him to all, even Dad who pats his head when no one is looking.

A Liseldun puppy, 10 weeks old.

WITH STYLE AND GRACE

by Karen Elvin

Each spring, the friends of the Norwegian-American Museum of Decorah, Iowa hold a benefit style show and brunch in Minneapolis to raise funds for the Museum. A lovely meal of traditional Norwegian delicacies is served and beautiful models show off the latest fashions. The Norsk theme of the event is emphasized as the gorgeous models carry precious antiques from Norway and the early Norwegian immigrants' homes and wear the beautiful traditional costumes of Norway.

One year, the planning committee for the event invited Minnesota's own Olav Wallo to take part in the style show with a live artifact that was his well-known trademark—a Norsk Elghund. He and the dog were to stroll down the elevated runway used by the models to give the guests a view of a true Viking and his faithful Elghund.

Chosen to accompany Mr. Wallo was Don and Marilyn Rotier's well-trained Obedience winner, DuCharme's Dukke av Framlo, Am. Can. UD, holder of the most Obedience records for the breed at that time. It was thought that the charming Dukke, who was well used to public appearances, would be best suited to this kind of performance.

The day of the style show arrived and Dukke was chauffeured to the large downtown department store restaurant by her owner, Marilyn. At the door reserved for guests and style show participants, Marilyn found that the security list read "Mrs. Marilyn Rotier" and "Dukke the Dog." Like a true star, Dukke was given a dressing room of her own, complete with air conditioning and a chandelier while the hard-working models were crowded into a single warm room to make quick changes in close quarters.

Exactly on cue, Olav and Dukke began their trip down the 80-foot carpeted runway, the well-trained dog walking perfectly at heel. As they moved along, the odors of the delicious foods on the plates of the spectators wafted up to the talented Elkhound nostrils and Dukke's nose began to twitch and twist as her gaze moved from plate to plate.

The crowd could see the desire in her eyes as she and her companion walked by the temptations of lefse, sill, meatballs, puddings and cookies. But Dukke, ever the lady, controlled her impulse to leap into the lap of plenty and kept to their pace with head up and tail wagging.

Halfway down the ramp, Dukke paused to search the crowd for a glimpse of her beloved Marilyn. Tilting her head from side to side, she seemed to be taking a bow. At the end of the runway, her pirouette was accompanied by that charming tilt of the Elghund ears as she searched for her mistress in the crowd. To the 375 ladies present, it was an irresistible sight. They rose to their feet clapping and cheering and as Olav and Dukke made the return trip, dozens of hands reached up to pat and hug her. She captivated their hearts, especially the several ladies in the group who owned Elkhounds too.

The next year, Mr. Wallo was asked to repeat his performance in the style show but the two-legged models threatened to strike if the scene stealing dog returned.

Thom Thom Cintor Tia, tree climber.

HOW RUGGED IS THE ELGHUND?

by Olav Wallo

It was spring and the ice was breaking up in Nine Mile Creek. Big ice chunks were floating with the stream.

Now I discovered that three of my Elghunds were missing—Kaisa and Tortaasen Ola had dug themselves out of the big run and of course, when that happened, Kongen had forgotten his guard duty and he could not resist going along on a hunting trip. The only thing for me to do was find the runaways and get them back into the enclosure. We have too many roads and super highways around our place.

Coming through the ravine, I could hear some barking down by the Nine Mile Creek, but it did not sound like any of my dogs when they are on the hunt. I ran toward the sound, and sure enough, there were Kaisa and Ola looking across the stream. On the other side was Kongen hanging desperately to the bank with his two front feet but unable to scramble out of the stream's rushing water. His hindquarters were submerged in the ice-cold water. How long he had been hanging there I would never know, but it must have been for some time.

I called to him to try to come back so I could help him out of the ice-jammed current but his strength was fading. He no longer barked, but was crying in a helpless way. Then I understood—he was stiff and frozen, unable to move. The raging creek was 25 feet wide and too deep to wade, giving me no chance to get across at that point. The nearest bridge was a quarter of a mile away.

As I ran toward the crossing, I hollered to Kongen, "Hang on! I am coming!" Running through the deep slush and snow along the creek slowed my step but finally I reached the bridge. The bridge seemed so long now, and on the other side the creek bank was deep in snow. I stumbled headlong into it but struggled up to run on again.

Racing toward the stranded dog, I could see he now had only one foot on the bank. His cries for help were heartbreaking. I was out of breath and my heart felt like it must burst, but I was his only hope. If I failed, he would be swept downstream with the icy flow and drowned.

Suddenly a great ice chunk hit him and he was torn from the bank to float free. I raced on ahead to a tree close to the water. Putting my arm around the trunk, I tried to stretch my arm out so as to catch him when he was swept by, but I saw that my reach was too short. Loosening my grip on the tree, I clung to the bark with my finger tips. Reaching out, I was just able to get hold of his front paw. The paw was wet, muddy and slippery but with the greatest of effort, I pulled him towards me and grabbed his front legs. Just as I strengthened my grip on the tree, thinking the dog was saved, I saw a big iceflow heading right for us. How could I hang on to the dog

251

with the ice pounding against him? My arm felt numb and my heart was pounding. If I let go, that would be the end of him. I knew I must pull him toward me and at the same time move the mass of ice to loosen its grip. It worked! The ice swung out and was carried on by the rushing stream.

With my own strength gone, it seemed impossible to pull Kongen up the bank but somehow I dragged him to a dry spot close to the bank. His body was shaking and trembling all over. It seemed he would shake to pieces. I found a clump of marsh grass and tried to rub him to start the circulation going. I rubbed him hard and fast but it was not enough to overcome his chill. I had to get him home. To carry him that far was impossible. I prayed that Bill Sherpet was at home in his house right by the bridge.

On the run again, I found Bill home and told him what was happening. Bill grabbed a blanket and we were on our way back to Kongen. As we ran toward the spot where I had left him, we saw that Kongen was slipping toward the creek and his pitiful cries were louder. He knew he was in danger of sliding into the icy water again and he could not help himself. His legs were frozen; he was helpless.

Bill made a 60-yard dash, and grabbed the dog's hind leg and pulled him back from danger. Wrapping Kongen in the quilt, the two of us carried him back to Bill's house. From there we put the dog into the car and were on our way home to where the big fireplace was blazing with warmth. We placed the exhausted, frozen dog on the bench before the warm fire. We turned him over and over in front of the healing warmth as if roasting a pig. The main thing was to get the blood circulating as fast as possible since the pain of frostbite can be excruciating when the circulation starts again.

The dog shivered and shook so hard I thought the bench would be shaken to pieces. But, the shaking was like a passing storm and little by little, he quieted down until finally all we heard was a subdued whimper. Then he fell into a sound sleep. We put him in the big easy chair with a pillow under his head. I called my veterinarian and told him the story. He told me to bring the dog in as soon as possible.

Kongen and I must have slept for nearly two hours after our ordeal. When he awoke in the chair, he looked quite surprised and got off to come over to where I sat. He placed his great head in my lap and looked at me with those beautiful eyes that reflected gratitude and deep devotion.

In a moment, he was looking around for some food. I told him, "You're supposed to be very sick, and here you are looking for grub." After he was well fed, he crawled up on the chair and slept soundly again.

That very evening he took over his regular guard duties, barking loudly when anybody drove up to our house. He has a rule which he strictly enforces. You can bring things into the house, but don't try to take anything out with you. Yes, the Elghund is rugged. No wonder he has adapted so well to the many lands where he has found admirers.

252

Testimonial to a Departed Friend

Years have rolled by since that never to be forgotten day. I was his devoted friend. We two were comrades. He was the best guard dog I ever had—smart, dependable.

However, there was one thing that got him easily offended. When I came home from a California trip, he was very cold. He just ignored me. I tried to be friendly, but he was not the same friendly trusting Kongen as before. The third day after I came home, I put my hiking boots on. Then he came to life. We were going on a long hike. That he loved. On our way back, I found a shady place and lay down flat on my back. When Kongen discovered that I was down, he came running, crying in a sad way, licking my hands and face. I did not move. Before long, a bee landed on my nose. I had to use my hand to brush the bee away. Then Kongen came to life, barking in a glad way, pulling my arm to get me up and when I put my arm around his neck, all was forgiven and forgotten.

Before my next trips away from home, I would take my suitcase outside and we would sit down and have a long talk. Then, when I came back, he would be very glad and happy. No, he was not a champion. I could not put a choke chain over his neck and jerk him around and demand absolute obedience. It would not be right. Do the dogs have any rights? We put the choke chain on and demand absolute obedience. We are the commander; the dog is the slave. Little do we know or appreciate their feelings or their thoughts.

Kongen was good hearted and generous. A lost dog, long, lanky, boney and hungry came around. Now what would Kongen do to the poor critter? I had a sack of dog biscuit open. Kongen took the poor hungry dog over to the sack. When the dog was full of feed, he found a place in the sun and slept for some time until the animal warden came to pick him up.

September came and it was time for a checkup for Kongen and Kaisa. They were fourteen years old now. It sure was a shock to me when the veterinarian informed me that Kaisa had a very low pulse and he recommended some pills. Kongen got the same result. No long hikes, no steep hills to climb. These were sad days for all of us. On the first of October, I found Kaisa dead in her bed; she had died in her sleep. The sixth of October at three o'clock in the morning, Kongen barked loud three times. Then I knew he was saying farewell to me. I turned on the light and there he was sitting, bright eyes so happy to have me with him. I sat on the floor and he put his head in my lap. I stroked his head and told him he must not die—I would be so lonesome. He raised up and looked at me, his tail wagging, then he lay down. A little later, he started shivering; then, a deep sigh, then no more. He was the last link of the many beautiful Elghunds I had imported from Norway. The King is dead; Long live the King.

Mo av Hestehov, CD, with friend. Bred by Sandra D. Speiden, and owned by her with Donna W. Germelman.

Your Responsibilities as a Dog Owner

If dog lovers are to retain the right to keep dogs as pets, we must be willing to supervise, train, control and clean up after them. When you acquire a dog, you acquire responsibility.

1. Provide an enclosed area where the dog can safety exercise or be prepared to walk the dog on leash at all times. Pick up all dog excrement.
2. Provide companionship and training for your dog to enable him to develop his greatest potential. Make him a part of your family. Why have a dog if you don't want it with you?
3. Provide adequate health care for your dog. Have your veterinarian immunize him annually against infectious disease. Do not be misled by the term "permanent shots"—no shots are "permanent." Be guided by your veterinarian's advice.
4. Provide proper nutrition for your dog. Good nutrition begun by the breeder must be continued by you.
5. Brush and comb your dog regularly. Bathe him when necessary and keep his nails cut short so his feet stay healthy. Give him a weekly check-up to catch health problems before they become too serious to manage.

Don't buy a dog and neglect him. Like you, he needs Love, Care, and Affection. The reward is a friend that accepts you as you are.

BIBLIOGRAPHY

ALL OWNERS of pure-bred dogs will benefit themselves and their dogs by enriching their knowledge of breeds and of canine care, training, breeding, psychology and other important aspects of dog management. The following list of books covers further reading recommended by judges, veterinarians, breeders, trainers and other authorities. Books may be obtained at the finer book stores and pet shops, or through Howell Book House Inc., publishers, New York.

BREED BOOKS

AFGHAN HOUND, Complete	Miller & Gilbert
AIREDALE, New Complete	Edwards
AKITA, Complete	Linderman & Funk
ALASKAN MALAMUTE, Complete	Riddle & Seeley
BASSET HOUND, New Complete	Braun
BLOODHOUND, Complete	Brey & Reed
BOXER, Complete	Denlinger
BRITTANY SPANIEL, Complete	Riddle
BULLDOG, New Complete	Hanes
BULL TERRIER, New Complete	Eberhard
CAIRN TERRIER, New Complete	Marvin
CHESAPEAKE BAY RETRIEVER, Complete	Cherry
CHIHUAHUA, Complete	Noted Authorities
COCKER SPANIEL, New	Kraeuchi
COLLIE, New	Official Publication of the Collie Club of America
DACHSHUND, The New	Meistrell
DALMATIAN, The	Treen
DOBERMAN PINSCHER, New	Walker
ENGLISH SETTER, New Complete	Tuck, Howell & Graef
ENGLISH SPRINGER SPANIEL, New	Goodall & Gasow
FOX TERRIER, New	Nedell
GERMAN SHEPHERD DOG, New Complete	Bennett
GERMAN SHORTHAIRED POINTER, New	Maxwell
GOLDEN RETRIEVER, New Complete	Fischer
GORDON SETTER, Complete	Look
GREAT DANE, New Complete	Noted Authorities
GREAT DANE, The—Dogdom's Apollo	Draper
GREAT PYRENEES, Complete	Strang & Giffin
IRISH SETTER, New Complete	Eldredge & Vanacore
IRISH WOLFHOUND, Complete	Starbuck
JACK RUSSELL TERRIER, Complete	Plummer
KEESHOND, New Complete	Cash
LABRADOR RETRIEVER, New Complete	Warwick
LHASA APSO, Complete	Herbel
MALTESE, Complete	Cutillo
MASTIFF, History and Management of the	Baxter & Hoffman
MINIATURE SCHNAUZER, New	Kiedrowski
NEWFOUNDLAND, New Complete	Chern
NORWEGIAN ELKHOUND, New Complete	Wallo
OLD ENGLISH SHEEPDOG, Complete	Mandeville
PEKINGESE, Quigley Book of	Quigley
PEMBROKE WELSH CORGI, Complete	Sargent & Harper
POODLE, New	Irick
POODLE CLIPPING AND GROOMING BOOK, Complete	Kalstone
PORTUGUESE WATER DOG, Complete	Braund & Miller
ROTTWEILER, Complete	Freeman
SAMOYED, New Complete	Ward
SCOTTISH TERRIER, New Complete	Marvin
SHETLAND SHEEPDOG, The New	Riddle
SHIH TZU, Joy of Owning	Seranne
SHIH TZU, The (English)	Dadds
SIBERIAN HUSKY, Complete	Demidoff
TERRIERS, The Book of All	Marvin
WEIMARANER, Guide to the	Burgoin
WEST HIGHLAND WHITE TERRIER, Complete	Marvin
WHIPPET, Complete	Pegram
YORKSHIRE TERRIER, Complete	Gordon & Bennett

BREEDING

ART OF BREEDING BETTER DOGS, New	Onstott
BREEDING YOUR OWN SHOW DOG	Seranne
HOW TO BREED DOGS	Whitney
HOW PUPPIES ARE BORN	Prine
INHERITANCE OF COAT COLOR IN DOGS	Little

CARE AND TRAINING

BEYOND BASIC DOG TRAINING	Bauman
COUNSELING DOG OWNERS, Evans Guide for	Evans
DOG OBEDIENCE, Complete Book of	Saunders
NOVICE, OPEN AND UTILITY COURSES	Saunders
DOG CARE AND TRAINING FOR BOYS AND GIRLS	Saunders
DOG NUTRITION, Collins Guide to	Collins
DOG TRAINING FOR KIDS	Benjamin
DOG TRAINING, Koehler Method of	Koehler
DOG TRAINING Made Easy	Tucker
GO FIND! Training Your Dog to Track	Davis
GROOMING DOGS FOR PROFIT	Gold
GUARD DOG TRAINING, Koehler Method of	Koehler
MOTHER KNOWS BEST—The Natural Way to Train Your Dog	Benjamin
OPEN OBEDIENCE FOR RING, HOME AND FIELD, Koehler Method of	Koehler
STONE GUIDE TO DOG GROOMING FOR ALL BREEDS	Stone
SUCCESSFUL DOG TRAINING, The Pearsall Guide to	Pearsall
TEACHING DOG OBEDIENCE CLASSES—Manual for Instructors	Volhard & Fisher
TOY DOGS, Kalstone Guide to Grooming All	Kalstone
TRAINING THE RETRIEVER	Kersley
TRAINING TRACKING DOGS, Koehler Method of	Koehler
TRAINING YOUR DOG—Step by Step Manual	Volhard & Fisher
TRAINING YOUR DOG TO WIN OBEDIENCE TITLES	Morsell
TRAIN YOUR OWN GUN DOG, How to	Goodall
UTILITY DOG TRAINING, Koehler Method of	Koehler
VETERINARY HANDBOOK, Dog Owner's Home	Carlson & Giffin

GENERAL

A DOG'S LIFE	Burton & Allaby
AMERICAN KENNEL CLUB 1884-1984—A Source Book	American Kennel Club
CANINE TERMINOLOGY	Spira
COMPLETE DOG BOOK, The	Official Publication of American Kennel Club
DOG IN ACTION, The	Lyon
DOG BEHAVIOR, New Knowledge of	Pfaffenberger
DOG JUDGE'S HANDBOOK	Tietjen
DOG PSYCHOLOGY	Whitney
DOGSTEPS, The New	Elliott
DOG TRICKS	Haggerty & Benjamin
EYES THAT LEAD—Story of Guide Dogs for the Blind	Tucker
FRIEND TO FRIEND—Dogs That Help Mankind	Schwartz
FROM RICHES TO BITCHES	Shattuck
HAPPY DOG/HAPPY OWNER	Siegal
IN STITCHES OVER BITCHES	Shattuck
JUNIOR SHOWMANSHIP HANDBOOK	Brown & Mason
OUR PUPPY'S BABY BOOK (blue or pink)	
SUCCESSFUL DOG SHOWING, Forsyth Guide to	Forsyth
WHY DOES YOUR DOG DO THAT?	Bergman
WILD DOGS in Life and Legend	Riddle
WORLD OF SLED DOGS, From Siberia to Sport Racing	Coppinger